KEEP YOUR AIRSPEED UP

KEEP YOUR AIRSPEED UP

the story of a
TUSKEGEE AIRMAN

HAROLD H. BROWN AND MARSHA S. BORDNER

THE UNIVERSITY OF ALABAMA PRESS   TUSCALOOSA

The University of Alabama Press
Tuscaloosa, Alabama 35487-0380
uapress.ua.edu

Inquiries about reproducing material from this work should be
addressed to the University of Alabama Press.

Typeface: Scala Pro

Manufactured in the United States of America
Cover image: Harold H. Brown in 2001 with a restored P-51;
photograph by Chris Zuppa, courtesy of the *Minneapolis Star Tribune*
Cover design: Michele Myatt Quinn

Cataloging-in-Publication data is available from the Library of Congress.
ISBN: 978-0-8173-1958-8
E-ISBN: 978-0-8173-9140-9

For our parents, John and Allie Brown, and Arthur Boyd and Phyllis Stanfield. And for Lawrence "Bubba" Brown, who played an integral role in our narrative and in our lives.

CONTENTS

ILLUSTRATIONS

PREFACE

I MET HAROLD BROWN IN 1987 when he came to Clark Technical College in Springfield, Ohio, as the Interim Vice President for Academic Affairs. I was new to my position as Dean of Arts and Sciences, and he was my first real boss in this capacity. I was attracted to his leadership style immediately—he was levelheaded, balanced in his response to people, focused on solving problems, and just plain fun to be around. I wanted to be an administrator just like him.

Over time, he began to share stories about his life. This was long before he became famous as a Tuskegee Airman, but the stories just stuck with me. I was fascinated and began to record his interviews, to read oral transcripts, to tape his lectures, etc., all the while knowing that Harold's was a story that had to be told—from the beginning of his parents' migration from the Deep South in 1919 to his growing up years in Minneapolis to his being a Tuskegee Airman in World War II. Parts of his story, often neglected, are his military career after World War II, his role as a pioneer in community college education as a second career, and finally, his love for the game of golf.

Harold's story, like those of other Tuskegee Airmen, remained largely unknown until 1995 when Bob Williams, a close friend of Harold's, finally got his movie, *The Tuskegee Airmen*, produced. Other events, such as the awarding of the Congressional Gold Medal to the Tuskegee Airmen in 2007, brought this group of men farther into the limelight. By 2012, when George Lucas produced *Red Tails*, the Tuskegee Airmen had begun to be known in many circles around the United States and the globe as overlooked heroes of the war.

Harold and his fellow Tuskegee Airmen had, indeed, gone on with their lives after the war, and in large measure had met with great success in government, in the private sector, and in academe.

The movies and other media coverage brought attention back to the war years and made them larger than life in some respects. In reality, the Tuskegee Airmen's flying experience in World War II lasted only from July 19, 1941, when the first aviation cadets entered Preflight Training at Tuskegee Institute,[1] to the end in late April 1945, when the 332nd Fighter Group, the only black fighter group of the war, flew its final bomber and reconnaissance escorts for the Fifteenth Air Force.[2]

During these years, the men fought for the "Double Vs," an expression coined by the editors of one of the black newspapers of that day, the *Pittsburgh Courier*—for Victory against Hitler's fascist regime and Victory against racial segregation at home.[3] What did these years mean for our country, and why did the experience of this group "catch fire" after that first movie?

Daniel Haulman, Chief of the Organizational History Division of the Air Force Historical Research Agency, has written frequently on the Tuskegee Airmen and spends a great deal of his time debunking myths about the airmen. He is quick to point out that "whether the 332nd Fighter Group was better than others is debatable. . . . In terms of aerial victory credits, the black fighter pilots were roughly equal to the white ones. Considering that the starting line for the Tuskegee Airmen was farther back than their fellow pilots, and that they finished at roughly the same line, one might conclude that they came farther in less time. Unquestionably, they climbed a steeper hill, because of the racial bigotry of the time."[4]

One of the most remarkable facts about the Tuskegee Airmen was that they achieved what they did even before the military was desegregated. President Truman ordered desegregation of the military in 1948 and that order was implemented in 1949. Before that time, "segregation was not just by tradition, but by law," as Harold mentioned many times in his public talks and lectures. The 1896 "separate but equal" doctrine stood throughout the war; the general belief was that equality could be achieved through separate facilities, separate equipment, and separate training. The problem, of course, was that nothing was ever equal. And yet these men not only persevered, but achieved equal or better results than their white counterparts.

As Haulman concludes, the true significance of the African American pilots was more far-reaching than simply flying as well as their white counterparts: "If the Tuskegee Airmen had not performed well in combat, the U.S. military might never have been integrated. The integration of the U.S. armed forces was the first step towards the integration of American society, and laid the foundations for the civil rights movement that resulted in equal opportunity, by law, for all Americans regardless of race."[5]

This book is the story of my husband, one of those Tuskegee Airmen, an African American man who, through dedication to his goals and vision, rose through a miasma of racial segregation to great heights of accomplishment, not only as a military aviator, but as an educator and as a human being.

MARSHA S. BORDNER, PHD
2016

ACKNOWLEDGMENTS

THIS BOOK HAS BEEN IN THE MAKING for over five years and has had many supporters. These include:

Dr. Daniel L. Haulman, Chief, Organizational Histories Branch, Air Force Historical Research Agency, Maxwell Air Force Base, Alabama, who spent an untold number of hours providing research assistance and reviewing the manuscript for historical accuracy.

Friends Karen H. Harris, Donna Lueke, Sandy Trout, and Terry Wheaton, who spent many hours editing the manuscript.

Sons Seth Bordner, who offered editorial advice early on, and Jonathan Bordner, who offered many hours of assistance on photographs.

Friends and family who provided occasional editorial suggestions as well as moral support:

Jo Brown (Bubba's wife), Tom Wiese, Linda Hertenstein, Dick and Karen Coffin, Greg Reed, Sonny and Sheryl Goings, Jeff Sondles, Connie and Fritz Cedoz, Alison Falls, Dave and Mary Caracci.

LaVone Kay, Marvona Welsh, Brad Lang, and Ken Mist of the Rise Above Project.

Grandsons Dashiell and Simon Bordner, who always provided comic relief.

Transcriptionists Vicki Martin-Dillon and Trish Channels.

The book is largely based on countless interviews, oral histories, and tapes. To mention just a few: "Oral History Memoir," American Airpower Heritage Museum of the Confederate Air Force, 1995, Bruce Boitz-Furu, interviewer; "Minnesota's Greatest Generation," Minnesota Historical Society, 2003, Thomas Saylor, interviewer; "Veteran: Harold Brown," transcribed by Allison Lewis Kimmel, court reporting student, at Clark State Community College, 2010, Becky Wiggenhorn, instructor; "Meet Seniors Who Served Our Country," in *Serving Our Seniors*, 2014, Sue Daugherty, interviewer; Preparation for Commencement at Heidelberg University, 2014, Angie Giles, interviewer.

KEEP YOUR AIRSPEED UP

– – – – – – PART I

THE EARLY YEARS

So there I was, a thousand feet above the ground over Nazi-occupied Austria in a P-51 Mustang, climbing away from the total wreckage of a German locomotive I had just shot up, when my airplane's engine stopped. Bailing out was my only option. I landed in deep snow. When I looked up, all I could see were two men with rifles pointed at me.

It is interesting what goes through a person's mind in such dire circumstances. First, it was hard for me to accept that this was happening to me. I kept telling myself that it just couldn't be true. Then it hit me: "There's a war going on. Here you are and you are the enemy. You just got caught. What do you think is going to happen to you?" I continued to think: "This is absolutely crazy to be in this situation. Here I am, only twenty years old, and me of all people, with this face, parachuting down into Austria. This is the last place I need to be, in the middle of a war. How did I ever get here to begin with?"[1]

MY STORY ACTUALLY BEGINS IN MINNEAPOLIS, Minnesota, some twenty years before jumping out of that plane.

I'm sure it really began with my parents' journeys from the deeply segregated South of the early 1900s all the way up to Minneapolis, Minnesota, where I was born in 1924.

I wasn't simply born with confidence and a vision for myself at an early age—that was built into me by my parents and those in our family who came before. I've always had a passion for learning, for setting goals and achieving them, for being as good or better than others in like circumstances around me.

As the years went by, I developed several passions. Among them was the passion for flying, which I developed as a young teenager, and later, a passion for higher education in the community college sector.

I

MY FAMILY AND ANCESTRY

MY BROTHER, LAWRENCE, OFTEN REFERRED TO as Bubba, because I couldn't pronounce "brother" as a small child, was born five years before me. He and I were shaped by the stories that were passed down about our great-grandparents, our grandparents, and our parents.

One of the interesting familial characteristics for me and for Bubba was our mixed racial heritage. It was a topic to which we often returned throughout our lives. Bubba, in particular, was adamant that there was only one race—*human*. He was extraordinarily proud of his family, which included two young girls from China who had been adopted by his son and daughter-in-law.

Bubba could never understand why any ethnic group self-identified as Italian American, Chinese American, or African American. Growing up, Bubba recalled: "We were just kids. . . . It was not like it is now. . . . People are so worried about what background they came from that it is almost self-segregation."[1] We often teased each other about having such a mixed racial background that we were like "mongrel dogs."

THE MATERNAL SIDE OF MY FAMILY

My great-grandfather by blood and Bubba's through family relationship was Jewish. (Bubba had a different birth mother than I.) His name was James Abrams and he was born on July 4, 1843, in South Carolina. Bubba often talked about a picture of Ole Man Abrams, as he was called, in which he has a big white beard and looked just as Jewish as he could be.

Ole Man Abrams married a woman named Louvenia Kidd in 1878 in Shelby, Alabama. We assumed that she was black. James and Venia, as she was called in some records, had eleven children, one of whom was my grandmother, Tina Abrams (Heath and later Lassley). Bubba and I both thought it was unusual for a Jewish man to marry a black woman, but according to Bubba's research, there was a significant number of cases where Jewish people would leave their clans and marry outsiders.

Late in life, Ole Man Abrams came to Minneapolis to live with his daughter, my grandmother Tina. Bubba recalled Abrams sitting on the front porch cussing in Yiddish at Jewish passersby. While the north side of Minneapolis in those years had a large Jewish community, it was clear that Ole Man Abrams had no interest in seeking out others of his ethnic background. He died on October 3, 1930, in Minneapolis. I can remember, at six years old, his death and funeral, and the coffin being at the house. A cousin and I peeked, and could barely see in the coffin—but there he was, with a long white beard and long white hair.

Back in Alabama, my grandma Tina had been married when she was very young to a much older black man, Adolphus Heath. We referred to him variously as Mr. Heath or Ole Man Heath. Census records reveal that Tina was born in 1884, while Mr. Heath was born around 1855, making him nearly thirty years her senior. Tina had five children with Mr. Heath. She was seventeen years old when she gave birth to her firstborn, Allie, my mother. According to what Bubba and I had been told, Mr. Heath had a big barn, a beautiful horse, and a fancy carriage. Ma talked about Ole Man Heath hitching up his horse and buggy, and riding up and down the street, just as proud as could be. Ole Man Heath had divorced his first wife and had married Tina when she was fourteen or fifteen. Apparently, his first wife subsequently burned their barn down, twice. Years later, my mother recounted: "That ole heifer came in there 'again' and burnt that barn down."

Several members of my family were rebels, and Grandma Tina was certainly one of those. Even though Mr. Heath was the head of household, she defied him and took her oldest child, my mother Allie, and left Alabama for the North. They eventually ended up in Minneapolis.

The Paternal Side of My Family

John A. Brown, Bubba's and my father, was a man of few words and told us little about the family's past. He had to be pressed to share any details about his family or our history. I sometimes wondered if he felt some shame about the role that slavery had played in his and our past.

Dad once shared with us that his father, Albert J. Brown, was the product of a master-slave relationship. In family documents, Albert is listed as a carpenter, indicating he was "skilled." The 1900 census reveals that he was born around 1844.

Dad also told Bubba and me that his mother was a Native American woman with long black hair. Her name in family and census records was Eugenia. Census data indicate that she was born around 1855.

Based on what our father had told us, Bubba and I never doubted that Eugenia was Native American. We had no idea what tribe our grandmother came from, but we were told that she lived for some time in Jenifer, Alabama, and ended up in Talladega, Alabama. Both Jenifer and Talladega are located in Talladega County. The name "Talladega" derives from a Native American (Creek) word meaning "border town."[2] We just assumed that our grandmother was a Native American from that area.

My mother, Allie, knew of John's family in Talladega. I recall her telling me: "The Browns lived in a big white house. I remember seeing this Indian woman sitting out there combing this coal black hair and rolling it up in a great big bun and pinning it up on her head."

During the years that I was a graduate student at Ohio State University, I was amused by the number of times that I was approached by students from India, who looked at my straight black hair and slightly hooked nose and inquired if I was Indian. I would laugh and say, "Yes, but not the kind of Indian you're thinking of. I am partly Native American Indian."

My wife, Marsha, trying to track down my roots, convinced me to take a DNA test to settle the issue of my heritage. The test showed my ancestry to be 58 percent Sub-Saharan African and 41 percent European (overwhelmingly from Great Britain)—but no part Native American. The DNA results largely explain my father's fair complexion and my straight hair. I was surprised to get the news and still do not absolutely believe the test—after all, my dad said his mother was Native American, so it's hard to believe that what he said was not true. As I was later to find out, however, the claim to have an ancestor who was Native American is common in many African American families.

In "High Cheekbones and Straight Black Hair," Harvard Professor Henry Louis Gates Jr. notes that it is quite common for African American families to claim that they are descended from Native Americans. Gates quotes Nina Jablonski, an anthropologist, about why African Americans likely have this

Figure 1. John Brown as a young man.

tendency: "Everyone wants to feel good about their ancestors. Having a Native American in one's background is ennobling and elevating, but having physical traits associated with European subjugation is not." The Native American has long been romanticized as the "noble savage," while black Americans have been cast as the "ignoble savage."[3]

The few other details that Bubba and I knew about our father's family background were that Dad was the youngest of nine children, and was the tallest and the fairest. Most of the other children were much shorter and were more brown skinned or had light brown skin. But Dad was fair, and had straighter hair than the others.

MY FATHER, JOHN A. BROWN

Dad was born on September 13, 1892, in Talladega, Alabama.

After finishing high school, he attended Talladega College for one year. Talladega College is Alabama's oldest private historically black college and was founded to provide a school for the children of former slaves. Perhaps his going to college, unusual for most blacks at that time, indicates the prominence of the Brown family or that the original "master" had provided resources for his offspring.

Figure 2. John Brown in uniform.

Dad enlisted in the US Army on April 27, 1918, in Talladega at the age of twenty-five and was discharged approximately eight months later on December 24, 1918, shortly after World War I had ended in November. He did not serve overseas. His discharge from the military lists his occupation as "farmer."

Dad returned to Talladega after his military service. He was not much of a talker, but he occasionally told us stories that would resonate for Bubba and me for the rest of our lives. Perhaps the most memorable was the one that led to his leaving Talladega. Dad told us of going into a hat shop to try on a hat. He decided that he didn't like it or it was too big. Anyway, he put it back on the rack, but the owner said, "Now, John Brown, you know better than that. When you try on a hat, you just bought it."

Dad said, "But I don't want the hat."

"Well, it makes no difference. You now got yourself a hat."

When my dad refused to buy it, the owner called the sheriff, who came down and had a talk with young John Brown. Dad insisted that he didn't want the hat—that it just didn't fit right.

The sheriff finally said, "Okay, but don't let it happen again." That was when Dad decided that he was going to get out of Alabama.

At that time in the South, blacks like my father were denied privileges allowed to whites of any socioeconomic level. Benjamin O. Davis Jr., who would one day be the Commander of the 99th Fighter Squadron and who lived at Tuskegee Institute as a boy in the early 1920s when his father was a faculty member there, recounted in his autobiography that there was one store in Montgomery, Alabama, that actually "bent the segregation laws and let some of the Tuskegee faculty shop with a special degree of freedom from insult."[4] He and his family chose not to shop there, but he became painfully aware of the rigid segregation laws of Alabama through experiences like this.

Pulitzer Prize–winning author Isabel Wilkerson, in *The Warmth of Other Suns*, documents how Jim Crow laws persisted for all blacks, even those who were well educated, long after my father had left the South. She describes a black physician in Louisiana in the 1940s who could not try on suits in a department store. Instead of suffering that humiliation, he would send his wife into the store, while he sat in the car waiting for her to bring several suits for him to inspect. He would tell her which ones to buy.[5] Traditions such as this persisted well into the 1960s. Young colored women, for example, could not try on hats in department stores in Atlanta at that time.[6]

So in 1919, my dad was certainly not allowed to try on a hat and then refuse to buy it. He faced a choice, as did nearly every black family in the South until the end of the 1970s: Stay in a Jim Crow caste system "as hard and unyielding as the red Georgia clay"[7] or migrate to the North.

The reasons for leaving were quite clear. For some, the sharecropper system seemed remarkably similar to slavery. The sharecropper, a tenant on the plantation owner's land, had to take the planter's word at "settlement" time that he was credited fairly when the crops were sold. By the time the planter subtracted the "seed, the fertilizer, and the clothes and food—from what the sharecropper had earned from his share of the harvest, there was usually nothing coming to the sharecropper at settlement."[8] Many sharecroppers ended up in even deeper debt to the owner.[9]

There were various other reasons blacks in the South wanted to leave. There were "typists wanting to work in an office. Yard boys scared that a single gesture near the planter's wife could leave them hanging from an oak tree."[10] The choice of picking up and leaving had to be difficult, but by the 1970s, "nearly half of all black Americans—some forty-seven percent—would be living outside the South, compared to ten percent" when, what historians would later call the Great Migration, began.[11]

Dad left Alabama to go work for a man in Michigan. This man, formerly from Alabama himself, had told Dad that if he ever wanted a job, he would have one for him in the lumber industry. Dad ended up in Manistee, Michigan, home to a booming lumber industry in the 1880s and continuing into the twentieth century. Although many Americans probably think of African Americans living in urban centers like Detroit, it was not unusual to find pockets of African Americans in rural Michigan. The Manistee Forest was a huge source of lumber. "There was actually a black logging company that employed fair-complected African Americans."[12] There was certainly a lure to the area for those who believed that they could make money as lumbermen.

After Dad left Alabama for Michigan, he sent a letter back to folks in Talladega telling them that there were jobs in Michigan and that he was coming back with tickets and money for those who wanted to relocate. Dad's actions were a real economic threat to the ruling class in the South. The planters preferred the Negro sharecroppers to white labor on the plantations, because of "the inability of the Negro to make or enforce demands for a just statement or any statement at all. He may hope for protection, justice, honesty from his landlord but he cannot demand them."[13]

Dad went back twice to take Alabama blacks up to Michigan. He had the conductor stop the train outside of Talladega, where he would pick the people up, and they would all travel back to Michigan. Bringing blacks out of Alabama to the North as Dad had done was fraught with risk. In Alabama, there were so many blacks leaving "that the state began making anyone caught enticing blacks away—labor agents, as they were called—pay an annual license fee of $750 'in every county in which he operates or solicits emigrants' or be 'fined as much as $500 and sentenced to a year's hard labor.'"[14]

After the first time that Dad returned for laborers, the sheriff said that if he ever came back to town, he'd shoot him. The consequences for blacks that challenged white Southerners at this time were severe. "Across the South, someone was hanged or burned alive every four days from 1889 to 1929."[15] Crimes included making "boastful remarks," "trying to act like a white person," or insulting a white person.[16] Yet Dad returned. His courage and determination were sources of real pride for Bubba and me.

Dad moved on to Minnesota sometime in 1919; it is not clear exactly when he arrived or even why he journeyed so much farther north than most other migrants. Most blacks followed three main tributaries out of the South, often determined by the railroad and bus paths of the day. There was the coastal route to cities like New York and Boston; the central route to cities like Detroit,

Chicago, and Cleveland; and a later route to the West Coast.[17] There were very few African Americans who migrated as far north as Minneapolis in those years. Yet our dad was never daunted by a challenge.

Dad was part of a movement, generally described as beginning around 1915, which spanned five decades. "The period between World Wars I and II was one of unprecedented changes for the Negro population. During this period there occurred the greatest single mass migration in American history. While the Negro population in the North was only 1,578,336 at the time of the 1910 census, the 1940 census showed 2,960,899 living there."[18] The overall population of African Americans in the North had almost doubled in only thirty years. Our dad (and both his future wives, Bubba's mother and my mother) was part of this great migration.

The Importance of Work in the Life of John Brown

One of Dad's earliest jobs in Minneapolis was as a fire knocker on the railroad. The trains ran by burning coal. The coal had rock and other materials in it that didn't burn. These cinders had to be taken out of the train after the firebox had cooled. When the trains came in after a long run, they were taken to the "round house," where Dad and the other fire knockers went down under the train, opened the firebox, and took all the slag and cinders out.

The business with which both Bubba and I most associate our father, however, was Archer Daniels, which had begun in Minneapolis as Archer Daniels Linseed Company in 1902. It was known after 1923 as Archer Daniels Midland, currently a global food-processing corporation.[19]

Dad began as a pressman in the linseed oil factory. I can remember so well that Dad reeked of linseed oil from working that press. In this operation, the workers would put linseed between two burlap sacks and then press it with steam. This helped extract the oil from the seed. The process was scorching hot, so the workers wore shorts and were often bare-chested while they worked.

Dad worked twelve-hour shifts and was glad to have the job. He was well respected at work. In Bubba's words, Dad "was very smart. Very quiet, but very smart. Everybody liked him. They thought he could walk on water. He never cussed, was always at work—he never took a vacation because he thought the guys might realize that they could run the place without him."

Dad eventually became a supervisor after a strike occurred at the company during which he was thrust into the limelight. In the 1930s, labor unions were very popular and strove to change work practices, such as reducing the long work hours of its members. Dad consciously decided not to join the union forces, for two primary reasons. First, he attended a union meeting and determined he did not respect its leaders. He, therefore, could not follow them. He also believed he had the best job of anybody that he knew and had some status among the laborers with whom he worked.

Dad's shift was at work when the strike started, and as a result, he and the other workers were locked in. He and his shift just kept working for several weeks until the strike ended. While Dad was locked in at work, the wife of one of the owners came to our house and brought a big basket of food for the family. She told us to contact her if we needed anything. Some of the strikers even came to the house to try to intimidate our mother, Allie. This was definitely a mistake on their part, for no one "messed with Allie Brown," as Bubba put it. Taking no chances, Bubba also went to the basement to get his .22 caliber one-shot rifle in case it was needed. Nothing happened, but it was in that time the unions were "making their stand."

After the strike ended, Dad was made a supervisor. As shift foreman, our dad got jobs for the young men in the neighborhood to shovel linseed out of the grain cars before the formal pressing process began. Dad got jobs for most everyone but his own sons. It was clear that he had higher expectations for us, or as Bubba once remarked, "I guess he wanted us to be more than that."

Occasionally, our mother would take us down to pick our father up from work. Some of the workers were heard to say: "There goes John Brown with his nigger wife and kids." The workers clearly believed Dad was white. Bubba later wrote in his autobiography that once when workers made snide remarks, "Dad was so livid that he bit his pipe stem off. But in the workplace he was the boss so his employees couldn't say too much about him if they wanted to keep their jobs."

Dad worked for the Archer Daniels Midland Company until he was forced into retirement at age sixty-five. His death certificate lists him as "supervisor/retired." He received a pension that seemed generous, but it had no provision to deal with inflation. At first, the $147 a month seemed more than adequate, but over the next thirty years until his death, it was not. Both Bubba and I regretted not approaching the Archer and Daniels families for an increase in the amount. We felt that the family would have rewarded our father based on his service to the company.

Dad was not ready to retire and resented being forced to do so. He had worked his entire life and was suddenly cast out of the work force that had given him a purpose for living.

Dad as a Role Model for Bubba and Me

Our dad was a man of honor and of compassion. Dad would not vote because he feared that jurors were selected from the list of voters, and he would not serve on a jury at any cost. He refused to serve on a panel that could send someone to prison for life or have them executed. Even though capital punishment had been abolished in Minnesota in 1911,[20] it was still a hotly debated topic during Dad's lifetime. In fact, executions reached the highest levels in American history in the 1930s.[21] Dad would not be responsible for convicting someone else of a crime. He did no wrong and expected the same of others.

Dad's reputation in the neighborhood was well known. He would walk into a pool hall and a hush would fall over the crowd. The thugs would suddenly clean up their acts. The bartender would say: "Okay, guys, Mr. Brown is here, so watch your language." And no one swore until he had gone. Virtually everyone, including our mother, Allie, always referred to him as "Mr. Brown."

Dad had strong convictions about any number of things. One, in particular, was his feeling about the South that he had left behind. Bubba had received a football scholarship to Alabama State University for the 1937–38 school year. While other friends of Bubba's from Minneapolis ventured to Alabama for higher education, Bubba was not among them. Dad had seen enough of the South. His son would definitely not head south to school.

While it was quite common for black migrants in the North to head south for holidays and summer vacations,[22] that was not true of our dad. In his later years, we offered to take him back to the place of his birth, Jenifer, Alabama, but he said, "I don't want to see Alabama, not even on the map."

We grew up in a time when the expression "spare the rod and spoil the child" was not some cliché. The use of belts for beatings was common. Yet our dad never, ever spanked us; he didn't have to. I can remember when Bubba would misbehave and Dad would say to him—and Dad was a big guy— "Lawrence, if I were you, I wouldn't do that again." Bubba later shared: "That was worse than a spanking or beating for either of us. As a man of few words, Dad always spoke very softly, and in order to hear him, you had to listen. You had to be right there looking at him when he talked."

Bubba and I also grew up in a time when people were not openly emotional. Dad was a devoted family man, but he never uttered words like "I love you." Love was shown through action, not words. Both of us knew how much our father loved us, but he seldom showed emotion. Both Bubba and I remembered when I had my tonsils taken out and my throat was really sore.

On this rare occasion, Bubba was sent out to get ice cream. As Bubba remembered: "We never got ice cream! *Never* got ice cream." Yet at this one moment, all three of us ate ice cream; Dad fed me himself and we all enjoyed this special time.

Dad's fierce independence manifested itself in a variety of ways. He told our ma and us that we would never live in the Project, located in the center of the black community in north Minneapolis. "There were all those colored folks down there." He wanted no part of government housing. He told us that he would not take a handout; he was too proud. We never did live in any home that was supported by the government.

Even when Bubba and I went off to war, we remained the focal point of our father's and mother's lives. It is impossible to imagine the anxiety our parents must have felt, when, in 1945, they received two telegrams within weeks of each other—each with bad news. The first said that Bubba was "grievously injured." The other said that I was "missing in action." It was not clear if one or both of their sons might be dead.

When we finally both got home, Ma wanted a picture of Bubba and me with our father. This led to one of our funniest memories of Dad. As Bubba recalled, "We were their lives, I guess. Ma always wanted to talk about her two boys. She wanted a picture of the three of us. I got the camera and we went outside and stood beside Dad. I got the pictures developed and brought them back and gave them to Ma. She was bragging about them and she took them over to show Dad. After he looked at them awhile, he said: 'Allie, come here.' So Ma walked over and he mumbled something to her and she said: 'What did you say?' He mumbled something again and she said, 'Tell the boys what you just said.' He mumbled some more and then she said, 'You know what this fool said? He wanted to know who is this old white guy standing here with the boys.'" (The Southern custom is that if I say something to you that doesn't make sense, you then say, "Do you know what that fool said?" It would be automatic. It wasn't meant to be a derogatory statement.)

One of the most touching stories about our dad came after his death in 1986, just before his ninety-fifth birthday. When Bubba and I began looking through his possessions, we found his overstuffed wallet. Looking inside, we found multiple pieces of paper. Every time that I had moved, Bubba had given our dad my new address and phone number on a small slip of paper. We also found a few slips describing changes of address for Bubba as well. He kept them all. Nothing was more important to Dad than his sons; he had kept pieces of both of us in his wallet.

Figure 3. From left to right:
Bubba, Dad, and me, 1945.

We found one other piece of paper in Dad's wallet: a record of his monthly pension payment and his death benefit. This was valuable information to Dad; he needed to know the amount he had to support his family and to cover his death.

MY MOTHER, ALLIE BROWN

My mother, Allie, was born in Sylacauga, Alabama, to Adolphus and Lavinah Heath on October 26, 1901. She was the oldest of five children.

Ma had to conform to the expectations of life in the Deep South. Her heart was broken when her parents pulled her out of school in the sixth grade. She clearly wanted to learn, but she was needed to work in the cotton fields. She talked about carrying that great big long bag as she and the others picked cotton from morning to evening.

Ma's experience was apparently common for black children in the rural South. In Mississippi, for example, "Colored children only went to school

Figure 4. My mother as
a young woman.

when they were not needed in the field." Colored children "didn't start school until the cotton was picked, which meant October or November, and they stopped going to school when it was time to plant in April. Six months of school was a good year." Children would walk to a "one-room schoolhouse that . . . had to suffice for every colored child from first to eighth grade," the highest grade for a colored child in those years in rural Mississippi.[23]

When she was just fifteen, Allie and her mother, Tina, fled Alabama for the North. There are many possible reasons for why they left. Surely, the thirty-year age disparity between Tina and Mr. Heath and also his basic personality may have played into the decision. Or perhaps more likely, the decision was influenced by the mind-numbing nature of picking cotton all day.

In the South, picking cotton was "one of the most backbreaking forms of stoop labor ever known."[24] In the 1920s, the gold standard of payment for cotton picking was fifty cents for a hundred pounds of cotton. "It took some seventy bolls to make a single pound of cotton," which meant that a person "would have to pick seven thousand bolls to reach a hundred pounds. It meant reaching past the branches into the cotton flower and pulling a soft lock of cotton the size of a walnut out of its pod, doing this seven thousand times and turning around and doing the same thing the next day and the day after that. The hands got cramped from the repetitive motion of picking, the fingers fairly locked in place and callused from the pricks of the five-pointed cockleburs that cupped each precious boll." Work began "the moment the sun peeked over the tree line to the moment it fell behind the horizon and they could no longer see. After ten or twelve hours, the pickers could barely stand up straight for all the stooping."[25] No wonder my mother found it heartbreaking to be pulled out of school to pick cotton.

When Ma and my grandmother, Tina, left Alabama, they went without the younger siblings. They eventually settled in Minneapolis, Minnesota. Ma never shared the details of their trip.

My mother, much like her mother, Tina, had a rebellious nature. She was fiercely protective of children all of her life. When Ma was sixteen or seventeen years old, she vowed to go back to Alabama for her younger siblings. She had saved enough money to buy tickets for herself and her siblings. Ma was money-smart from an early age and even saved money for clothes for her sisters and brother. She went south via the train system and directly to the school. She picked up her two sisters, Vivian and Evelyn, as well as her younger brother, Cozell. She took them to the train station where they went to Nashville, on to Chicago, and finally back to Minneapolis. They were gone before Mr. Heath even knew Ma was back in town.

If Ole Man Heath had known that Ma had come for her siblings, he would never have let the children go. Ole Man Heath was already angry because his wife and daughter had left him. They were his kids after all. Ma took appropriately sized clothing for her sisters, but picked child-sized clothing for Cozell, who would have been about five or six. He was twice the size of the clothes that she had brought. He had to squeeze his feet in sideways to make his shoes fit at all. This was a favorite story of our family.

Alma, the second oldest child in Ma's family, stayed behind in Alabama. She married and had two children, Edna and Grace. They remained in Alabama for some time, but eventually Alma came to Minneapolis and then later sent for her daughters.

Alma ran a house of ill repute in Minneapolis and later one in Chicago. Ma used to tell me to never go down to her house, but I used to run errands for Alma, who was nice and always kind to Bubba and me. It was obvious that something was going on when she sent me down to the courthouse with an envelope, which I assume was a payoff. When I was in junior high school, there were a few occasions when she would get a call and shut everything down.

ALLIE BROWN, THE PERSON BUBBA AND I REMEMBER

Ma was a "determined" woman in many respects. She refused to marry Dad until he went down to Cincinnati and picked up Bubba and brought him back to live with us.

Dad had met and married Bubba's birth mother, Harriet Drake, at an earlier time, but she died of tuberculosis when Bubba was only two years old. Ma told me that she helped care for Dad's first wife before she died. After her death, Dad had taken Bubba to Cincinnati to be with his mother's people. Bubba remained there for a short period until Dad came back for him when he and Ma were married.

Ma was always bringing in and taking care of someone's kids. She did that all of her life. She raised Eugene, who was the son of one of dad's brothers. She also asked to take in the then school-aged boy Prince Rogers Nelson, who was to later become the rock legend Prince. His family lived in the same neighborhood in Minneapolis. Ma asked to raise Prince when his mother was having difficulty keeping him in line. Ma, however, was not needed this time.

Ma was fiercely protective of children and would not hold her tongue when she saw injustice. One time she saw a young girl who had been beaten with a cord from an iron by her father. This very strict father was also the minister of their church. The girl came to Sunday school, and when my mother saw the welts on her back, she confronted the reverend: "Did you beat this girl this way? You call yourself a pastor? You aren't fit to be the pastor of anybody. You ought to be ashamed of yourself."

The girl's mother said, "Now, Mrs. Brown, this is a family affair."

"Family affair nothing!" Ma replied. "You sat by, and if you were a big enough fool to let this man beat your daughter like that, then you are a bigger fool than he is."

Ma was obstinate and very determined once she decided she was going to do something. She used the money she had earned cleaning houses, a job she had gotten after working at a bottle factory, to pay off the $3,500 that she and Dad owed on the home on Olson Boulevard. Dad would not have thought it possible to own a home; he would have simply assumed that they could never afford one. But Ma was not a woman to be told "No." She saved the money, bought the house, and then told Mr. Brown that they owned a home.

Ma was the one in charge of the household finances. She took his paycheck each week and cashed it, giving Mr. Brown tokens to ride the streetcar to work. In their later years, when Ma and Dad were well into their eighties, Bubba remembered how Ma held the purse strings but did not understand or trust banks. At one point, she and Dad sold the cabin they owned on Lake Sullivan for $10,000. Ma had promised Bubba that she would take the check to the bank, which she did. However, instead of depositing it, she had the check cashed and placed the money in her purse. Ma definitely did *not* trust banks.

Ma remained religious through most of her life. She had become a Seventh-Day Adventist when I was a child of eight or nine. Bubba remembered her watching Bible study slides, including Bible verses and pictures that illustrated the verses, frame by frame, with a small slide projector and screen. He had to have the equipment repaired time and time again, because Ma would not spend money for a new one. While I was in the war overseas, Ma sent me Bible verses on a regular basis—many of which I kept. After Dad died, however, Ma lost interest in life itself. God had always answered her prayers, but He did not keep Dad alive.

2

MY EARLY LIFE IN MINNESOTA

BUBBA AND I NEVER KNEW EXACTLY HOW our parents came to live in Minneapolis, but there is research that indicates that those migrants who traveled the farthest to begin new lives were often the most successful. "The general laws of migration hold that the greater the obstacles and the farther the distance traveled, the more ambitious the migrants. 'It is the higher status segments of a population, which are most residentially mobile,'" wrote sociologists Karl and Alma Taeuber in a 1965 analysis of the census data on the migrants.[1] Another migration scholar, Everett Lee, wrote: "As the distance of migration increases, the migrants become an increasingly superior group."[2] While we certainly could not prove that our parents were "superior" as people, we felt that the values and work ethic passed on to us from them contributed to our eventual success.

I was born on August 19, 1924, in Minneapolis, Minnesota, five years after Bubba. My earliest memory is living on Bradford Avenue. Figure 5 is one of only three pictures on a tintype that show me as a young child.

I am not a person who speaks openly about my feelings, but suffice it to say, my mom was my hero. She worked whatever jobs she could get to help keep our family clothed and fed. One of my earliest memories was of Ma washing bottles in a local bottle factory located a few minutes from home. I was left alone beginning at age four, not uncommon in those days when parents were working, and remember sitting alone in front of a big bay window. Before he left for school, Bubba would print my name at the top of a tablet. I would then print my name, Harold H. Brown, over and over until it was

Figure 5. A tintype of me
as a young child.

perfect. This habit of practicing something until it was as near to perfection
as possible became routine for me the rest of my life. This has been especially
true for activities for which I have had a passion—such as flying airplanes and
playing golf.

OUR NEIGHBORHOOD

In Minneapolis, we had very little segregation. We were not segregated by
neighborhoods or by schools. As a matter of fact, the only time that we really
experienced segregation was in the big hotels and in a few very nice restau-
rants—places we couldn't afford to go to anyway. So, in reality, segregation for
me was a pretty minor thing.

The neighborhood Bubba and I grew up in was not merely integrated, it
was quite ethnically diverse. A Swedish family lived right next door to us and
right behind them were two Mexican families. My friend Emanuel's mother
worked in a kitchen with a dirt floor making tortillas on what looked like an
open fire but was actually a small furnace. She made tortillas all day. Emanuel

and I would grab peppers and wrap tortillas around them. To this day, I love tortillas.

Across the street was a Polish family and on the corner was a Jewish family. On the Jewish Sabbath Day, the family would ask the kids in the neighborhood to do tasks, like lighting a jet burner, because they were not allowed to perform labor on the Sabbath.

Bubba's memories of Bradford Avenue also explain why ethnicity had little relevance to those who lived there. In one house near our family home, there was a duplex with a Hungarian family upstairs. The father was a tailor and as Bubba once shared, "Of course, he dressed very well. Everybody else wore the blue-collar stuff. Downstairs was a Jewish family from Poland. Families from the Ukraine inhabited two other houses nearby. Another home housed a Scandinavian family. Yet another nearby building was a house of ill repute. Across the street was a big apartment building. Most of the people living there were guys from the old country who were working to get enough money to bring their families back here."

In fact, as he reflected on those days, Bubba shared, "We may have been a bit better off than most of the other families in our neighborhood. We had a furnace in our house, while most others had coal stoves that required bringing in coal and wood and taking the ashes out. We were all poor and unsophisticated, and we were learning together. We were no threat to each other. We weren't going to steal anything because there wasn't anything to steal. In fact, we didn't have any keys to the house."

Bubba went on to clarify that skin color had no meaning in their family and community. He said: "You didn't use the 'N' word [nigger] or the 'B' word [black]. One was as bad as the other. In the community, if we called anyone who was a half a shade darker than we a *black*, it was a fight. Labels still bother me. Today I have grandkids, two who are Chinese. I don't think of them as part of an ethnic group. They are part of the family."

Our family was the only African Americans living on the block. Others lived in a six-block area of north Minneapolis and a significant series of blocks in south Minneapolis. According to a documentary in DVD format, *The Heart of Bassett Place*, the African American population in Minneapolis was 4,000 in the 1920 census.[3] The overall population of Minneapolis in 1920 was 308,582.[4] That means that African Americans made up only a little over 1 percent of the Minneapolis population.

Migrants from the South such as my parents prospered in the North for a variety of reasons. Journalist Isabel Wilkerson writes:

According to a growing body of research, the migrants were, it turns out, better educated than those they left behind in the South and, on the whole, had nearly as many years of schooling as those they encountered in the North. Compared to the northern blacks already there, the migrants were more likely to be married and remain married, more likely to raise their children in two-parent households, and more likely to be employed. The migrants, as a group, managed to earn higher incomes than northern-born blacks even though they were relegated to the lowest-paying positions. They were less likely to be on welfare than the blacks they encountered in the North, partly because they had come so far, had experienced such hard times, and were willing to work longer hours or second jobs in positions that few northern blacks, or hardly anyone else for that matter, wanted.[5]

That characterization fits my parents fairly accurately.

DAILY LIFE

During the time I was growing up, many families shared intergenerational homes, and that was true of us as well. We lived on Bradford with our grandparents, Tina Heath and her second husband, James Lassley, who lived downstairs, while my immediate family lived upstairs. Grandpa Lassley carried a pocketful of pencils to try to impress others, but he couldn't read or write. He did, however, own a 1929 Model T Ford, which no one else on the block could afford. He worked at Ford Motor Company and all its employees could buy cars at a much-reduced rate and pay for them by having a small amount taken out of each paycheck.

In those days, there was virtually no money for toys, so children played outside all day. I can remember some winter days ice skating from early morning until dusk.

As children, we moved from one house to the next. Bubba recalled being able to see five of the houses we had previously lived in from our home at 605 Olson Boulevard, the last one we lived in before Bubba and I went into the service. Bubba remarked, with some humor: "We didn't move far, but we moved often. It might be said that we invented urban renewal." We probably moved each time that our parents could find a cheaper place to rent. The houses were all old and they had rodents and bed bugs ("trained" bed bugs, Bubba would jokingly say, that would go across the ceiling and drop in the bed). One of

Bubba's favorite memories of living in one of these homes was the time that he and Ma chased a rat out of the house when I was only a baby.

The house on Olson was a thirteen-room mansion that had been owned by a doctor. The mansion had been located in what had been a wealthier neighborhood of Minneapolis in earlier years (when Olson was known as 6th Avenue). There were two fireplaces and a furnace with steam heat. Bubba and I slept in what had been the maid's room. Our family initially rented this home from a Jewish man, who later offered Ma the opportunity to buy it. Bubba once remarked that buying a home was "light-years away from any family in the area. Renting was a way of life." Yet this was the house that Ma bought.

As a family, we were not well to do, but we were typical of the neighborhood. We were fortunate that Dad virtually always had work. Only once, during the middle of the Depression, was he laid off.

For the first few years of our schooling, Bubba and I attended Blaine School, the closest school to our home on Bradford. We lived on the fringe of the black community, but we were definitely a minority among the white children at Blaine. As we recalled it, we were never made to feel or actually felt different from the other children.

More than anything else at that time, I wanted my own bicycle. But that was never to be, because as was common among minority families, clothes were a higher priority. Bubba remarked that when minorities came in, the salesmen knew: "They usually went top shelf." Each year at Easter Ma would buy each of us boys an outfit at Rothchild's, a well-known department store in Minneapolis. The type of clothing might vary, but the clothing itself was always "first class."

Every Christmas each of us would receive new boots (hopefully with a knife pocket at the top), a pair of corduroy pants, one shirt, and a sweater or jacket if last year's jacket had worn out. We also got two pieces of fruit, either apples or oranges. Ma always went first class at Christmas when it came to clothing, but she would never purchase toys on her slim budget.

Our diet was typical of African Americans of that time. From the days of slavery and beyond, black people had always been given the waste of the animal. Dishes were full of that which was fat and tasty, but often not healthy. This led to so many African Americans being overweight and diabetic. Throughout my adult life I've watched my weight carefully, as I have seen the price others have paid for an unhealthy diet.

Bubba and I were raised Seventh-Day Adventists. Our parents had become members when we were children. Church was on Saturday, and Ma insisted that both of us attend. The church followed the Old Testament food laws. Pork was never allowed in our house. I can still hear my mom say: "Swine ye shall not touch." Seafood that crawled on the bottom (that did not have scales) was not allowed. I also never ate catfish, both because of my home life and because I saw raw sewage dumped into the Mississippi River in Minneapolis. The largest fish were close to the dump sites. No one, to this day, has ever been able to talk me into eating catfish, even those raised on freshwater farms.

I was also glad we didn't eat pork because one dish that was common was chitterlings (the intestines of hogs). The odor of chitlins being cooked could be smelled two blocks away. The idea of eating a pig's intestines was disgusting then and remains so for me now. Even though the insides of the hog were washed many times over, I still believed that it was impossible to get all of the fecal matter out of the "wrinkles," as they were sometimes called.

Being five years older, Bubba never chose to spend time with me. At Bubba's memorial service in 2012, I recalled a specific time in our childhood with fondness and told the crowd gathered to celebrate Bubba's life: "There were times when Mom would tell Bubba, 'You have to take your brother with you.' This was bad news, like mixing oil with water, and Bubba would respond with the exact same words each time: 'Mom, do I have to drag him along?' And Mom's response was always the same: 'If you want to go, you have to take your brother.' It was always the same, like a broken record! So off we would go. Now you must understand that I had a special position that I had to maintain with respect to my brother. It was six paces behind and slightly to the right. This made it easier for Bubba to see me. Of course, Bubba would complain the entire time with the exact same threat, 'Come on, Harold, keep up, or I'll take you home!'" (I was thinking, "Keep this up and one of these days—pow!").

One of the most embarrassing moments of our early life occurred when I was just beginning kindergarten. Bubba was in the fifth grade, and he often took me to school. One day Mom really blew it by giving me one of her homemade laxatives. (Homemade dynamite might better describe it.) One can easily guess what happened. I had this horrible accident, and it was ugly! Bubba was called out of class to take me home. I assumed my normal position, six paces back and to the right. Bubba screamed: "Don't get too close to me!" So I backed up about ten paces to the right, crying all the way home. I even felt a little sorry for Bubba for having to take on that task. At the same time, I felt a little payback pleasure for all the difficult times he had given me.

As we grew older, we did not spend time together. I was delighted when Bubba left for the war. Shortly after the war began, in the spring of 1942,

Bubba was drafted into the service. As Bubba went marching off to war, I went marching straight to his closet and claimed all of his clothes. Bubba had some sharp clothes. I was the best-dressed guy at the high school prom in June 1942!

Bubba and I did not communicate a single word to each other for almost three years during the early part of the war. This was to change drastically in 1945, when we saw each other for the first time after that long absence and became best friends, which I recount later in "The War Years."

THE PHYLLIS WHEATLEY COMMUNITY CENTER

The center of life for the community and for Bubba and me was the Phyllis Wheatley Community Center. In the early twentieth century, "settlement houses," or community centers, had become a worldwide movement. They were typically found in urban areas across America. Social workers and volunteers would move into blighted neighborhoods to help uplift the poor and disenfranchised, and to "Americanize" the flood of immigrants arriving in large numbers.[6]

The Phyllis Wheatley House was the first agency in the Twin Cities to focus on the needs of the African American community. It was named in memory of the eighteenth-century enslaved woman who became the first African American woman to publish a book of poetry.

The Wheatley, as it was affectionately called, opened in October 1924, shortly after my birth. A well-educated black woman from Dayton, Ohio, W. Gertrude Brown, became the first head resident. Brown had graduated from Columbia University and had studied at the University of Chicago. She looked at our neighborhood and wondered how she would sell the idea of a community center—not only to the immediate community, but to the entire city of Minneapolis.

Bubba described some of the needs for the Center: "There were domestic workers coming into town through the railway stations, and hustlers would try to pick them up and take them to seedy hotels. She [Brown] thought they could solve this problem by having this community center where these young women could go until they could find themselves a place to stay. As it turns out, it became the harbor for everything."

Bubba identified another disenfranchised group: "The University of Minnesota would not allow minority students to live on campus in the dormitories. If the guys who came to the university didn't know someone there or some minority family didn't accept them, they came as roomers to Wheatley. Some of them were football players." Bubba further elaborated: "The house also furnished rooms free to minority graduate students as long as they each took responsibility for one of the house's clubs. . . . At Phyllis Wheatley, people were hired on the basis of whether they could do the job or not, not because of their color." Furthermore, "that graduate student group provided us with role models who were much more sophisticated than we were and who had much, much more experience academically than we did."

Bubba remarked that he and I went to the Wheatley House when it was a smaller place initially, but it "became the best community center anywhere in the country at the time." He stressed that it was for "Everybody. The community. The neighborhood. It wasn't for minorities or just for women." In a poignant reflection on Miss Brown, Bubba said that the Center "was for anyone who lived within the sound of her voice."

Miss Brown was passionate about selling the Center. She made a habit of going to every house in the neighborhood and telling the families what this place was supposed to be about. It was the forerunner of the NAACP; the Urban League started there. She had other programs like Head Start and a nursery school. There was a health clinic and a dentist there. Drama and cooking classes were offered. The sports program became the best in the city. The Center also had a camp for recreation. The name of Wheatley was not only known in the neighborhood, it was known in the city and the state. Miss Brown promoted the Wheatley Community Center to everybody.

The role that Miss Brown and the settlement house played in our lives cannot be understated. It was a place of safety and comfort. As Bubba shared, "The worst punishment that you could get was to be banished from the Wheatley House. It was a way of life." It was a home away from home. It was also a place where we learned discipline and respect. When we reached the door, we'd better wipe our feet, we'd better take our hats off, and when we saw Miss Brown, we'd better greet her appropriately or she was right down on us.

Very near the Wheatley House there was about a five-and-a-half-block area that contained a skating pond, tennis courts, horseshoe pits, two outside restrooms, a bandstand, and both football and baseball fields. There was also a volleyball court, swing sets, and teeter-totters. Both Bubba and I remembered hours of skating and other outdoor activities that filled our lives in those years.

A friend of ours, during a speech given many years later, described the Wheatley House as follows:

In 1929, the new Wheatley House opened and became the most profound influence on Minneapolis blacks for the next three decades. Phyllis Wheatley provided summer camp each year, giving low-income families the opportunity to get away from the city. Our greatest exposure to black professionals came about due to discrimination in housing. Students attending the University of Minnesota, and entertainers like Marian Anderson, Paul Robeson and Bill "Bojangles" Robinson were obliged to stay at the Phyllis Wheatley House. We were inspired by the success of these individuals.[7]

3

MY LOVE AFFAIR WITH A PLANE

AFTER OUR FAMILY MOVED INTO OUR HOME on Olson Boulevard, my life took a turn that would be significant in my discovery of airplanes and my goal of becoming a military pilot.

My mother, like so many others, saw abilities in her son that were not necessarily apparent to others. She saw in me the potential to be a pianist and started me on piano lessons when I was eight. These lessons continued until I was about eleven when I started to have a love affair with an airplane. I announced to Ma that I no longer wanted to take piano lessons because I had decided to become a pilot.

This was during the Depression so airplanes were still quite new. Even though none of us could afford to fly in one, everyone in my neighborhood would stop and stare up in amazement when a little yellow Piper Cub, going about sixty miles an hour, would fly over our houses. Of course, Ma immediately objected to the idea of my flying. She assumed that this was nothing more than a young child's fantasy. It took a few months of refusing to practice my piano for my mother to give up on the idea of my becoming a pianist. She finally resigned herself to the fact that it was not to be.

I began to read everything I could find about flying. I came across a book in the local library entitled *The Life of an Army Air Corps Cadet: Randolph Field, West Point of the Air.* It told the story of a cadet at Randolph Field in Texas. I spent days at the library reading and rereading this book until I almost had it committed to memory. Some of my friends began to tease me by calling me

"Lindbergh." Some even said: "Hey, Lindbergh, they won't even let you wash those planes, much less fly one."

During my youth I almost always had a job and I saved my money. I started by delivering papers when I was twelve years old. I was one of a few boys who delivered the black weekly newspapers. There were several of them. The most prominent were the *Chicago Defender*, the *Pittsburgh Courier*, the *Kansas City Call*, and the *Cleveland Call and Post*. The paper cost ten cents and we received two cents for each paper we sold. This was also the year I began building model airplanes, small balsam wood models that were propelled by the use of rubber bands that turned their propellers. My paper route supplied sufficient funds to cover the cost of my new hobby.

Another factor influencing my love of flying was a popular movie, *The Dawn Patrol*, released in 1938. Starring Errol Flynn and David Niven, the movie took a deeply romantic perspective on wartime flying. It portrayed two fighter pilots flying dangerous missions during World War I. Their courage and chivalry in the air sparked an even deeper passion in me about becoming a fighter pilot, an interest that never faltered as the years went on.

In the summer of 1941 when I was sixteen, I went to work at Abe Roseler's Drug Store as a delivery boy. I eventually became a soda jerk, serving ice cream and malts to local customers. I worked twenty hours per week for twenty-five cents per hour. When I had saved thirty-five dollars from my meager five dollars per week salary, I talked my Uncle Cozell into taking me out to Wold–Chamberlain Field (now the Minneapolis–St. Paul International Airport), where I signed up for flying lessons at seven dollars per lesson. My lessons were in a yellow Piper Cub J-3, a cheap and popular little tail dragger that is still flown today. In it I learned the basics of air flight. I had hoped that by the time I had spent the first thirty-five dollars for five lessons that I would have saved additional money for more lessons. However, it didn't work out that way, so after taking just five lessons, I was forced to quit, never completing the program.

Of course, when Ma discovered that I had spent my hard-earned money on flying lessons, she was furious. But Dad told her: "He has to earn the money, so he can spend it any way he chooses." The flying lessons convinced me more than ever that becoming a military pilot would be my goal in life.

I attended North High in Minneapolis, a large school of almost 3,000 students, with a preponderance of those students being Jewish. As I looked back in later years at my 1942 yearbook, I saw very few black faces, even though the school abutted the area where many black and other minorities lived. There were far more black kids who could have gone on to high school, yet in those days many of the minorities dropped out. Some joined the Civilian Conservation Corps (CCC), a public relief program created by the Roosevelt Administration to employ youth for the preservation of natural resources. In fact, the CCC had appealed to me, but when I asked Dad about joining, he just looked at me—he didn't even open his mouth to reply. I got the message loud and clear.

One of my black classmates, Oscar Pettiford, however, went on to become one of the most recorded bass-playing bandleaders/composers in jazz. His family, a total of nine, lived on the north side of Minneapolis. The entire family made up a band. His father played drums, his mother played piano, one sister also played the piano, and a younger brother played trumpet. Oscar played a bass fiddle. He played with many of the jazz artists of the day, including Coleman Hawkins, Dizzy Gillespie, Duke Ellington, Charles Mingus, and Miles Davis to name a few. Oscar left the United States and moved to Europe, where he continued to make a name for himself. I was able to make contact with him around 1959 while I was doing short-term Alert Duty for the Strategic Air Command in England. We agreed that the next time I came to Europe, he would show me Europe like I had never seen it before. Unfortunately, I missed that opportunity. He died at thirty-seven years of age in 1960.

Graduation from High School

In June 1942, when I was only seventeen, I graduated from high school. Figure 6 is my graduation photo.

Several of my friends, one other of whom was black, also yearned to be pilots. Figure 7 is our picture in the 1942 North High yearbook with a caption that read: "Keep 'em Flying." To my knowledge, none of the others went to flight training.

During the summer of 1942, I had two important experiences: First, I took the exam to get into Tuskegee Army Flying School, and second, I enrolled in the National Youth Administration Program, which was designed to help young people get jobs.

In the National Youth Administration Program, there was a variety of vocational training options available, and I, of course, enrolled in the aviation program: Power Plant and Air Frame. During the mornings, we learned about the engine (Power Plant), and in the afternoon, we actually built two gliders (Air Frame). A friend and I were assigned the rudder assembly. We built it

Figure 6. My graduation photo, 1942.

Figure 7. Yearbook photo of the Aviation Club. I am the third from the left.

and then carefully sanded it to make sure that it was absolutely perfect. Near the end of the four months of training, we finished building the glider. The next step was to get our glider out to an open area to determine if it would actually fly. The glider was attached to a truck that pulled the glider in tow as it sped away. On its first flight, the glider was released from the truck and flew a short distance before settling back down to earth. It flew! On its next flight, an airplane was used to tow the glider up to an altitude of over 1,000 feet before it was released. It then flew almost thirty minutes before eventually landing. We reveled in our success.

While I was pursuing my interest in flying, I was aware of the growing involvement of the United States in World War II; however, I was not propelled into flying for this reason. I was simply interested in flight training and knew that the easiest way to learn how to fly and to get good training was in the military. The fact that the war was going on was somewhat incidental to the whole idea of flying. War or no war, for me it was learning how to fly that was important. As a matter of fact, the war was so far away—it was way over there—that it didn't impact my decision at all.

I had never doubted that by the time I graduated from high school, the issue of letting black men fly would be resolved. Nonetheless, I was keenly aware in my teen years that there were very few black pilots. During my high school years, many of my friends told me that I wouldn't be able to get into the military, but my response was always: "By the time I'm ready, all the problems will be solved and I'll walk right in." I never doubted that I would be accepted into the military; my confidence served me well.

THE BLACK PRESS AND OTHER SUPPORTERS OF BLACK MEN'S RIGHT TO FIGHT

At the end of the 1920s and well into the 1930s, it was simply assumed that black men had no place in an airplane. They should stick to more menial occupations. Benjamin O. Davis Jr., who would become the legendary leader of the Tuskegee Airmen, wrote in his autobiography that in 1929 when he was just seventeen: "I still wanted to fly airplanes, but the harsh reality was that there was no way for a black man to become a professional pilot. The United States then offered few career opportunities of any kind to black people. Blacks took many jobs that whites did not want: redcaps in railroad stations, waiters, Pullman porters, dishwashers, street cleaners, garbage handlers, elevator operators, car washers. If educationally qualified, they could become doctors, lawyers, ministers, businessmen, and teachers, but only where there was little or no mixing with whites."[1]

The issue of blacks being able to fly became the center of a major debate in the late 1930s. I followed the arguments. The debate centered on the complexity of flying machines and the belief that black men were just not intelligent enough to fly something so mechanically complex. I can remember reading that *Pittsburgh Courier* every week. We lived in a segregated society by law and by tradition, so this discussion was a challenge to the general thinking of the time. The *Courier* began publishing articles about the unfair position being taken by the military power structure in its staunch refusal to train black pilots. This position violated the general government policy of "separate but equal."

The general command of the military stuck to its position of "no black pilots" based on a position paper, "The Employment of Negro Man Power in War," prepared by the Army War College in November 1925, seven years after World War I. The report undertook the evaluation of the fitness of black soldiers for service in a future war. It concluded that the American Negro, on the evolutionary scale, "has not progressed as far as the other sub-species of the human family. . . . His mental inferiority and inherent weaknesses of character are factors that must be considered with great care in the preparation of any plan for his employment in war." In essence, Negroes were cowards, were inferior, completely incapable of higher learning, and lazy. The report even detailed that the size of the Negro cranial cavity as "smaller than the white."[2]

The report was a "classic example of the pseudoscience that both characterized and solidified American whites' perceptions of blacks in the interwar years. Narrowly focused on the performance of the black officers and soldiers of the 92nd Infantry Division in the 1918 Meuse–Argonne offensive, it provided ample justification for the War Department to apply racist policies much more broadly throughout the armed services."[3] I later studied mathematics in some depth through my college training, and had even taught statistics. The report was not only cruel; it was flawed. The sample included men who were illiterate and could not even sign their name beyond a simple "X." These men clearly could not have flown an airplane. The report made generalizations about all black men based on a flawed sample of these few.

The general attitude expressed in the report was nothing new to me. People had used derogatory words about us all my life. But this was different. The military establishment was using this report as evidence to keep us from participating in flight training.

Some far-thinking congressmen concluded in 1939 that it would be wise to have a large pool of pilots from which the Army Air Corps could draw flying trainees, especially if the country went to war. In that year, the Congress established a new program called the Civilian Pilot Training (CPT) program.[4] Anyone who completed the CPT program and had achieved "pilot" status needed only to complete the more advanced training required to be a military pilot. Thus the forty weeks it would normally take to fully train a pilot would be cut in half to only twenty weeks by using CPT graduates. The program would be established in colleges all around the country. In fact, "By the end of 1939, nearly ten thousand students were enrolled in CPT programs at 437 colleges and seventy vocational institutions throughout the country."[5]

Due to effective lobbying, the CPT program was extended to include six predominantly black colleges.[6] Up until this point, blacks had been systematically barred from pursuing a career in aviation. "A 1940 Bureau of Census publication listed exactly 124 licensed Negro pilots in the entire United States . . . only seven of whom held commercial pilot ratings."[7]

It was thought at the time by the black community that the inclusion of six black colleges in the CPT program would lead to including blacks for participation in the Army Air Corps Flight Training Program. It soon became clear that that would not immediately happen. Even though there were many successful black graduates of CPT programs, the myth that black trainees could not learn to fly still persisted. The military power structure indicated that learning to fly a relatively simple "Piper Cub" trainer, such as those used in the CPT program, did not prove that blacks could learn to fly a more complicated fighter plane and use it as a fighting weapon.

The whole matter of training Negroes was a political hot potato. There were generals saying that blacks were untrainable—that it just wouldn't work. They could make up any number of reasons to deny us admission. For example, they might ask: "Well, what if you have to make a forced landing at a base other than your home [meaning black] base? There's no way a black pilot could order a white mechanic to repair his airplane." They had 10,000 reasons and more for denying us the right to fly.

The black weekly papers, led by the *Pittsburgh Courier*; the NAACP, led by Walter White; A. Philip Randolph, head of the Brotherhood of Sleeping Car Porters, the most powerful black labor union in America at the time; and numerous presidents of historically black colleges and universities began a crusade to open military flight opportunities to black Americans.[8]

In 1940, our country had an election coming up. President Roosevelt was running for his third term. Wendell Willkie was the Republican candidate for president. Roosevelt thought he was assured of the black vote. But Willkie "was working hard to entice black voters back to his party."[9] Roosevelt was a smart politician, however, and would not let Willkie steal the black vote from him. In October 1940, "President Franklin D. Roosevelt's administration announced that blacks would be trained as military pilots in the Army Air Corps. The War Department promoted Benjamin O. Davis Sr. to be the first black general in the U.S. Army and Judge William H. Hastie, the first black federal judge, as a civilian advisor to Secretary of War Henry L. Stimson."[10]

In January 1941, "The War Department announced plans to create a 'Negro pursuit squadron,' whose pilots would be trained at Tuskegee, Alabama."[11] It was understood from the outset that the Negroes would be trained on a segregated base and in a segregated unit. In 1941, another significant event occurred at Tuskegee Institute in Alabama. Eleanor Roosevelt, wife of the President, was attending a board meeting of the Julius Rosenwald Fund on the campus of Tuskegee Institute.[12] While at this meeting, she decided to visit the CPT program at Kennedy Field to see how it was going. When Mrs. Roosevelt arrived at the airfield, she met Chief Alfred C. Anderson, head flight instructor of the program. Anderson was a pioneer in black aviation and "was the first black pilot to earn a commercial transport pilot's license in 1932."[13] Mrs. Roosevelt caused quite a stir by requesting that Anderson take her up for a ride. The story of her flight became national news and brought a spotlight to the issue of black men in the air.

No one will ever know how influential this event was, but many of us Tuskegee Airmen believed that Eleanor was the conscience of the President. We could only speculate that there was a conversation in which Eleanor prompted the President to continue his support of the black airmen. Some even believed that she was the catalyst for the creation of the Tuskegee program itself, although the War Department had created the program five months before her storied flight with Chief Anderson.

My earlier belief that the situation for blacks as pilots would resolve itself had come to pass. I was sixteen years old when the President made his announcement, and I turned seventeen that following August. The way had been paved by those with the courage to stand up to the military's resistance to allowing black men to fly.

The Tuskegee Experiment Takes Flight

"In March of 1941 the AAC [Army Air Corps] would begin accepting applications from prospective aviation cadets for a proposed all-black pursuit squadron."[14] The squadron would only "require about three dozen pilots."[15] The chance of being selected for flight training was extremely limited from the outset.

The first class of aviation cadets entered Preflight Training in July 1941, and the first phase of military flight training began in August 1941. It consisted of thirteen trainees.[16] They were what many, at that time, would consider the "elite of black America; they were all college students or graduates, at a time when fewer than 2 percent of African American adults held college diplomas."[17] One of the trainees, Benjamin O. Davis Jr., son of the black man who had been named a brigadier general the prior year, was a West Point graduate. These men led the way for other young black men, like me, who did not have college degrees, but who would follow in their footsteps in the next few years. Five of the thirteen successfully completed the flight program in March 1942, while eight were "washed out" or cut from the program.[18] Other classes began to graduate every five weeks.

I can say with great satisfaction that after this beginning, our group went on to serve outstandingly in North Africa and Sicily as the first black fighter squadron. Later, the 332nd Fighter Group, the Red Tail fighter pilots, served with distinction in the Fifteenth Air Force stationed in Italy, escorting bombers as they flew into enemy territory.

4

BUBBA'S EXPERIENCE IN THE MILITARY

Bubba was born on September 7, 1919, and graduated from high school in 1937.

Bubba's experience in the military, which may not have been typical of all African Americans, was still much closer to that of other black men during World War II than mine. His story, in stark contrast to mine, illustrates what ultimately drew us back together as brothers and friends.

It may not be commonly known that more than a million black soldiers were in uniform during World War II.[1] In contrast, the Tuskegee Airmen, pilots and support staff, were made up of nearly 1,000 pilots and about 14,000 support personnel.[2] That means that the Tuskegee Airmen represented only about 1.5 percent of all those black men in service to their country.

After high school, Bubba went to California to see the world and to find work. In 1942, Dad called Bubba and told him to get home because draft letters were being sent to the house. At that time, every able-bodied man had to sign up for the draft. The United States was now at war, and Bubba was the perfect age to be drafted. In fact, he was drafted in June 1942 (when I was getting ready to graduate from high school).

The Needs of the Military Came First

Like me, Bubba initially had a great interest in flying and later recalled: "I wanted to fly. I just felt that I would rather be flying. You didn't know much about military flying, but you just knew that you wanted to fly. It was just

Figure 8. Bubba's high school graduation photo.

something that we all got into." The needs of the military, however, took precedence over Bubba's interest in going into flight training. He shared: "The military was planning the invasion of North Africa and they needed 'donkey troops.' Who did they put in the donkey troops? Minorities. Except for where Harold was, the minorities were the service troops. After all, we weren't smart enough to fly planes or shoot rifles." As Bubba wrote in his later years, the military needed service troops "to act as stevedores to move all supplies and ammunition to the soldiers on the front lines. You didn't have to be anything but warm and upright to be a stevedore."

Rick Atkinson, winner of the Pulitzer Prize, confirmed Bubba's observation in Volume II of his *Liberation Trilogy*: "In the summer of 1943, only 17 percent of black soldiers were high school graduates, compared with 41 percent of whites. . . . Consequently, blacks were shunted into quartermaster companies for duty as truck drivers, bakers, launderers, laborers, and the like.

By January 1944, 755,000 blacks wore Army uniforms—they made up 8.5 percent of the force—but only two in ten served in combat units compared to four in ten whites."[3]

In Bubba's case, he and his friend, Earl Miller, who was drafted at the same time, were well educated. They had graduated from North High School in Minneapolis and already had some college education. The military needed men who could organize and run the donkey or service troops. As Bubba once remarked: "When they were forming these service troops, they needed guys who could read and write to make these things work. You can't have a total complement of donkeys. You got to have a donkey master."

The minorities from the South were mostly uneducated and illiterate so the Army had to find people who were more sophisticated to handle the administrative requirements of the outfit. Being fairly well educated, Bubba was not typical of the other blacks in his outfit. "Basically, I was segregated inside a segregated outfit. I had been to college; only six of us had. I could type, but very few others could. And then I was the color I am (light skinned). I just didn't fit anywhere. I was from Minnesota, but I might as well have been from Mars."

Bubba had been told when he applied for flight training that he would be called to be a Tuskegee guy when there was an opening. He remembered: "Boy, I was waiting for that call." He waited and nothing happened. Before he left the States, he decided to apply for a leadership role through the Officer Candidate School (OCS); he knew his ability should qualify him to get in very easily.

Bubba later wrote: "I was top dog in the underclass, but I knew I couldn't get any higher than that underclass in the military. That Officer Candidate School situation brought it home to me. The Army was short of officers, so they were trying to get anyone with any leadership ability into OCS. Of course, there weren't too many officers of color at that time."

In January 1944, the reality of the leadership situation for black men was stark: "The U.S. Army had 633,000 officers, of whom only 4,500 were black. The U.S. Navy was worse, with 82,000 black enlisted sailors and no black officers; the Marine Corps, which had rejected all black enlistments until President Roosevelt intervened, would not commission its first black officer until several months after the war ended."[4]

Attitudes about the leadership capabilities of black men from the War College's 1925 study, "Employment of Negro Man Power in War," remained pervasive in the 1940s and sabotaged Bubba's interest in becoming an officer. That study repeatedly states: "The Negro, particularly the officer, failed in the

World War."[5] The War College study makes clear that blacks were not believed to be capable of leadership of their own troops, much less the leadership of white troops.

An August 5, 1942, Office of War Information report, "White Attitudes Toward Negroes," indicated that most of those surveyed did not believe that Negroes were as intelligent as whites.[6] In the South in particular, the belief was that Negroes should be led by white officers, and if Negro officers were to be employed, they should be minor officers, who had close contact with the Negro troops. The top officers should be white.[7]

Bubba's situation was further complicated by the quality of the white officers that the minority troops generally received to lead them. When they formed companies, the minorities, as Bubba recalled, "got the blond guys [Caucasians] who were misfits; they were stuck leading minority outfits and they knew why they were in this minority outfit."

Bubba singled out his company commander in particular. This man had flunked OCS (Officer Candidate School) three times. "Before the war he had been a parts runner in a lumber yard in Lameda, Texas, and belonged to the National Guard. He chewed tobacco and needed a bath all the time. Ugh. But he was my boss. And that bastard stood over me." Bubba's desire for a leadership position in the army was simply discounted by that company commander. Bubba had given his Officer Candidate School (OCS) application papers to him. Much to his chagrin, Bubba found out that the captain had not even submitted his paperwork. "Now what do I say to this guy? You dumb SOB. You didn't send it in."

Bubba even filled out another form to expedite the process and finally volunteered for the infantry; by that time a minority infantry, the 366th, had gone overseas. "That's how pissed off I was at the whole system. The blond-haired officers were worried that if I were to leave the organization, it would bring down the effectiveness of the place."

When Bubba confronted the captain, the captain responded: "'I understand that you want to go into the infantry.' I said 'yes' and he wanted to know why. I didn't want to tell him that he was an asshole, but he knew that I thought that. He looked at me and said, 'You know, Sergeant, your request is denied. Dying is too good for you.'"

As time went on, Bubba was told that his orders from the Air Corps were going to go through, but this group of men "still wanted me to lead the unintelligent guys—the illiterate guys—that couldn't read or write. . . . They didn't know anything about keeping records and making things work properly. They weren't going to let me go out of that outfit because I was doing things the way they should be done."

Bubba finally got his okay to go into the Air Corps in June 1943. He had been overseas since October 1942; the invasion of North Africa was in November 1942. By the time he heard from the Tuskegee project, he knew what war was about. He also realized the danger if he did not pass flight training: "The problem was that if you washed out, you didn't go back to your original unit; instead you went to the infantry, because they needed bodies there. So I said no thanks to the Tuskegee group." The percentage of guys that washed out was well over 50 percent in the early years.

Bubba remained a staff sergeant for the remaining time he was in the military. He went into the military in June 1942, made staff sergeant in December 1942, and was still a staff sergeant in September 1946 when he was discharged.

MILITARY LIFE ON THE GROUND

Bubba's experience on the ground in the army was very different from mine in the air. It was simply something that, as an airman, I could not relate to. The men on the ground, as Bubba recalled, were always in a precarious position. Bubba's whole battalion supplied ammunition to the front. "Our guys would take our tanks with their small guns, or pea shooters, as we called them, and get them ready for battle. The Germans were in the mounds up there, and in fifteen minutes, they appeared with tanks with much bigger guns. The British were there with us and they saved our butts. Everybody is a part of the battle depending upon what the hell happens around you."

When asked if he was ever in danger, he indicated: "Yes. If you are in the theatre of combat, you are always in danger. If the guys in front that you are supplying with stuff don't hold their position, you become the front. The chances of being killed in that war were tremendous. You had the best soldiers in the war, the Germans, fighting you. You also had a German Air Force that was pretty good at that time."

Bubba and the others who went to war together had very little training. "We were an ordnance company, so we handled all of the ammunition that the American troops used in North Africa. You would think that they would have taught us something about what we were handling, but we had never even seen any of it until we got on the ship going to the invasion of North Africa. They didn't care about us at all. We were at the bottom of the barrel. Just statistics. Just bodies, I guess."

Both Bubba and I had encounters with the German people—some good and some bad, but we both had experiences with Germans that would make it difficult to demonize the entire race for the sins committed by Hitler and those committed to his ideology.

Bubba sometimes talked about his interactions with German POWs. He indicated that there were 30,000 of them in North Africa at one point. He further said: "The German officers all spoke at least one language besides German. The best soldiers in the world, by far. No competition."

In one particular case, he was assigned to speak with a German lieutenant, "a little beady-eyed, blue-eyed, blond guy." Bubba had been selected to speak to this lieutenant based on his limited education in Spanish in high school and in college. The lieutenant was only required to give his name, rank, and serial number. Yet he was cocky enough, even while a prisoner, to tell Bubba: "In six months you guys will be following the horses in Berlin as prisoners." Bubba continued to try to interrogate him, and as he was finally ready to move on, the lieutenant "dug into one of his pockets and pulled out a wallet. From it, he retrieved photos, and he showed me his family. In our broken Spanish, he told me he'd been in the war since 1939 (we were having this discussion in 1943). He told me he was ready for this war to be over so he could go home. It occurred to me that he was thinking about the same damn thing I was thinking about and maybe we weren't so different from each other after all."

Bubba and I, both in the same war, had no contact until February 1945. We had not seen each other for almost three years. That reunion is told later, as part of my experience shortly before I was shot down and became a POW.

------PART II

THE WAR YEARS

I was sitting in seat 28A on Flight 937 en route to a conference on academic programming in the growing movement of two-year technical colleges. We were smoothly cruising at 30,000 feet. The steady drone of the jet engines was quietly reassuring as I stared out at the passing landscape. I was reminded of another time, when I was seated in my P-51 carefully searching the surrounding sky for every aircraft that might be waiting for an opportunity to attack the bomber formation we were assigned to protect. There would be many such missions, and they all began with my dream of becoming a military pilot.

5

I JUST WANTED TO FLY

Since childhood I had wanted to become an aviation cadet and eventually a military fighter pilot. The advent of war made that dream a possibility. I wanted to fly, and I wanted to be a Tuskegee Airman.

In those years, the only group training military fighter pilots was the US Army Air Corps. There was a lot of luck that went into being selected for the program for young black men. There was also a lot of rigor that went into being successful during training and ending up being a fighter pilot.

Initially, the Army Air Corps preferred college graduates for flight training, but over time there were not enough applicants to meet the needs of a nation at war. Consequently, the restrictions became fewer and high school graduates like me could apply. So, during the summer of 1942, at seventeen years of age, I took the physical and mental tests to become a cadet in the Air Corps. I was the only black man taking the mental test in Minneapolis on that summer day. The test measured our general knowledge in a variety of subjects, including math, physics, and English. Mathematics and physics were my favorite subjects in high school, which helped me on the test.

Many of the black men that my brother Bubba and I knew did not take the mental test because they had either dropped out of school or felt they couldn't hack it. Of the 104 young men who sat for the test in Minneapolis on that day, including some freshmen from the University of Minnesota, I scored fifth highest.

After passing the mental test, I was scheduled to take the physical exam. I flunked it! I was underweight for my height. I weighed a quarter pound below the minimum requirement of 128.5 pounds. I was given a week before I could take the retest. The doctor who had weighed me asked me if I liked milkshakes, to which I responded: "I'm a soda jerk. I serve shakes and malts all day." He said: "What I am going to suggest will be easy for you. Drink a chocolate malt with an egg in it, morning and night, for three days before the retest . . . and don't have a BM." On the day of the retest I weighed 128.75 pounds. I passed the test—then ran for the bathroom.

Even though I had passed the exam, my treatment was different from that of the white men who had passed. The whites were sworn into the Army Reserve, and their service time began immediately. Because they were now in the Reserve, they could not be drafted. Black men in the pool, in contrast, could be drafted before being selected for flight school.

My papers were sent to Washington, DC, to be part of a pool from which I might or might not be selected for flight training. The black candidates were part of a quota system that initially required only about three dozen trained pilots to fill out its full complement. As A. Todd Moye notes in *Freedom Flyers*: "The War Department had limited black opportunities in military aviation by creating a single all-black pursuit squadron in 1941 (and three additional squadrons in 1942)."[1]

One characteristic of the military experience for black men who wished to be pilots was the wait. We took the exam and then we waited, and we waited, and waited a little longer. Earlier in the selection process, there were a number of guys who waited six months to a year for their call, and during all of that time they were in jeopardy of being drafted by the army. They were fair game. I was luckier than most; I only had to wait for four months.

THE BEGINNING OF FLIGHT TRAINING

In December 1942, I received my letter to report to Fort Snelling, in St. Paul, Minnesota. At last I had been selected for flight training! I was over the top with excitement. The letter meant something entirely different for my parents. They had been through this process with my brother, who had headed to North Africa within a couple of months after being drafted. They knew that he faced great danger.

I reported to Fort Snelling to voluntarily enlist in the military. My letter indicated that within two to three weeks I would be sent to Biloxi, Mississippi, for additional testing and six weeks of basic training. I had never been in the South, so before I departed, my mother gave me daily lectures on how to behave. She knew that as a Northerner, I had experienced very little overt discrimination and that I was unprepared for what I would experience in the South.

My mom's advice shocked me. It was: "Now when you go south, treat people very respectfully. It's 'yes ma'am' and it's 'no ma'am.' You may even have to step off the curb and onto the street to let white people pass you by, but you do it and don't you open up your mouth."

I responded: "But, Ma, you mean I have to step down onto the street just to let white people pass?"

She spoke sternly: "Listen to me, boy. You have never been in the South, but I have. I know how those people are in the South. You listen to me or you will get yourself into a whole lot of trouble."

I left Minneapolis for the long train trip to Mississippi. Because I was traveling day and night, I was given tickets by the military for the Pullman sleeping cars and for my meals. My journey took me first to Chicago and then on to Nashville. In Nashville, I crossed the Mason–Dixon Line and needed to find my next train among the multiple tracks at the station. I approached a ticket agent and asked which track my train would come in on. The agent politely directed me around the corner to the next window and told me that I would find help there.

To my amazement, the same agent appeared in the window and said: "May I help you?" It all seemed very odd, until I looked up and saw the "Colored" sign above the ticket booth. It finally hit me that this was what my mother had been talking about.

The ticket agent now gave me the number of the track I should be looking for.

I then approached a black conductor and told him: "I have a ticket for a Pullman."

The conductor responded: "First time south, son?"

"Yes, sir."

"Do you see those two cars behind the locomotive? That's where you sit."

I saw only black folks in those cars. I threw my duffel bag in a corner, and I took a seat among them. No sleeping berth for me. All the soot and smoke from the locomotive came through those cars. By the next day, I was filthy. It didn't matter if I was wearing a uniform or not; if I had a black face, I sat behind the locomotive.

The next morning a peddler came through the car selling fruit and snacks. That was what was available. It had been made abundantly clear to me that I was not welcome in the dining car. For black travelers in this era of American history, there was no guarantee that we could even get food during a trip on the railroad. The great dining car was reserved for whites and partitioned off from us by a curtain.

As I arrived in Biloxi, I saw other guys who were arriving from other parts of the country. I was one of approximately six hundred black men who successfully passed the initial test and were selected from the pool to begin preparation for flight school. The group of us who had just arrived was taken to Keesler Field by truck. When we arrived at the Air Corps field for basic training, I was shocked by what I found. We black men were isolated on one side of the field, completely segregated from everyone else. It was a rude awakening. I found myself right down in the bowels of the South, in Biloxi, Mississippi.

After some regular boot training and about halfway through basic, we were retested with the same exam that we had taken initially to determine if we were eligible for flight training. It seemed odd at the time, and we were surprised we had to take the same test again. The white recruits were not required to repeat the test. I would estimate that the retest washed out approximately half, or three hundred, of those blacks who wanted to be airmen.

I was in Biloxi for only six weeks, but I experienced segregation in ways that were new to me. In the theaters in the South, blacks had to sit up in the top section. Among Negroes at the time, this was called "Negro Heaven." I also learned that there were separate drinking fountains for blacks and whites. Even the restrooms were segregated. If we weren't allowed to drink out of the same faucet, we surely weren't allowed to sit on the same stool.

I had one experience that was particularly chilling. We didn't have many opportunities to go into town, but one day we had a leave so I walked into town with Robert Murdic, from Franklin, Tennessee; he graduated from Tuskegee one class behind me. Fortunately, Robert had some acquaintance with how to behave in the South. In the white section of town we walked past an old white man sitting on his porch. He said, "Hey, come over here, you two little nigger boys. I want to talk to you."

I said to Robert, "Did you hear what he just said? Did you hear what he called us?"

Robert said, "Harold, just keep walking, just keep walking. Don't say a word. Don't look back. Pretend you didn't hear him. Keep your damn mouth shut. Keep walking, keep walking."

We walked on until we came to the colored part of town. We were walking on pavement until we came to a railroad track. We went across the track and the difference was stark—dirt road and shanties sitting up on cinder blocks. When Robert saw how shocked I was, he said: "Harold, like I told you, you are in the South now. This is the way it is. The people who live here are poor. They don't have much of nothing."

We stayed for a while and visited a few of the joints but were soon on our way back to the base. We walked a different way, however, to avoid the old man on the porch. My experience with him was a reminder of my ma's warnings about the South.

TUSKEGEE

There had been many reasons why black men were not allowed to become military pilots. One of those was that there was no place for them to train. That changed in 1941 when Tuskegee, Alabama,[2] about 40 miles east of Montgomery, was chosen as the site for the fledgling flight training program. During the early years when the legendary hero B. O. Davis Jr. first came to Tuskegee, it was a difficult place for training. It was a segregated hierarchy, with all white officers running a black base. They followed the same customs as the segregated society outside the base, with the white officers having their own club and eating facilities.

The first class, 42-C, entered the US Army Air Corps in July 1941. The six "who passed the primary phase of flight training at Moton Field began basic flight training at TAAF [Tuskegee Army Air Field] on November 8, 1941, as scheduled, even though the facility was only two-thirds complete. The cadets lived in a hastily constructed tent city, and another cluster of tents served as their Corps of Cadets headquarters, day room, and classroom."[3] "TAAF's commanders faced a nearly impossible administrative task. The commanding officer of any other army airfield the size of TAAF, even in the midst of chaotic wartime expansion, could expect to be responsible for one, perhaps two, phases of pilot training. TAAF, in contrast, housed preflight, basic, and advanced fighter training programs and an artillery liaison pilot training program. Whereas most other bases of its size either taught pilots to fly or trained pilots for combat—an important distinction—in the first two years of its existence TAAF would be responsible for organizing a fighter squadron and sending it directly into combat."[4]

By the time I got to Tuskegee in 1943, most of the difficulties the first classes had faced had been resolved. This was because Colonel Noel Parrish, a new white commander, had taken over and he had a whole different philosophy from early commanders. When Colonel Parrish first arrived at Tuskegee, he was the training officer and, as such, took all of his orders from the base commanders. He wasn't in a position to do anything except follow those orders. As time went on, there were so many complaints about the discriminatory way the base was being run that Colonel Parrish was elevated to base commander and made a full colonel. Nearly all the Tuskegee Airmen were very fond of Colonel Parrish and had a great deal of respect for him because of the dramatic changes he made once he was in command.

There were actually some benefits to being in a segregated Air Corps. As much as I hated segregation, I think that we were probably better off in a segregated unit at the time because there had been so much resistance to allowing minorities to join the Air Corps. Many of us also believed that there were those within the military power structure that were just waiting for us to fail. If we had been integrated, it would have been easy, having two or three of us distributed throughout all of the training units, to wash us out for any reason. We would have been nothing more than just another individual casualty of the difficult training program, but in a segregated unit we knew that some of us would successfully complete the training.

By being segregated, we were also given the best opportunity to showcase our flying skills and our air discipline—something that would not have happened in an integrated unit. As a group of black pilots, we represented all blacks in our country. We had the burden and the opportunity to prove that we could succeed in aerial combat. Being segregated allowed us to prove to the nation that we were worthy of the responsibility with which we had been entrusted.

Furthermore, I had several very good white instructors who clearly had my best interests at heart. There were a few of the guys who felt that they had lousy instructors who gave them a particularly difficult time. But I'll just call it the luck of the draw. I was very fortunate. I had good instructors and I was quite happy being in a segregated unit.

College Training Detachment (CTD)

I began my first educational experience at Tuskegee Institute in the College Training Detachment, a program created for men with no college background. When the military was not getting a sufficient number of men with a college education, it reduced the requirement to a high school diploma, assuming the applicant could pass the intelligence and physical tests.

The other trainees and I lived in dormitories. We were classified as "aviation students." When we finished the four-to-six-month training, we were "aviation cadets" and were officially in the aviation program. The length of time an aviation student studied the curriculum was dependent upon the score that he made in the regular and frequent testing. I stayed in the program for a few days past four months.

The curriculum at Tuskegee was college level and was rigorous. It included coursework in geography, English, history, physics, mathematics, and the current Civil Air Regulations. Physical training was required each day, including calisthenics and marching in formation. We marched everywhere, to and from the mess hall, and to and from classes. The CTD program required homework, study, and testing. I can't recall anyone actually failing the College Training Detachment. As aviation students, we wanted to be aviation cadets in the worst way and were highly motivated. Having gone this far, we did not need anyone outside ourselves to motivate us.

Graduation day from CTD finally arrived. Four months had seemed like an eternity, since it stood in the way of what I had dreamed about since I was a young man—becoming an aviation cadet in the US Army Air Corps. The only visible change was that my cap now had a propeller on it, but wearing that new insignia and being called an aviation cadet meant the world to me.

6

FLIGHT TRAINING
In the Air at Last

FLIGHT TRAINING FOR AVIATION CADETS LASTED approximately forty weeks and was broken into four parts consisting of Preflight, Primary, Basic, and, finally, Advanced Training.

The training was the same at every air base. Each ten-week session was made up of 2 five-week periods. A student was in lower Preflight for the first five weeks and then upper Preflight for the remaining five weeks. Classes graduated every five weeks and were identified by the year and a letter of the alphabet to represent the month, beginning in January. My class was 44-E, which meant that I would graduate in 1944 in the month of May.

On the final day of CTD, we new cadets waited eagerly for our trip to Tuskegee Army Air Field (TAAF), about six miles north of the Tuskegee Institute, where we would begin Preflight Training. The big 6-by-6 army trucks arrived in front of the dormitories on the campus of Tuskegee Institute. At the designated hour, we boarded the trucks with our few belongings. This would be the first time most of us visited TAAF.

When the trucks arrived at our TAAF barracks, home for the next ten weeks, we were surprised to be met by a large group of upperclassmen cadets. As we stood to leave the bus, they shouted: "Okay, you dummies, off the trucks and fall into formation! You will stand at attention, eyes forward, and don't utter a word. You will only speak when given permission. Do you understand?"

We all responded in unison: "YES SIR!"

The upperclassmen continued: "You are lower class, Preflight cadets, the lowest thing on this base! Your new name is 'Dummy.' You will be assigned to an upperclassman, assuming that an upperclassman can find one of you worthy of that honor. Do you understand?"

"Yes sir," we responded.

"Welcome to the life of a Preflight cadet," I thought to myself with some disappointment.

"The good news," I told myself, "is that you are now an aviation cadet. You can hear and see the aircraft flying every day. It's exciting and real, and you know that if you are lucky enough, you, too, will soon be an upperclassman, enjoying all the success of actually flying."

"Welcome to the life of a U.S. Army Air Corps cadet," I thought to myself with renewed optimism.

Preflight almost seemed to be an extension of CTD. We were awakened early in the morning; we dressed, made our beds, and fell out into formation for reveille, when the flag first went up. We then marched to breakfast with our designated group. We marched in formation, sometimes at double time, to all activities.

Our group had a highly regimented schedule of activities, such as calisthenics and classroom studies. We had coursework in aerodynamics, physical sciences, and a course in weather. We also had to learn Morse code. My favorite visits were to the flight line where all the aircraft were parked. It was fun to hang out around the aircraft—to touch them—to feel them—to climb into the cockpit. It was the first time for many of us to actually be around airplanes. Our days were completely filled from morning until retreat was sounded in the evening, when the flag came down. The evening was our time, but a lot of that time was filled with activity with or for our assigned upperclassmen.

Occasionally the upperclassmen found time to haze us. After a full day of flight, they might stop by our barracks, order us out of our bunks, and tell us to fall into formation. The hazing would consist of a variety of physical activities, such as push-ups and squats against the wall. Other times, after they had completed their night flying, the upperclassmen would awaken us, pull the sheets off our beds, knot them, and throw them in the showers. We had to retrieve them, unknot them, and make our bunk so that a coin would bounce off the stretched sheet. Fortunately this wasn't a regular occurrence.

Many popular figures and entertainers stopped by during our time at Tuskegee. Joe Louis and Lena Horne visited while I was there. Duke Ellington and his band stayed for a couple of days. There were big dances to which local girls were invited. After all, we were *pilots*. We were the elite of the elite.

PRIMARY

Preflight was the last phase before actual flying, and all cadets looked forward to its completion. We were then on to Primary. Few of us knew that Primary would wash out a significant percentage of the Class of 44-E.

On the first day we were bussed to Moton Flying Field, a couple of miles from campus. Our class was made up of sixty students. We were met by Director Jackson, Chief Pilot Charles Alfred Anderson, and the group of pilots who would take us through the approximately sixty hours of flying time in the bi-wing PT-17 (Primary Trainer) Stearman. The PT-17 was the first of four planes to be used in our training. The other three were the BT-13 (Basic Trainer), the AT-6 (Advanced Trainer), and the P-40 (Transition to Fighter Aircraft). Our instructors in Primary were all black and came out of the Civilian Pilot Training Program.

The first day was orientation to the Primary Training Program. Each cadet was assigned to an instructor, who introduced him to the airplane, inside and out. The PT-17 was a two-wing aircraft with two open cockpits. Its fuselage was blue and its wings were yellow. It looked something like a World War I plane, but that was where the similarity ended. It was a much more advanced aircraft.

When I met my instructor, Mr. Gilbert A. Cargill, a soft-spoken gentleman from Cleveland, Ohio, I immediately liked what I saw. That was good, because we would spend the next ten weeks together. The next few weeks were crucial to us cadets. It was the period during which our flying skills would need to become sufficiently proficient for our instructor to allow us to fly solo. This was a very big step in our flying career.

Our experience as cadets varied from person to person. During each bus trip back to the campus, there was extensive chatter about how the day had gone. The conversations ranged from very high to very low. It was tough to hear some of my classmates talk about how badly things were going for them and that they were certain they would never solo. I, on the other hand, was delighted by everything that was going on.

Like almost all pilots, I can remember quite vividly what it was like to solo for the first time. I had completed seven and a half hours of dual instruction with Mr. Cargill. I had landed the aircraft and he told me to taxi over to the

Figure 9. PT-17 Stearman. Courtesy of the USAAF.

wind "T," which played a vital role for pilots. The T showed us the direction the wind was blowing as we looked down on it from the sky. The T, sitting on a pivot, would swivel as the wind changed. We did not have runways to land on nor radio communication; we landed on nothing more than a large field that could accommodate several airplanes practicing takeoffs and landings at the same time. It was important to make sure all of the planes were landing in the same, and proper, direction. The wind T allowed this to happen.

I followed Mr. Cargill's instruction and taxied over to the wind T. When we arrived with the engine still running, Mr. Cargill climbed out of the front seat (where the instructor normally sat), and pulled his parachute out. He left me in the backseat (the seat from which the plane normally was flown when we flew alone). He said, "It's yours. Do you think that you can fly this airplane alone, and land it without crashing it and killing yourself?" He then lay down on the ground near the wind T, using his chute as a pillow. "I'll be waiting here for you," he said. I knew then that I was being soloed.

It is difficult to fully describe that first solo flight because so much was going through my head at the time. "My God, I am on my own. Can I really land this plane?" At the same time, I had a strong belief that, "Yes, I can fly this plane and I can land it alone! This has been my goal and I am ready." My first solo flight turned out to be completely uneventful as I flew around the traffic pattern and performed a normal landing.

I taxied back over to the wind T, where Mr. Cargill was waiting. He commented, "Well, you landed it okay. Take it around one more time to make sure you know what you're doing and so I can see that the first landing wasn't just pure luck."

I again took off, flew around the traffic pattern, and made another good landing. I didn't mention it to Mr. Cargill, but it was really the second landing that convinced me I was ready to fly solo, now completely confident in my ability to fly the aircraft. Pilots soloed as early as possible. It wasn't unusual to solo under ten hours. As a cadet began to approach eleven or twelve hours and hadn't soloed, the instructors would begin to look at him suspiciously, since flying solo was the most important test required to become a pilot.

The next major milestone for an aviation cadet was the initial "check ride," which occurred at twenty hours. That was when a different instructor, someone other than your regular instructor, took you up to test the progress you had made. When it was time for my check ride, I was scared to death I might flunk out. I wasn't sure what I would be asked to do, but in retrospect, there were only so many things I could be asked to do with such limited flying experience.

My first check ride was with Chief Anderson, who is perhaps best known for taking the first lady, Eleanor Roosevelt, up on a ride when she visited Tuskegee. My check ride occurred after I had accumulated seventeen and a half hours of flying time and involved nothing more than basic flying skills, including straight and level flight, holding altitude within prescribed limits, making shallow turns in a 30-degree bank while maintaining altitude, and making medium turns at an approximate 45-degree bank. To make the turns, I had to maintain the wings at their proper degree of bank in reference to the horizon. In time, this would become second nature, but this was my first real test of that skill. I also had to demonstrate comparable skills in shallow and medium dives, and climbs. All went well and I passed my twenty-hour check ride.

The next twenty hours of flying included more difficult maneuvers, like simple aerobatics, making abrupt climbing turns in which the aircraft nearly stalls (called chandelles), and flying loops and barrel rolls. I also had to perform steep dives and climbs, figure eights, and in general, demonstrate more precision in all phases of flying. I flew my forty-hour check ride with Mr. Charles R. Foxx, who was known to be a tough instructor. I really sweated this check ride, even more than the first one. Foxx really put me through my paces, but I passed again.

During the final twenty hours of flying in Primary, we cadets practiced every maneuver that the aircraft was capable of safely performing, including a variety of aerobatics such as barrel rolls, slow rolls, loops, snap rolls, and spins. One of our favorites was to see who could make the most turns while spinning the aircraft; we would then brag to our classmates: "I got sixteen turns. How many did you get? Tomorrow I'll break sixteen and get eighteen."

We would sneak up a few extra thousand feet and put it in a spin, spiraling straight down—just let it wind up and spin. We'd look out and watch the world spin around, an exciting view and exciting feeling. When we had enough and were approaching that very hard earth, we would pull out by directing the plane in the opposite direction of the spin. If we were spinning to the right, for example, we would move the stick to the left, causing the left aileron to come up, while simultaneously pressing the left rudder. Then we'd dump the nose and point the aircraft straight down, picking up airspeed. This way we regained complete control of the aircraft, and brought the nose up to level flight. It was no big deal, and we did it over and over.

Aerobatics in the PT-17 were just plain fun. I can recall the first time I did a snap roll on top of a loop. I went up into the loop, and by the time I was on my back, I was pretty close to a stall. I snatched the stick back, full left or full right rudder, and it snapped on me. I let it snap once back to one full roll. Then it continued the roll out of the loop. We loved to do this maneuver. The final check ride came at sixty hours, which I passed without any problems.

During the Primary phase of flying, about a third of the class was washed out by not flying solo or by not showing continuing improvement in flying skills on the twenty-, forty-, and sixty-hour check-rides. Forty of our original class of over sixty cadets completed Primary flight training.

BASIC

We were eager to begin Basic, the next phase of our training. We flew the BT-13 Vultee aircraft, a bigger and more powerful aircraft than the Stearman. It had a single 450 HP engine, a glass canopy, and fixed landing gear. It was affectionately known as the Vultee Vibrator (Vultee being the name of the company that made the BT-13) and Vibrator because it constantly rattled.

While Primary Training was designed to produce pilots with fundamental flying skills, Basic Training was focused on introducing a basic pilot to the flying skills of a military pilot. This included flying in formation, which required a high level of flight discipline; the fundamentals of combat flying; improved aerobatic skills; and night flying (with flying in night formation as well). The transition from a biplane, the PT-17, to a single wing BT-13 was easier than I expected. It only took a few hours of dual instruction to make the transition. Most of my classmates had very little trouble, but a few cadets did wash out at this point.

Our instructors in Primary had all been black and had themselves flown only the Piper Cub and the PT-17. They were not military pilots. The instructors in Basic and later in Advanced were all white. The techniques of flying became more complex in these military planes, and the black pilots had not been trained in the techniques of flying them. It had generally been assumed that black men were not intelligent enough to master the more sophisticated aircraft.

My Basic Training instructor was Lieutenant Whitaker. By his very distinct accent I could tell he was a good ole' Southern boy. I had a good relationship with Lieutenant Whitaker and thoroughly enjoyed flying with him. In addition to formation flying and aerobatics, he taught us simple cross-country flying, which consisted of flying outside the local area. This required basic navigational skills, which came very easily to me. In addition to fundamental dead reckoning (flying from Point A to Point B by using heading, time, and distance), he introduced us to the fundamentals of radio navigation (flying by listening to a radio tone). Finally, we learned night flying, including simple cross-country.

Basic training of about sixty hours of flying time included routine check rides to ensure that we were meeting military flying standards established for this phase of our training. Successful completion of Basic Training produced much more than a person who could fly a plane. We were now well on our way to becoming military pilots capable of performing a variety of tasks at a high skill level.

As cadets, we had little time off, but on one occasion we were able to go up to Atlanta, Georgia, for a couple of days of relaxation. Atlanta was about a two-hour drive from Tuskegee. When I was walking down the street and a white couple came along, I stepped off the curb into the street until they had passed, just as Ma had said. That wasn't a pleasant experience, but I did it.

After the passage of the Civil Rights Act of 1964, I went back to Atlanta and walked down Peachtree Avenue without moving to the side for anyone. What a breath of freedom it was to walk down the street like any other person! How things had changed over those many years.

Advanced

The final phase of preparing the other cadets and me to be military pilots was Advanced Training. The aircraft we flew was the AT-6. This aircraft was really

Figure 10. BT-13. Courtesy of the USAF.

neat. It was similar to the BT-13 in that it was a single-engine airplane; only it was powered by a larger, 650 HP engine. It had a variable pitch propeller and retractable landing gear—the first airplane we had flown that had landing gear that retracted up into the body, making it much more aerodynamic and fast. It could carry a .30 caliber machine gun, which we used during the gunnery phase of training. Successful flight training in this aircraft prepared us to be introduced to current fighter aircraft, which in our case was the P-40. The AT-6 was the last aircraft we flew with two seats for dual instruction.

In Advanced, we began with thirty-seven cadets. Only thirty of us would graduate. We entered this final phase of flight training happy and excited, eagerly looking forward to the challenges we would face these last ten weeks before graduation. It hardly seemed possible that after sixteen months of continuous testing in class and seemingly endless check rides, the end was in sight. But all of us entered with the fear of not completing the training.

The routine at the beginning of this phase of training was much the same as in the others. The first day was orientation, and we were assigned instructors and provided with schedules. Then we were introduced to the AT-6. The transition from the BT-13 to the AT-6 was relatively simple for most of my classmates and for me. This training was about putting the final touches on the military combat pilot. Formation flying now included formation take-offs and landings. Cross-country flights were longer and included night cross-country. Formation flying became more frequent and precise.

We were also introduced to instrument flying, which included classroom hours and flying hours "under the hood." Flying under the hood meant that a piece of canvas was pulled up over the back of our seat and covered the interior of the cockpit so that all visibility to the outside was blocked. The only reference to where we were in relation to the earth was our instruments. An instrument instructor was on board to guide us.

We also learned about flying at high altitudes requiring oxygen masks. On one such mission our goal was to take the AT-6 as high as it would fly to reach the maximum altitude. Somewhere over 20,000 feet above sea level, our indicated airspeed approached "first stall"; at that point we were at maximum altitude. Above that, this airplane would no longer fly. It so happened that I reached 23,000 feet before my airplane stalled, making me tops for the mission. On the way down from altitude, all of us had a ball performing every aerobatic maneuver we were ever taught.

The last training event was learning the gunnery aspects of combat flying. We flew to Eglin Field in the Panhandle of Florida on the Gulf Coast to learn this skill. The target we were assigned to hit was a long sleeve pulled by a cable about 200 feet long attached to another AT-6. A flight of four AT-6s with color-marked bullets would attack the sleeve on individual gunnery runs. After each AT-6 group in the formation made approximately three runs, all the aircraft would land. The holes in the sleeves were then counted by color and were added to compute the score. These trips to Florida required us to stay at Elgin for three or four days at a time. Flying home was always a big deal. We flew a sixteen-ship formation over the field, the only time that we flew in a formation that big.

Unfortunately, we cadets were soon to hear the ugly rumor that ten of us would be washed out of class 44-E. I thought to myself: "What a shame to have to face a 'numbers game' at this, our final phase of training." Everyone had an overriding fear of washing out. The fear came from knowing that we could wash out for reasons other than our ability to fly. We never took anything for granted. We could be asked to go on a check ride without cause. That was not the case in Primary, where we had scheduled check rides, but was true for Basic and Advanced, where the quotas kicked in.

Figure 11. AT-6. Courtesy of the USAF.

I was particularly fond of one of our flight instructors, Mr. Robert A. Dawson. Flight Officer Dawson had gone to the University of Minnesota before entering the US Army Air Corps Flight Training Program and becoming a flight instructor. Dawson hadn't been there long when I arrived. Since I was also from Minnesota, we had an instant connection.

At our first briefing in Advanced, the instructors were hazing the group, and loving every minute of it. Dawson asked, "Is there anyone here from Minnesota?" Of course I raised my hand.

He proceeded to question me: "Have you ever attended the University of Minnesota, and do you know the fight song?"

My response was: "No, I did not attend the University of Minnesota, but yes, I do know the fight song."

In reality, I had heard it many times but didn't know all of the words. Nonetheless, I responded, "Yes!" That was a big mistake.

He immediately shouted, "Okay, Dummy Brown. Get up on that table and serenade me with the song!"

I quickly jumped up on the table, but the thought occurred to me: "My God, what have I gotten myself into? This could be my first step toward being washed out."

I began to sing. I felt that no one had a worse singing voice than I, but I had to begin: "*Minnesota, hats off to thee. To thy colors true we shall ever be. Firm and strongly united are we—Rah, Rah, Rah!*"

I had forgotten the remaining words so I stood there looking like the biggest ass in the world. Dawson was laughing and calling me the biggest dummy in the training program. I was ordered off the table and back into formation. I spent a very long and fretful night.

The next day on the flight line, Dawson saw me and took me into a room where he confirmed that the rumor about ten cadets being washed out was a fact. Most importantly, he gave me some very sound advice: "Harold, when you come down to the flight line, have sharply pressed flight coveralls, not a speck of dirt on your shoes; stand sharply at attention when spoken to and don't behave in any way that will provide any of the instructors an excuse to give you a check ride."

Because there was only one training base for black pilots and it operated under a quota system dictated by Higher Command, there were restrictions on the whole program throughout our training. That also explained the high washout rate. Dawson told me that the instructors were told that only a certain number could come out of the program, and therefore, "We whittle 'em down. A guy comes in with dirty shoes or shoelaces untied, and we tell him to get his parachute. We're going for a check ride." That could be it. Sometimes a guy came out okay, but many times, that was it. He got his pink slip and he was washed out.

Dawson further told me: "Remember, this is not about flight proficiency. It's about numbers. And ten of your classmates must go." He added: "I washed out better pilots in this program than I've seen graduate in other programs, but there is nothing we can do about it."

What had begun as a joke about the University of Minnesota fight song ended with Dawson's really looking out for my best interests. His advice was some of the best I was given in all of my training. I adhered to these principles of disciplined behavior and impeccable dress for the rest of my training. Nearly ten washed out of Advanced, just as Dawson had predicted. This clearly demonstrated the kinds of obstacles we faced throughout the training. There was no sense of fair play—just a numbers game.

The great irony, however, was that the 332nd Fighter Group and the 99th Fighter Squadron suffered continuously from a shortage of pilots. It was not by accident that numerous black pilots flew 70 to 75 missions. In fact, "Many of them flew more than one hundred missions before returning stateside,"[1] while the white pilots routinely flew 50 missions and rotated home. There clearly was a need for replacement pilots like me, but the quota system restricted us from meeting that need.

7

THE TRANSITION TO WAR

WHEN MY CLASS AND I WERE about halfway through Advanced Training, the need for more pilots reached a peak. An emergency requisition for pilots was sent through the chain of command from the 332nd Fighter Group. For the first and only time in the history of the Tuskegee Airmen, a group of fifteen cadets of the thirty in Advanced was selected to fly the P-40, which served as our introduction to single-engine fighter aircraft, before graduation. I was in this group. We wrapped up our training two weeks early in the AT-6 and began flying P-40s.

Normally, cadets finished the program, were commissioned with pilot wings, and were sent home for seven to ten days of leave. They then came back to Tuskegee for twenty hours of flight time in the P-40. But we fifteen cadets, by flying the P-40 early, had completed combat fighter training by the time we graduated from Tuskegee in May 1944. Flying a P-40 signified a major change in our status as young pilots. We had moved from the "T" or Trainer designation to the "P" or Pursuit designation (later changed to "F" for Fighter in jet aircraft). At last, we were flying real "fighter" planes and were not just in training.

Our group of fifteen was certainly excited, but we were told: "You are not yet commissioned, so if you goof up this airplane, we will wash you out. Don't you dare lose control while landing and ground loop it [drag the wing tip and spin]." I remember this experience with some ambivalence: "Here we are. Great to be selected. But we could go from sugar to shit in a hurry."

Among the cadets, we joked about why our particular fifteen were selected, but those in our group, of course, believed that we were the top fifteen pilots. It was a big deal all around the airfield for us cadets to be flying the P-40. Other class members were heard to say: "Oh, man, those guys are flying the P-40s, and they're nothing but cadets." At only nineteen years of age, I was basking in the moment. To add to my excitement, I was selected as the first one to fly the P-40. What a thrill. The choice to be first could have been alphabetical, since Brown is at the beginning of the alphabet, but I clearly believed in my heart that it was because I was the best pilot in the group.

Flying a P-40 for the first time was breathtaking. When I climbed in and looked at that long nose stretching all the way to the prop, all I could think was, "Wow! Am I ready for this?" We were also moving from a plane with 650 horsepower to one with just over 1,200.

There were other dynamics related to flying the P-40. When I got in that plane for the first time, it was a very hot day in May. Because of its huge engine, it was very easy for the P-40 to overheat. It was impossible to see over the very, very long nose, so I needed to "S" turn the aircraft as I taxied. I was constantly in a left or right turn, just so I could see what was in front of me—a whole new experience, but relatively simple to do. So I taxied out and got to the end of the runway, where there was a big water truck. After I revved the engine up, checked it out, and checked the mags (which generated current for the engine), I was ready to go. Just before I took the runway, the water truck sprayed a lot of water into the air scoop in the front of the aircraft, right behind the prop. The aircraft had a liquid-cooled engine, so the water was cooling the air that was sucked into it. After I was hosed down, it didn't take more than twenty or thirty seconds for them to tell me I was cleared to go.

I was used to hearing the roar of the T-6 and could tell just about how much throttle was required at takeoff by its unique sound. That was the roar I thought about when I pushed the throttle up on the P-40 for my first takeoff. I started down the runway with the "right sound," but I noticed I was going relatively slowly. I asked myself: "What in the world is going on?" I looked down and my instruments told me I was only using half power, as it indicated 30 inches of mercury on my manifold. My ears had told me I was at full throttle. That was a little embarrassing, since I didn't even have full throttle on the airplane and here I was, rolling down the runway trying to take off. I immediately pushed the throttle all the way up to the stop. At that point it ran up to over 50 inches of mercury. Now that was full throttle! The takeoff was uneventful and the aircraft was pretty easy to hold on the centerline. When I got to sufficient airspeed, I just rotated the aircraft normally, as I was used to doing.

The flight was pretty much uneventful. On the first flight we were only supposed to fly around to get accustomed to the airplane, because it did not fly like any of the others we had flown. It was much more powerful, and we were flying at a much higher cruise speed. We normally cruised at about 150 to 160 miles per hour in the T-6. In the P-40, I was cruising at something close to 220 to 230 miles per hour. That took a little bit of getting used to. We were just flying around and boring holes in the sky, doing a lot of steep turns. We were told not to do any aerobatics on our first flight. The only maneuver that we were asked to do was to go up to approximately 8,000 feet, pull the nose of the aircraft straight up, then take our hands off the controls, pull the throttle to idle, and watch to see what happened.

That sounded a little shaky to me, and so instead of going to 8,000 feet, I decided it was better to get a little extra room beneath me, so I went up to 8,500 feet. When I pulled the aircraft straight up and the airspeed slowly bled off, I expected the aircraft to act very violently—dropping one or the other wing dramatically and causing a loud stall warning to sound. But it didn't. It just sat there, a very stable, docile airplane. The warning horn was sounding; the aircraft behavior was gentle. Instead of violently moving to the left or the right, the nose of the aircraft just slowly fell until it was well below the horizon, at which time it started into a steep dive, picking up speed as we went. After the aircraft reached cruising speed, I simply eased back on the stick, bringing the aircraft to level flight once again. That was a rather interesting experience, simply because our instructors didn't tell us what it was going to do. They wanted us to find out on our own.

It was time to bring the P-40 in for my first landing. I came in, circled the field, and got into the traffic pattern. As I turned base leg (the crosswind turn before final approach into the wind), I started to lower the landing gear. The cockpit had three small indicator lights, small pictures of the airplane with its wheels lowered, which we called selsens. When the gear went down and locked into place, the selsen showed a little wheel on each side of the aircraft, so that a pilot could see that the wheels were properly in place for landing. As a further indication that things might not be right (that the gear was not down and locked into place), when the throttle was pulled back below idle speed, there was a warning horn that would sound if both landing gear were not in proper position. We had two systems to tell us whether or not the gear was down and locked: the indicator selsens and the warning horn. As I turned on to the final approach, I noticed that the right selsen indicator did not show the

Figure 12. P-40. Courtesy of the Library of Congress.

gear down and locked. As I was coming down final, I pulled the throttle all the way back to see what would happen. The warning horn sounded.

I added full power to the aircraft and aborted the landing. I called in to Major Robert Long, our flight instructor, who was always on the radio when the cadets were flying. I told him, "Sir, I got a problem. The right sensor indicator shows the right gear is not down and locked, and I'm getting a horn."

He instructed me, "Okay, get out of the traffic pattern and pick up some speed. After you get some speed, I want you to make some very, very hard left and right turns. When you go into a very hard left turn, you are putting a small amount of G force on the aircraft. Maybe that will be sufficient to force the gear down into the locked position."

I did what he said. I turned from the left to the right and nothing happened. I flew around for a short time while Major Long tried to figure out what he wanted me to do next. Other than what we had tried, there wasn't much more we could do.

Major Long instructed me: "Okay, Harold, I want you to come down the final approach with the left wing low and land the airplane on the left gear and the tail wheel. Hold the left wing low as long as possible, and as the plane slows up, it will gently roll over to the right gear. This will minimize the damage if the right gear collapses."

I thought to myself: "It would be a task to land the airplane normally with both landing gears down and locked, considering this is my first flight in the plane, and now he is instructing me to land on one main gear and the tail wheel." I was nothing but a cadet, so I followed his instruction and brought the plane in left wing low, right wing high. The touchdown was very smooth. I held this position until the airspeed was so low that the aircraft just rolled over onto the right gear. I braced myself for the expected collapse of the right gear, but that did not happen. I brought the aircraft to a halt and the maintenance crew immediately ran out and put the landing gear pins into the gear to prevent it from collapsing.

It just so happened that both gear-down indicators had malfunctioned, giving a false reading that the right gear was not down and locked, when in reality it was. I was the big man on campus, flying around with all the fire trucks out on the runway and a large crowd of people close by watching to see the catastrophe in the making. However, the event really became uneventful because there wasn't anything wrong. I flew the aircraft precisely as I was instructed, for which I was commended when I got out of the plane. Nonetheless, landing a P-40 for the first time on the left wheel was quite an experience.

While I was in the air on the first flight, some of the other cadets were photographed. Figure 13 shows six cadets standing confidently in front of the P-40 as they prepare to take their own flights. None of them, of course, could foresee what would happen to them in the future. Three of the six would die before the war was over.

In left to right order in figure 13, the men and a quick summary of their experiences in the military are as follows:

RICHARD BELL—as described more fully later, died at Walterboro in flight training within three months after the photo was taken, never making it overseas.

WENDELL HOCKADAY—as described more fully later, died when his plane crashed into the Alps in 1945 on the same day that George Iles was shot down.

GEORGE ILES—as described more fully later, was shot down and reunited with me in a POW camp. He would return to the United States with me in June 1945.

Figure 13. Six cadets in front of the P-40. Courtesy of the Air Force Historical Research Agency.

JIMMY LANHAM—shot down an Me-109 on April 15, 1945, and shot down another Me-109 on April 26, 1945; the latter was one of the last aerial victories of the Tuskegee Airmen during the war.[1]

SAMUEL J. FOREMAN—was "reported missing over northern Yugoslavia at 1100 hours"[2] or 11:00 A.M. on January 21, 1945. I was later told that Foreman was at the tail end of a flight when he disappeared. Foreman had a tendency to lag behind and had been told on more than one occasion to keep up. His flight group assumed a German plane had snuck up from behind and shot him down. Since no one saw anything, he was listed as missing in action. He was later listed as killed in action.

ROBERT W. WILLIAMS—shot down two FW-190s on March 31, 1945, for which he earned a Distinguished Flying Cross for heroic actions on that day.[3] After returning from the war, Williams, a good friend of mine, went on to coproduce the 1995 HBO film *The Tuskegee Airmen*.

Figure 14. File photo taken several weeks before my graduation from flight training.

GRADUATION AT LAST

On May 23, 1944, I at long last graduated from flight training in the class of 44-E and received my wings. I remember that day fondly. Here I was, nineteen years old and a brand-new, freshly minted second lieutenant. I had wings on my chest. I was the hottest thing to ever say good morning to the sun, or so I thought.

On exactly that same Tuesday in May, while I was walking on air with my new wings, assault troops were sweeping to the English seaside into various marshaling areas in preparation for the invasion of Normandy.[4] A week later, on June 6, 1944, the Allies invaded the Normandy coast. All of us in flight training expected that the Allies would invade the Continent. After all, the only way to get to Berlin was to cross the Channel. We didn't realize until much later about the sacrifices—the loss of lives—that the invasion of Normandy entailed. The liberators had sent eight assault divisions ashore and "had suffered 12,000 killed, wounded, and missing, with thousands more unaccounted for."[5] Newspapers like the *Stars and Stripes* focused on the victories, not the loss of life, and that's what we read. Besides, at nineteen years of age, I

Figure 15. A night on the town in Chicago. From left to right: an unidentified woman, Thomas Jefferson, me, an unidentified woman, Bob Williams's brother, an unidentified woman, Bob Williams, George Iles, and George Iles's wife.

was wrapped up in my own flying and had other things on my mind.

We had a one-week leave after graduation before going to Walterboro, South Carolina, for combat fighter training. On the first night, four of us went to Chicago for an evening of fun. We spent our time in the nightclubs. We were in uniform, and we were ushered into the clubs and given all the amenities. "Please come in. Let me shake your hand." We were all reasonably young—nineteen, twenty, twenty-one, twenty-two, and we were treated like heroes.

That kind of recognition, which came after being a commissioned pilot, really affected me. I have been asked if it went to my head. My only truthful response is: Yes! I *loved* it. *Absolutely.* I was the greatest thing that ever walked down the street. There was a certain amount of cockiness that went with such recognition, although I think I was reasonably reserved compared to some of the other guys.

After a night in Chicago, I departed for Minneapolis to visit family and friends, where I also received a hero's welcome. Being a black officer was just unheard of, and a pilot on top of that. We knew that we were among a very select group of people.

Combat Fighter Training in Walterboro

After graduation and a few days off, the fifteen of us who had flown the P-40 were sent to Walterboro, South Carolina, about forty-eight miles from Charleston. The other fifteen cadets in our class who had not flown the P-40 returned to Tuskegee for more instruction in that aircraft.

Our training at Walterboro lasted about two months and consisted of 60 to 70 hours of training in fighter aircraft as the final preparation for our overseas assignment as replacement pilots for the 332nd Fighter Group. Earlier Tuskegee pilots had trained at Selfridge Field in Michigan. However, when the 332nd and the fighter pilots who had trained there had gone overseas in January 1944, the fighter-based training for all graduates coming out of Tuskegee shifted to Walterboro Army Air Field.

At Walterboro, we were trained in the P-47, affectionately known as the "The Jug," because to some it looked like a milk jug. It was otherwise known as the Thunderbolt. The Thunderbolt had a big, powerful 2,800 horsepower engine. It was not a pretty sight, but overall it was a great plane to fly. We were trained on this aircraft because the 332nd was flying it in combat overseas in June 1944, but by the time we got overseas, the 332nd Fighter Group had begun receiving P-51Cs from the white fighter groups who had moved to the newer P-51D model.

While at Walterboro, we spent a lot of our time flying in two-ship and four-ship formation. In addition, during many flights we would break up and fly a line formation, single file, one behind the other. We performed all kinds of aerobatics as we followed the leader. There were other times when we went up with our instructor in a two-ship formation and engaged in mock dogfights. We would turn in opposite directions, then turn back toward each other and engage. We were each trying to get on the other's tail by making violent turns, dives, aerobatic moves—you name it. We did everything that we could to keep the instructor from getting on our tail. Of course, the significantly more experienced instructors could fly the aircraft better than we. Most times they got on our tail and called to say: "Well, I got you in my gun sight; you just got shot down." Then we would start it all over again.

That was what fighter training was all about. We were constantly putting the aircraft through its paces, doing everything that it was capable of doing. We were learning the aircraft very thoroughly—how to fly it, and how to fly it the way we would if we were in actual combat and trying to get on an enemy's tail, or how to fly it if the enemy was trying to get on our tail and we were try-ing to evade him.

In addition to the many hours of formation flying, we also got in a certain number of night flying hours. We certainly didn't do aerobatics at night. We just got in very short cross-country flights, flying a designated route within about a 75-to-100-mile radius of the airbase. These flights were designed to give us some night flying navigation practice. This practice did not amount to much because the Americans, unlike the Brits, were not flying the heavy bombers at night in Europe.

Our training of about sixty hours lasted most of the month of June, through July, and into part of August 1944. By early August we were getting ready to be transferred overseas. At this point we were no longer flying. We had to get all of our equipment together for our deployment and then we were given a three-day leave. We could do what we wanted, but we didn't have enough time to go home, so we just goofed off in Washington, DC, for a couple of days.

FATAL ACCIDENTS

While at Walterboro, there were two fatal accidents in the class of 44-E, one during the time that I was there and one during the time that the second group from my class was in training. These were just the first two of many friends who would be lost during my time in the service.

The first accident occurred during late afternoon. It was the last flight of the day. Richard Bell, while flying solo, put his airplane into a steep dive from 30,000 feet.

Several of us were sitting around the barracks when we heard his aircraft coming down—making a high-pitched, extremely loud noise, obviously in a long vertical dive. He kept coming and coming, the sound growing louder and louder. One of the guys said: "Jesus Christ, is he ever going to pull it out?"

The roar of the aircraft told us that it was at maximum speed. It soon became obvious that a crash was imminent. Seconds later it hit the ground, completely vertical and at maximum speed. It sounded like a thousand-pound bomb had hit the earth. There was nothing left of the plane or the pilot except a huge crater. It was such a shame. Dick Bell was one of the best pilots in our group.

The P-47 might go through a period of compressibility somewhere be-tween 30,000 and 20,000 feet if a pilot reached a critical speed at this altitude. During such a period, the plane would not respond to back stick pressure.

When it entered the denser air below, the plane generally began to respond when the pilot pushed the throttle full forward and gently pulled the stick back to help bring the nose up. This compressibility issue was a flight characteristic of the P-47. No one will ever know if this tendency in the plane contributed to Bell's death.

The second group of pilots from the class of 44-E began training at Walterboro approximately three weeks after us. The second accident occurred during a night flight. George Cisco had landed his aircraft and was taxiing down to the end of the runway in order to pull off on to the taxiway. A second aircraft, flown by Ralph Turner, landed reasonably close behind Cisco. The Jug, the P-47 that Turner was flying, had many blind spots because of its big nose. Turner simply did not see Cisco. Turner assumed that Cisco had pulled off the runway and was on the taxi strip. Cisco was killed when the two planes collided.

Fighter Pilots

Over the years, I have often been asked what it took to be a combat pilot. In an interview in 2003 with Dr. Thomas Saylor, who interviewed many World War II vets from Minnesota, I chuckled at the question and simply told him that fighter pilots were taught to be "raunchy."

"Raunchy?" he asked. I told him that it just took an overabundance of cockiness. For me, that meant that I thought I was the greatest pilot to ever have said good morning to an airplane. I never thought I would ever get shot down. Reflecting on this, now I see why old men send young men to war. Young men believe they will live forever and will survive anything. That's the attitude a pilot has to have to fight and win a war. Fearless. As he gets a little older, he starts wising up and is less likely to want to go out and fight a war, unless he is sitting back as a general and sending the young guys out to do the fighting.

Years after the war at an air show in Oshkosh, Wisconsin, I met Chesley Sullenberger, the pilot who executed the emergency landing of US Airways Flight 1549 on the Hudson River. The jet was disabled by striking a flock of geese during its initial climb out of LaGuardia in January of 2009. This amazing example of extreme pilot proficiency is often referred to as the "Miracle on the Hudson."

My first question to Sullenberger was: "Captain Sully, I bet you were a fighter pilot, weren't you?"

Sully responded: "Why do you ask?"

"Because," I said, "it would take a fighter pilot's instincts to make the decision to land that plane perfectly in the Hudson. If you had hesitated, you would never have gotten that plane lined up and successfully landed on the river."

Sully responded: "Yes, I was a fighter pilot."

As pilots during World War II, none of us chose to fly single-engine planes in combat rather than multi-engined bombers. The military made those decisions, and such decisions occurred after a pilot had finished Basic flying and had gone into Advanced. At that point, the pilot went into advanced single-engine or advanced multi-engine flying, the last phase of flying.

Some decisions were simply based on physical size. Some pilots were just big, and cockpits in fighters were small. For example, a P-39 (the Airacobra, a single-seat fighter plane built by Bell) required that the pilot be no taller than 5-foot-11 and weigh no more than 200 pounds, just to be able to fit into the cockpit. General Chappie James was about 6-foot-4 and weighed about 250 pounds. He wanted to fly the P-39, but was told: "You just can't fit in, sir." Nonetheless, Chappie wanted to fly it, so the seat was taken out and he sat on the floor of the plane on a little pad, so the story goes.

Those men chosen to fly twin-engine planes had the same skills as those in fighters. The twin was a little bigger and the pilot had more throttles in his hands, but essentially it was still an airplane. He was a pilot. If he could fly a single-engine, he could fly a multi-engine.

The one thing I would say, finally, about fighter pilots is that they needed a lot of skill and a controlled recklessness. I can recall doing things as a fighter pilot that I wouldn't dream of doing today, such as buzzing the field, and then pulling out and rolling the airplane. I'm a little older, I'm a little wiser, and I now know, "Hey, if you miscalculate, you could kill yourself." But back then dying in an aircraft was perhaps the last thing on my mind. I always felt that I was good enough. So I rolled the thing over, after buzzing the field, no big deal about that. However, Colonel Davis put a stop to that foolishness.

8

THE TRIP OVERSEAS AND COMMANDER B. O. DAVIS

AFTER FIGHTER TRAINING, WE BEGAN OUR journey overseas for Northern Africa. We reported to the point of embarkation, Camp Patrick Henry, near Hampton, Virginia, in September 1944. After almost two weeks of waiting, we were loaded on to Liberty ships, small cargo ships that were mass-produced during World War II.

Liberty ships were cramped—not the best for traveling over the rough Atlantic, but perfect for carrying supplies. Because they had no armament, the Liberty ships had to be protected by destroyers. In our case, we traveled in a convoy of about a hundred ships. After we boarded the ships and got out from land some distance, we could see ships coming from many other ports all over the eastern coast. There was that one location as a rendezvous point for all of the ships.

We had about ten destroyers that were escorting our convoy across the Atlantic. The destroyers were very fast, extremely well armed, and equipped to handle submarine attacks. There was a lot of zigzagging and slowing and speeding up to avoid enemy submarines. There were several occasions when it was believed that a submarine had been sighted. In such cases, the destroyers immediately went to investigate.

Although we had no real trouble crossing the Atlantic, I had one very close call on board that ship. The quarters in such a small ship were particularly close. In a small bunk room, a group of eight or nine of my classmates were lying around BS-ing, making small talk, while Gentry Barnes, a classmate, was playing around with his .45 caliber automatic weapon. All of a sudden it discharged. It sounded like a canon going off in such close quarters. The bullet ricocheted all over. We were deadly silent for about five seconds . . . all of us frozen, not knowing where that bullet was going to wind up. We just sat there staring at each other.

Then finally someone said: "Anyone hurt?"

We went round the room. "I'm not hit." Another said: "I'm okay."

Everyone said the same thing. We assumed that no one had been hit, but then George Iles got up to walk and said that he had felt something strike his left boot. He looked down and saw that the bullet had entered the sole and had lodged there. There was this little hump toward the front bottom of his boot, which turned out to be the bullet from the .45. George kept those boots as a souvenir.

It seemed that we would never reach Ramitelli Air Field, but there was nothing we could do to speed up the journey. Unfortunately, the North Atlantic could get very rough in the fall season and we were on these little ships bouncing all over the place for thirty-two very long days. The return trip, in contrast, took only eight days.

At last we sighted land and passed by the Rock of Gibraltar, then arrived at Oran, Algeria, where we stayed for four days. Oran is on the north coast of Africa in the Mediterranean Sea. We off-loaded all of our gear from the ship and went to a local military base. We were given the freedom to go into town and sightsee around Oran. It was a little Arab town, with everything to cater to the soldiers that were there. There were bars, of course, with all the booze a guy could want..

The next step in our journey was to board a luxury liner that had been refitted as a troop carrier. In about four days we arrived in Naples, Italy, where we waited again for transportation to take us to Ramitelli Air Field. A week later, we finally got our stuff together and boarded trucks that carried us to Ramitelli. The time from our point of embarkment in Hampton, Virginia, to Ramitelli Air Field took more than fifty days—a journey that seemed interminable. Even though replacement pilots were urgently needed, it didn't seem like the military was in a big hurry to get us to our destination.

Once at Ramitelli, the fifteen of us were assigned to our squadrons. About half of us went to the 99th Fighter Squadron, a couple went to the 100th, a couple went to the 301st, and the remainder went to the 302nd. We were all divided up, but more of us went to the 99th Fighter Squadron, because it had the greatest need for replacement pilots.

The Germans had retreated to north of Rome near the Po Valley by the time

I arrived in Italy in late October 1944. The Allies had successfully launched campaigns in Northern Africa and Sicily and had marched into Rome in June 1944. They were constantly pushing the enemy back north. Ramitelli Air Field, on the Adriatic or eastern side of Italy, was about 30 to 35 kilometers north of Foggia, Italy, where the bombers and three groups of twin-engine P-38 fighters were located.

We had finally arrived. How did it feel? It was new and it was foreign and it was exciting. We looked forward to what we were going to be asked to do with a certain amount of apprehension, of course. We would be flying combat missions, escorting the heavy bombers from Italy up into Germany. There was always a certain amount of nervousness about taking off with full wing tanks on our aircraft, but it was exciting and was what we had trained for. It was an adventure to most of us, and it felt that way throughout most of the war. In later years, I could chuckle about the exuberance of youth; none of us ever believed that *his* plane would crash. We believed that we were immortal.

A Living Legend

I met the legendary Commander B. O. Davis for the first time when I reported for duty at Ramitelli Air Field. Although Davis had been trained at Tuskegee, by the time I arrived there in March 1943, he was already taking the 99th overseas after months of waiting for an assignment. Even though I had not yet met Davis, he was larger than life to all of us black men who followed in his footsteps. The stories of his persistence against all odds were legendary and greatly inspired all the men in his command.

All young black airmen, including me, had heard about B. O.'s years at West Point. During those four years, the young black cadet was given the silent treatment by his classmates and was spoken to only in an official capacity. He lived alone the entire time he was at West Point.[1] He graduated number 35 out of a class of 276 in 1936.[2] With a class ranking that high, B. O. should have had his choice of career paths. He requested the Army Air Corps but "received the same answer that all black Americans received in those years: The AAC is not accepting Negroes at this time."[3] He had to wait until the first class at Tuskegee was formed in 1941 to get that opportunity. He eventually became the leader of the Tuskegee Airmen.

The 99th Fighter Squadron, under B. O. Davis's leadership, had reached full strength by August 1942 and expected to be deployed shortly, but six months passed before deployment to North Africa came in early April 1943.[4] Arriving in Northern Africa, the squadron was gradually introduced to combat after being "attached," not "assigned," to the 33rd Fighter Group, Twelfth Air Force, under the command of Colonel William Momyer.[5] Normally, there were three fighter squadrons in a fighter group. In this case, the 99th was attached to the 33rd as a fourth squadron. The verb "attached" describes an unusual relationship between a squadron and a fighter group. The 99th could not stand alone within the organization of the Army Air Corps, so it was simply "attached." To "assign" the 99th Squadron would have meant that it was fully a part of the organization, and as a result the men would be on the same base, eating and drinking together. There would have been commingling at briefings. Because the lead squadron was typically rotated within the fighter group, it would have meant that the 99th would eventually have been the lead squadron. None of those propositions were acceptable to Colonel Momyer and the other white officers in charge.

For these reasons, the 99th Fighter Squadron had its own base some ten miles from the 33rd Fighter Group. When the Tuskegee Airmen flew missions, they would fly from their base to the other base for briefings, and then join the 33rd for missions. The situation was made even more difficult because the first Tuskegee pilots didn't have the benefit of flying with the old hands so they could learn from them. Normally, a new pilot flew with an experienced flier, but they were denied that opportunity. Spann Watson, one of the pilots in the 99th, remembered only one set of flight instructions from the commander of the 33rd: "You boys keep up."[6]

In September 1943, B. O. Davis was called back to the United States to take command of the 332nd Fighter Group, a larger all-black unit preparing to go overseas.[7] Soon after his arrival, there was an attempt to stop the use of black pilots in combat. Senior officers, including Colonel Momyer, had recommended that the 99th be removed from combat operations because it had performed poorly. B. O. was furious; he had never been told of any deficiencies with the unit.[8] He had only one option: to defend the record of the airmen he commanded before a War Department Committee.

Before this committee, B. O. refuted the charges in the reports that Colonel Momyer had submitted. He fully explained that the criticisms in the report were based primarily on a single mission in which some of the black pilots had acted out of inexperience and not incompetence.[9] They had allowed themselves to be engaged with German fighters when they should have stayed with the bombers. The committee was satisfied with the documentation that B. O.

provided. Without his representation in Washington, the Tuskegee experience could have ended at that point.

In February 1944, B. O.'s new 332nd Fighter Group was assigned to the 62nd Fighter Wing, Twelfth Air Force, at Montecorvino, Italy, near Naples. The group ended up flying P-39s on coastal patrol, nothing else. It was almost a noncombat assignment. During the whole time our guys were flying patrol, they had fewer than a handful of encounters with enemy airplanes.[10]

In March 1944, General Ira C. Eaker, Commander, Mediterranean Allied Air Force, requested that Colonel Davis report to headquarters. He described a plan to transfer the 332nd from its coastal patrol mission to bomber escort with the 306th Wing, XV Fighter Command. General Eaker made clear the contribution the 332nd could make to reduce the heavy losses of B-17s and B-24s. He told Davis that the command had lost 114 planes in February, the previous month.[11] The new assignment meant a change of equipment for the black airmen from the P-39 to the P-47. It also meant that they would be joining escort missions that were performed by the other fighter groups in the XV Fighter Command. Colonel Davis leapt at the opportunity for the 332nd to enter combat as fighter escort for the bombers.[12]

In April, General Eaker began to make plans for the 99th to join the 332nd, which B. O. had left in Italy the prior September. However, the 99th already had seventeen victories to its credit as part of the Twelfth Air Force and it could not join the 332nd until its role in tactical operations in May was complete.[13] In May 1944, the 332nd was transferred from the Twelfth Air Force to the Fifteenth Air Force.[14] The 332nd finally flew its first combat mission on June 7, 1944, coincidentally the day after the Normandy Invasion.[15]

The 332nd established itself at Ramitelli in June 1944 and "was soon joined by the 99th Fighter Squadron, making it a four-squadron fighter group and the largest in the theater."[16] Our fighter group began to get increased opportunities to excel in the air. We were sought out to help the Fifteenth Air Force when so many of its bombers were going down. With around ten men on each of those bombers, these were very heavy losses. The bombers were being lost because most of the time the other fighter groups providing protection were being drawn away from the bombers. One of the favorite tactics of the Germans was to send half of their force in to draw the fighters off, leaving a big gap in the defense and allowing the other German fighters to knock out the bombers at will.

When I arrived in Ramitelli as a replacement pilot, I was well aware of the history of the 332nd and its leader. The first time I met B. O., he came to greet our group of new arrivals. He welcomed us to the base and then his first directive was: "Your assignment is to protect the bombers, to get them to the target, and to bring them all home safely. You don't go off chasing fighters to get a victory for yourself." The bomber protection protocol was that as long as the German fighters were sitting out there, we were to simply let them sit. If they became an imminent threat to the bombers, only then would we engage them. Then B. O. made the remark that I remember so well: "You can go off and you can shoot down ten fighter aircraft, but when you come back, I'm going to ground you, and then I'm going to court-martial you. You will never fly again."

We had our orders and we followed them very, very strictly. B. O., being a West Pointer—well, we didn't argue with Colonel Davis. He was about 6-feet-2, slim as could be, and straight as an arrow, a really, really good man. Not surprisingly, he went on to become the first African American general in the US Air Force, which was formed from the US Army Air Force following World War II.

Because the 332nd was requested to assist in the protection of the bombers and because the Tuskegee Airmen, known as the Red Tails, stuck with their bombers, our reputation grew. Initially the bomber crews didn't know who the Red Tails were, but our guys didn't run off after individual victories and we became known for sticking with the bombers. There were many times heading back home that there were stragglers that started screaming for fighter cover. We'd send a flight back to find them and escort them back to friendly territory. In time, they called us the Red Tail Angels.

It has often been said that the Tuskegee Airmen never lost a bomber, a myth that got started by a journalist in March 1945 and was further perpetuated through an article in the *Chicago Defender* later that month.[17] Virtually all of the Tuskegee Airmen knew that bombers had certainly been lost. However, the Tuskegee Airmen lost significantly fewer bombers to enemy airplanes than the average of the other fighter groups[18]—very likely because we stuck with our bombers instead of seeking personal victories.

Over the years, I received several letters from former bomber pilots and crewmembers that verified the important role the Tuskegee Airmen had played in saving their lives. Some letters of thanks came from family members. Here are some excerpts from a letter written by William Martin of Darien, Illinois:

Dear Colonel Brown:

My older brother was a B-24 pilot during WW II, flying out of Italy, and told me the following story.

He was going on a mission one day, to Ploesti, or somewhere well east of Italy and, on the way in, lost one of his engines. He said this was not a problem because he could still keep up with the other planes in the formation. Ultimately they dropped their bomb load and turned back toward Italy. At some point soon after, he lost a second engine and started to fall back of the main formation. He said that this was what the German fighter planes were watching for . . . stragglers.

My brother said he immediately called for help. He knew that his plane was in the area where the Tuskegee Airmen were escorting bombers. He said within minutes of that call, 2 or 3 fighter planes arrived to protect him and escorted his plane until it was out of reach of German planes. He was always grateful for the protection he had been given.

My brother has been dead for over 15 years and is buried in Arlington Cemetery. But for the Tuskegee Airmen, he might have died 50 years earlier.

9

THE AIR FORCES, THE P-51, AND RAMITELLI AIR FIELD

THE UNITED STATES HAD FOUR AIR FORCES in Europe: the Twelfth and the Fifteenth in Southern Europe and the Ninth and Eighth in England. The Twelfth and the Ninth were "tactical" and the Eighth and Fifteenth were "strategic." The "tactical" air forces were tasked with supporting ground troops—strafing (low-level shooting), bombing, and hitting special targets just in front of the ground troops' positions. They provided what was called close escort. The "strategic" Air Forces bombed targets in an effort to destroy the infrastructure.

The Fifteenth Air Force sent bombers from the south in Italy northward into areas held by the Germans. The Eighth Air Force, stationed in England, flew the northern route and bombed targets as they headed west to east. The key to winning the war was the absolute destruction of the enemies' tools for waging war. To that end, we had to destroy every ammunition plant, every vehicle plant, all the ball-bearing plants, and all the oil refineries. If we succeeded, then the enemy couldn't wage war.

Winning that war required a huge military force in the skies. The Eighth Air Force was three times the size of the Fifteenth. At maximum effort, the Eighth Air Force could put 2,000 bombers and 1,200 fighters into the air, while the Fifteenth could put up 600 bombers and 400 fighters. That's a whole lot of airplanes.

On one of our missions while in route to our targets for the day, I saw the mighty Eighth Air Force in the distance. We were flying due north and their planes were about twenty miles ahead flying from west to east, crossing our path at a 90-degree angle. We could see the lead bomber group over the horizon, while the remaining bomber stream was stretched back to the other horizon. It appeared to me that the total bomber stream was probably 30 to 40 miles long. I have never seen so many aircraft in the sky as I did that day. It was an incredible sight.

THE FINEST FIGHTER AIRCRAFT IN THE WAR

As a fighter pilot assigned to the Fifteenth, my primary role was to provide escort for the bombers flying into German territory. I flew my first mission as a combat pilot in the legendary P-51 Mustang. We Tuskegee Airmen flew four types of fighter aircraft in the war: the P-40, the P-39, the P-47, and the P-51, but we enjoyed the greatest success by far in the P-51.

At an earlier stage in the war, the Germans were shooting down B-17s and B-24s at a very high rate. The Allied aircraft losses in the first three months of 1944 alone were devastating, with almost 800 heavies shot down.[1] Two factors began to change this situation. The P-47 and P-38, the two high-altitude fighters operational at that time, got outfitted with external wing tanks so that they could fly on longer missions, and the P-51, a long-range fighter, was introduced in the spring of 1944. The prototype for the P-51 had been rolled out in 1940, but it wasn't until the addition of the more reliable and efficient Rolls-Royce Merlin engine that the P-51 could be operational at high altitudes. When the P-51 became part of the inventory, it soon became the aircraft of choice for many pilots in both the Eighth and Fifteenth Air Forces.

In later years, Brad Lang, the son of a Tuskegee Airman who flies a restored P-51C for "The Rise Above Project," described the P-51 this way: "It's akin to driving a Ferrari or a Lamborghini, because it is very nimble, agile, and flies very fast. Its climb rate, acceleration, turn rate—all are excellent."

I was introduced to the P-51 in November 1944, just after I had arrived at Ramitelli. I had to be checked out in the C model before going into combat.

This included a few hours of reading the pilot's manual and learning all the P-51 systems, including various speeds for takeoff, cruising, and landing the plane. We also spent a few hours in the cockpit on the ground, to allow us to become familiar with the location of all the gauges and systems before actually flying the P-51. This took approximately one day. The next day I flew the P-51 for the first time.

I had already flown the P-40 and P-47, so I found no real surprises in my initial experience in the aircraft, yet the P-51 was certainly faster and more maneuverable than the previous two fighters. On my first flight I quickly discovered how the P-51 responded in turns. I could go 350 miles per hour, do a tight turn, hit the flap handle, and put 20 degrees of flap down. That immediately slowed the airplane down and allowed me to make a much tighter turn. I was almost immediately going in the other direction.

In later years, a fellow pilot asked me if I felt high G's, the force of gravity, when I performed this kind of turn. I told him: "You really felt the G's in that plane. In fact, you could pull G's tight enough that you would get a slight grayout, but it would only last a few seconds. I could turn so fast that the G's would close my eyelids. The P-51 was structurally designed to handle this level of stress."

Flying the P-51 was just plain fun. On my first flight in the P-51, I performed every aerobatic maneuver I knew; I really wrung the aircraft out. After a couple more flights, I was fully prepared to fly my first combat mission. Of course, I didn't know everything about the aircraft on my first combat mission, because I had only had about five hours of flying time in the P-51. However, as I gained more flying time, becoming more knowledgeable and comfortable in the P-51, it became abundantly clear to me that the P-51 was the finest combat aircraft fighting the war, especially among the conventional aircraft with reciprocating engines (propellers).

P-51C COMPARED TO THE P-51D

The black pilots generally inherited the older aircraft, the hand-me-downs, as the white pilots got upgrades in equipment. This was true of the P-47s, and later was true of the P-51Cs. We slowly started getting D's near the end of the war, but we were the last outfit to pick up the D models.

The D model was more advanced and provided much better visibility than the C. The difference was that the D had a bubble top. The C was a "straightback," which meant that the body of the aircraft formed a straight line from the windshield all the way back to the tail section. It was difficult to look around in the C, but with that bubble top, I could see out in every direction. It was also easier to get in and out of the D, because the whole canopy just slid back and I could just step over the edge into or out of the cockpit. With the C model, I had to fold that little canopy back over on itself and then climb in or out on the left. Then I had to bring the canopy back up over and lock it up. Figure 16 shows a P-51C as it looked in World War II.

Figure 16. P-51C. Courtesy of the Air Force Historical Research Agency.

I flew seventeen of my missions in the C and crash-landed one in Northern Italy. When my plane was down for maintenance or out of commission for some other reason, I flew the D. However, I was in the C when I went down while strafing in Austria.

Over the years I have been frequently asked why the tails of the Tuskegee pilots' airplanes were painted red. Some of the questioners tried to find symbolism in the color. In fact, one young German girl asked me if there was some relationship to the red in the Red Baron. In reality, our planes and our pilots, by extension, became the Red Tails as a way of distinguishing our fighter group from the three other P-51 fighter groups in the Fifteenth Air Force in Italy.

The other three groups were made up of white pilots and ours, the 332nd, was made up of black pilots. The color of the tails were as follows:

52nd Fighter Group, Yellow Tails
31st Fighter Group, Red-Striped Tails
325th Fighter Group, Checkerboard Tails
332nd Fighter Group, Red Tails

The color of the tails helped the bomber pilots easily recognize the group that was escorting them.

Figure 17. In
front of my tent
at Ramitelli.
Courtesy of the
Craig Huntly
Collection.

RAMITELLI

The Army Corps of Engineers created airfields throughout Italy in support
of the Fifteenth Air Force. This included the one at Ramitelli for the 332nd
Fighter Group.

The Corps laid down wooden platforms upon which tents were erected.
Wooden sides of approximately three to four feet were added to the platforms
and from those sides the canvas tops were attached. Italy was very, very muddy
when it rained, so the raised wooden platforms kept us high enough to avoid
the mud and rain.

There were usually four guys to a tent, but sometimes fewer. I shared a tent
with Charles Jamerson, one of the early black pilots in the 99th, and with a
ground officer. I remember an instance when Joe Gomer, who had graduated

a year before me in 43-E, was the only guy left in his tent; the other three had been lost in combat.

Each tent was heated with a five-gallon stove, which was connected to a large drum outside that fed a small amount of gasoline at a time. The cots were arranged around the stove. It was warm enough inside, but occasionally a stove started a fire, resulting in a destroyed tent. As far as I know, there is only one photo of me while overseas, shown in Figure 17.

It wasn't just in air combat where danger lurked for us young pilots. Pilots were often lost in training or non-combat-related accidents. One particularly tragic incident resulted in the death of Lieutenant Roland Moody. In late March 1945, a P-38 from another fighter group stationed south of Foggia was spraying mosquitoes around the Ramitelli Air Field. The plane accidentally dropped a fuel tank on Moody's tent. The tank burst into flames and he burned to death.[2] B. O. Davis was reported to be very displeased and was said to have called the group commander to complain of the negligence.

I would be remiss if I did not recognize and celebrate the "other" Tuskegee Airmen, the maintenance and support personnel, who made it possible for us pilots to fight the battle in the air. While the focus of most attention in recent years has been on the nearly 1,000 pilots, there were originally close to 14,000 ground personnel. We were our own self-contained air force. We had our own flight surgeons, our own military police, our own cooks, mechanics, radio men, armament men, etc.

IO

COMBAT

WHEN I ARRIVED AT RAMITELLI IN NOVEMBER 1944, the weather was lousy for missions. The "Personnel Narrative" of the *History for November, 1944, 332nd Fighter Group* stated that during November "an overcast of grey skies hung over the 332nd Fighter Group causing many stand down days."[1] The report also noted that I was one of the "fifteen new faces" added to the flying personnel of the 332nd Fighter Group. Many of the Tuskegee pilots flew well beyond the typical fifty missions flown by the white pilots, primarily because there was no one to replace them. In fact, Charles McGee had flown 136 missions by the time he had completed his tour of duty.[2] Our arrival provided much-needed relief for these men.

MY FIRST MISSION

We had one week of transition after arriving at Ramitelli to become familiar with the P-51 and then we were on our first mission. I have often been asked what my first mission felt like and if I was afraid. My response has been: "Fear? Not really. Once a pilot was airborne, he hooked up with his flight and focused on the mission. I was only one of sixty aircraft and I flew wing with an experienced pilot. For that first mission I flew with Captain John Daniels, who later died in a B-25 crash (Mitchell, twin-engine US light bomber) in 1945 near Tuskegee as his plane was returning from Chicago. Real nice guy. He was a good five or six years older than I, one of the older Tuskegee guys. He was well seasoned, having flown a significant number of missions before I met him. As we departed on my first mission, Captain Daniels simply said: "Just stick with me. Fly on my wing and don't do anything silly and you'll be okay."

While I wasn't afraid on that first mission, I did feel a reasonable amount of apprehension. Before this, it was all fun and games, but now I was going off on a real mission. Here's where it started settling in. The first thing I sweated out was that single engine. "Is this engine going to run the way it was advertised? Will it get me there and get me home?" We were aware that there were a number of guys who wound up either bailing out or crash landing strictly because of engine problems. They either parked it up in Germany, or if they were able to, they got it back over the bomb line up in Northern Italy so our first concern was the engine.

After the apprehension about the engine, I wondered if we were going to run into enemy fighters. That first mission was uneventful. In fact, we didn't see any enemy aircraft at all. We picked up our bombers and flew a normal mission. It lasted about six and a half hours, and by the time we got back, I was tired. I had been sitting in that little cramped cockpit, and then, my first mission was over. I was happy to have it behind me.

My Fourth Mission

My fourth mission was quite an exciting experience. We had taken off and were flying in formation when we hit some hazy clouds—they were thin but just enough for me to lose the horizon.

Our flight leader said to "Get in tight." He would fly on instruments and we would follow his lead. I started coming in and looked down at my instrument panel. I suddenly realized that I had "caged" one of my instruments, the "artificial horizon," on takeoff and had forgotten to "uncage" it once we were flying straight and level. Caging simply means that the spinning gyros by which the artificial horizon worked were locked in place. Once the artificial horizon was caged, it became inoperative. Caging was a way of protecting the artificial horizon when a pilot was doing turns and steep dives. In a dogfight, a pilot could really damage the artificial horizon.

I had a ways to go to get in formation and started coming in. I said to myself: "Oh, shit."

I contacted the leader: "Hey, lead, what the hell are you doing?"

He said: "I'm straight and level. Now I'm beginning a slight turn to the right."

I told him: "Man, it looks to me like you're in a steep turn."

I suddenly realized that I was developing a case of vertigo and called in to let all the other squadron pilots know to watch out for me. I didn't know up from down. We were up about 15,000 feet, so I took my hands off the controls, pulled the throttle back to idle, grabbed hold of the seat, and waited.

My airspeed was beginning to wind up and go faster, so I knew I was going down, but I didn't panic. I knew that I would break out at 10,000 feet where there was fair weather. We were over the Adriatic Sea, so I knew there would be no mountains to dodge. I could also see the needle and ball, another instrument on my panel, over to the right—indicating that I was in a tight turn. I dropped my wing tanks to ease my ability to stabilize the airplane.

When I broke out of the clouds, I regained my horizon and realized that I was in a tight spiral. It was a simple task to regain control of the aircraft, and I headed back to base. Since I had dropped my tanks, I could not finish the mission. I was never really afraid during this experience, since I had 10,000 feet of air space to work with. If I had been out over the water at night with only a few thousand feet of airspace, this episode could have been extremely difficult, if not fatal. I vowed that improving my instrument flying would be my highest priority.

MISSIONS IN GENERAL

Preparation for a mission was fairly routine. The night before, we would be told that we were flying the next day. About 4:30 or 5:00 A.M., the duty officer would wake us with the words, "Yep, we're flying today." Everybody immediately got up and got dressed for a long day ahead. We jumped on the waiting truck and went down to Group Operations for target and bomb group assignments. Our assignments were given in a big briefing room where there were as many as sixty to eighty people. We had four squadrons with anywhere from fifteen to eighteen aircraft in each, so we were putting up anywhere from fifty to seventy aircraft on each mission.

While some missions were fairly routine, others, such as traveling to a heavily fortified area like Munich, were not. In a case like that, we might be briefed that the Germans had eight hundred guns on the ground and could put up as many as six hundred fighters. Before such missions, tension definitely ran higher. Some of my fellow pilots might say: "If we get home today, this is going to be DFC day [Distinguished Flying Cross, a military award for bravery]. The only way we're going to get home is to fight our way out of the area."

After the briefing, we went down to our aircraft on the field and strapped ourselves in our airplanes. Each pilot had his own plane and mechanic. For those times when our aircraft was unflyable and being repaired, we would take a spare aircraft, but for the most part, I normally flew the one airplane.

I have frequently been asked if I felt anxiety before a flight. I felt a small amount of apprehension, primarily because we were carrying wing tanks loaded with fuel. This increased our gross weight and extended our takeoff run—often up to 80 to 90 percent of the runway. Once we had our planes started, the squadrons would assemble and line up, one squadron on each of the four corners of the runway. Then the lead squadron would take the active runway and the starter would fire a green flare into the air to start the mission. As the lead aircraft started his takeoff, there were two or three airplanes on the takeoff roll at the same time. One would be breaking ground with another about 100 to 200 yards behind him, and then another about 300 yards behind the second one. We put the aircraft in the air as quickly as possible with only a 5,000-foot runway to work with.

I can recall a particular instance when I was watching planes take off shortly after the other replacement pilots and I had arrived at Ramitelli. I had not yet been checked out in the P-51. Because we were new, we were taken up to the roof of the operations building to see a mission take off. Although we had seen crashes before, this is one that I remember particularly well. Five planes lost power on takeoff. The first came to a halt at the end of the runway. Two and three maneuvered to the left and right of the first plane, but number four ran into the one on the right. There was a big explosion—two fireballs. Number five went to the left and collided with the plane on the left, but with no explosion. The remaining aircraft continued taking off, because we still had a mission to fly. Those are the things that we really sweated as we approached takeoff.

I also remember vividly another takeoff accident involving a fellow classmate, Thomas L. Hawkins. During his takeoff roll out, Hawkins lost control of his aircraft and ran into a revetment area that provided a barricade of protection for other planes. He crashed into one of the parked planes, resulting in an explosion. Men in the area raced to his aid, but couldn't get close due to the heat. They could see Lieutenant Hawkins struggling to get out of his aircraft, but he was overcome and fell back in the flames.

Once we were airborne, we were all keenly aware of the danger of relying on a single engine compared to flying an aircraft with two engines. We frequently saw the other US fighter plane, the twin-engine P-38, in the skies. Those pilots flew the same kind of missions as those of us in the P-51s. While we were sweating out engine problems, we looked at the P-38s with envy. If a pilot was flying an airplane with two engines, he could lose one and still get home. It was not unusual to see a "feathered" P-38 in the sky. One engine would be shut down and the propeller would be "feathered" to keep it from windmilling, restricting forward movement. Those planes had a much greater chance of getting home.

In the final analysis, the engines sometimes ran perfectly and sometimes they malfunctioned. Engine difficulties were so common that I don't think we ever flew a mission that everyone in the squadron completed. If we experienced trouble, we would have to head back home by ourselves, and we just hoped that the engine would keep running long enough so that we could get into friendly territory. Under those circumstances, if the engine actually quit, we could at least bail out safely.

After landing our planes, we'd go to the end of the runway and move off onto the taxi strip. Typically the crew chief for each plane would be there waiting. He would hop on the wing and direct us to the revetment area, where our planes would be parked each night. Each pilot had his own crew chief, whose job it was to maintain the aircraft and have it ready to fly the next day. There were other guys, like the radio specialists and armament staff, who serviced multiple planes, but each plane had its own chief and no one messed with the crew chief. There were times when Staff Sergeant Brown, my crew chief, chewed my ass off for a bad landing. He would say: "Getting a little sloppy on that landing, sir." Or: "*What* kind of landing was that?" The chief began working on the plane the minute we got back and would work on into the night if need be. Staff Sergeant Brown loved that P-51, and I depended on him to keep the plane flying five to seven hours each day.

Immediately upon landing, we headed into debriefing with the Intelligence Office. We were offered two ounces of booze to settle our nerves. We could drink the alcohol there or save it to add toward a full bottle later on. I generally saved mine. We met with the intelligence officer of our squadron, who then provided the fighter group intelligence officer with information from our day's mission. We typically only reported when something unusual happened, like seeing a B-17 going down with no parachutes, or encountering enemy aircraft.

OUR TARGETS

The map of Central Europe shown in Figure 18 outlines the geographical areas of operational responsibility of the Fifteenth Air Force.

The responsibilities of the Fifteenth Air Force within this broad geo-graphical area were: (1) the destruction of the German Air Force; (2) the destruction of German fighter aircraft plants, ball bearing plants, oil refineries, rubber plants, and munitions factories; (3) the attacking of communication targets along the Brenner Pass route and in neighboring Austria; and (4) the weakening of the German position in the Balkans.

Germany's Achilles's heel was oil. The "Fifteenth Air Force in Italy would target refineries in Romania, Vienna, and Budapest, along with synthetic-oil plants in Silesia, Poland, and the Sudetenland."[3] "The Allied powers controlled more than 90 percent of the world's natural oil, compared to just 3 percent for the Axis."[4]

The Fifteenth Air Force selected its targets for bombing or other activity based on a stream of current target information provided by frequent photo-reconnaissance missions. The P-38 carried photo equipment in place of armament and required a small four- to six-plane fighter group escort.

Like all the other fighter groups, the 332nd flew bomber escort missions based on the strategic priorities of the Fifteenth. The longest flights required up to six or seven hours. I flew to a variety of locations shown on the map in Figure 18, including Regensburg, Brux, Bleckhammer, Innsbruck, Munich, Vienna, and Prague. I was later shot down while strafing in the Linz–Steyer area of Austria.

The bombers were all stationed in the vicinity of Foggia, Italy. This "locale placed heavy bombers within reach of every likely target in the [European] theater: Zagreb was 230 miles away, Sofia barely four hundred. Budapest, Vienna, Athens, and Munich lay within a five-hundred-mile arc; Regensburg, Bucharest, Ploesti, and Prague within six hundred miles; Blechhammer within 670; Marseilles within 730; and Berlin within nine hundred."[5]

The P-51 Fighter Groups, along with the other groups that provided bomber escort, the P-38 Fighter Groups, were mostly based north of Foggia. Figure 19 provides a visual image of the Fifteenth Air Force fighter and bomber bases.

The bombers, traveling a greater distance and moving at a slower rate of speed, were the first to take off. We could see them passing by our base an hour or perhaps an hour and a half ahead of us, depending on the winds. We would join them at our rendezvous point before they reached enemy territory and surrounded them above, below, and on both sides.

If it was a short mission, the fighter pilots might be assigned to provide the bombers with coverage into the target, over the target, for withdrawal from the target, and for getting them home. If it was a longer mission, one group

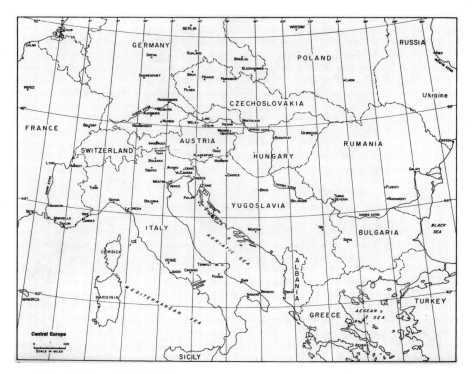

Figure 18. Map of Central Europe.

might escort the bombers to the target and another might pick them up after they had made their bomb run and escort them home.

If I saw enemy planes on a mission, I had one thought in mind. It was: "Today is the day. I'm going to get a couple of victories!" I looked forward to the day that I could actually engage an enemy aircraft. There were a few guys who didn't think that way and made no bones about it. They would say, "If I never see one, that's okay." I didn't tell them but I thought to myself: "It is best that you never run into an enemy plane or else you won't get back home. They'll blow you out of the sky." These guys were already defeated before they ever engaged the enemy.

Some missions were uneventful in terms of seeing or engaging enemy fighters, but on many missions the anti-aircraft ground fire, called "flak," was so thick that it looked like a black cloud hanging over the target. By 1944, "anti-aircraft flak had become the primary German defense. Flak was credited with destroying 6,400 Anglo-American planes in 1944 and damaging 27,000 others."[6] The loss of life in those bombers was immense. "In the first half of 1944, battle casualty rates for every 1,000 bomber crewmen serving six months in combat included 712 killed or missing and 175 wounded: 89 percent."[7]

I used to see those poor bomber guys hit the Initial Point (IP), the location where the bomb run began, and think that they'd be lucky to make it back out. They would turn into the target, and once they started in after the IP, they would fly a straight line. The pilot put the plane on autopilot, and the bombardier, who sat in the nose of the plane, took control of the plane. He would make corrections, to which the plane responded, as he lined up for the target ahead.

In my later years I met Bob Clemons, a navigator on a B-17, at a Minnesota air show. He described flak as follows: "Flak was terrifying, mostly because there was nothing we could do. At least we could shoot back at German fighters out in the open. We had thirteen .50 caliber machine guns on the B-17. There were ten of us on board, and all of us would shoot except the pilot and copilot. Once the bomb run began, however, we had to hold it steady. No evasive action. A bomb run could last five to twenty minutes. As navigator, I was sitting in the nose of the plane, right behind the bombardier, so I could see all that was going on. The Germans would saturate the area we were going to bomb. They knew our altitude because the contrails coming out of the exhaust of the airplane told them exactly where we were. The Germans mostly shot at us with 88 millimeter artillery shells. Those shells were lethal. They were half full of explosives and half full of junk—whatever else the Germans could find—steel, concrete, aluminum, cast iron. They went off either at impact or at our altitude. It was terrifying."

The Role of Fighter Pilots

Our job as fighter pilots was to escort the bomber formation up to the IP, where they would head through that black cloud of flak to the target. There was nothing that we could do by flying in there with them. Furthermore, the enemy fighters weren't about to go in there either, even if they saw our fighter planes around.

We would fly around the target, the black cloud, to the other side, where the bombers would exit the target area. While circling the black cloud, we paid close attention to any large explosion, signaling that a bomber was hit. If we observed any explosion, we announced it on our radio. Sometimes we might hear someone say, "Uh-oh, there's a 17 [B-17 American four-engine bomber] that just went down. Watch to see if there are any chutes."

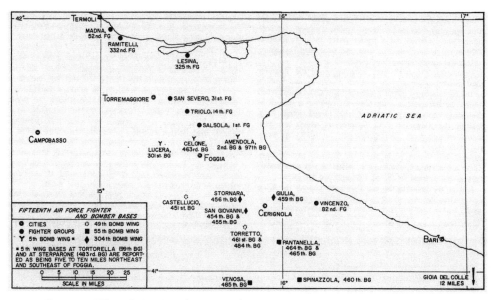

Figure 19. Fifteenth Air Force bases in Italy.

Enemy planes, if there were any, made every attempt to prevent the bombers from dropping their bombs. If that was unsuccessful, they would fly to the exit point and look for stragglers, planes that had been damaged over the target. The enemy planes looking for stragglers also had to deal with us because we were there to provide protection for damaged planes.

The bomber formation looked entirely different coming out of the target area after dropping their bombs. The formation, which was so beautiful going in, would come out raggedy, struggling to get out of the target area. Maybe a few airplanes had been lost over the target or a couple might have lost one or more engines or suffered other damage to their aircraft. There was a lot of hollering and screaming over the radio by those who needed help. The full realization of how serious this was occurred for me the first time that I saw the big explosion of a bomber and began seeing guys bailing out of their crippled bomber. I knew for the first time: "This is for real."

There were any number of occasions when bombers were in trouble and needed our help. We'd be halfway home and then we'd hear some poor guy up there saying, "I've lost two engines. Are there any fighters in the area? I need fighter cover, fighter cover!" And a leader in our squadron would say to a flight: "How's your fuel level? Why don't you go back and see if you can find that guy." So a flight would run back. Sometimes we'd pick them up, sometimes we didn't. If we picked them up, they'd be in the window waving at us, yelling, "Fighters! Fighters!"

Those bombers were so happy to see us. Oh, *man*, were they. Those were the guys that the enemy fighters were looking for. They were duck soup for the enemy fighters, who would just fly in and wipe them out. We Tuskegee Airmen had a reputation for losing significantly fewer bombers in comparison to other groups. That is why the bomber groups many times requested us for their fighter escort.

Of my thirty missions, perhaps during fifteen to twenty I saw no enemy fighters at all. On all the rest, they were sitting off over there and we could see them waiting. We would watch them and they'd watch us. Sometimes they would attack, sometimes they wouldn't. Out of all the missions when I saw enemy fighters, there were about six, maybe seven missions when they actually attacked the bombers. The other times they sat out and played games. They would come in, we'd turn toward them, and they would break it off and leave. We weren't in aerial combat every day.

Earlier in the war, the Germans were much more aggressive, attacking more frequently. The earlier Tuskegee pilots could make book that they were going to run into a fighter, and the only way they were going to get home was to outrun or outfight them. The Germans had some "hot rocks," some of the finest pilots in the world. It took all of our guys' skills to survive some of those battles. As the war went on, the more experienced German pilots were becoming fewer and fewer, and the Americans were getting better and better.

By the time I arrived in late 1944, we were far more in control of the skies and could come and go as we pleased. The Germans were definitely on the defensive and they were putting up fewer and fewer airplanes, while we were putting up more and more. In fact, "By July [1944], novice German fighter pilots typically received less than thirty flying hours in training before being hurled into combat, less than one-tenth the Anglo-American average; the life expectancy of a Luftwaffe pilot could be measured in weeks if not hours."[8]

There were a few occasions, however, late in the war, when the Tuskegee pilots did win some significant victories. One of the most memorable occurred on March 31, 1945, when twelve members of the 332nd Fighter Group shot down thirteen enemy planes. My close friend Bob Williams shot down two enemy aircraft and received a Distinguished Flying Cross for heroic actions that day.[9] Bob told me years later that he felt that the Germans they went up against were kind of desperate. They were less experienced and were just put up there for show. They simply didn't put up much of a fight.

While I never shot down an enemy aircraft, I feel content, in retrospect, with the thought that the enemy pilots I engaged are sitting home having a glass of wine just as I am.

THE "HEAVIES"

I have the utmost respect for the brave men of the heavy bomber aircrews. The Eighth Air Force, affectionately but accurately referred to as the "Mighty" Eighth, had a total strength of 200,000 people by mid-1944 and became the greatest air armada in history. At its peak, the Eighth could dispatch more than 2,000 four-engine bombers and more than 1,000 fighters on a single mission. The achievements of the Eighth Air Force did not happen without a high price in casualties. "Half of the U.S. Army Air Force's casualties in World War II were suffered by the Eighth Air Force (more than 47,000 casualties, with more than 26,000 dead)."[10]

Long after the war, I was invited to participate in an event called "The Gathering of Eagles" in Minneapolis, Minnesota. I participated with six other pilots with known reputations. One of these, Bob Morgan, aircraft commander of the well-known bomber *Memphis Belle*, remarked to me that it was nothing less than a miracle that he and his fellow airmen became the first bomber crew to successfully complete twenty-five missions—a full tour of duty. Morgan told me that he usually flew lead bomber and saw countless wingmen go down during those twenty-five missions.

Even though the number of bombers lost was high, the bombers also accounted for a large number of enemy aircraft losses. The bombers were well armed with ten or more .50 caliber guns. Many of the B-24s had two guns in front, two in back, two on top, two on the bottom, and one on each side. The B-17, armed with as many as thirteen guns, was called the "Flying Fortress."

However dangerous the work of the bombers, what they accomplished was absolutely critical to the war effort. It was essential that the infrastructure of Germany be destroyed so that the war effort could be crippled, thus bringing an end to the war. As the war effort evolved, the need for long-range fighter escorts for bombers became critical. Without such protection, the bombers would have continued to sustain heavy losses, and the war effort would have lengthened.

LETTERS OF THANKS

While the American public was largely unaware of the Tuskegee Airmen until 1995 when the HBO movie *Tuskegee Airmen* was aired, the bomber crews and their families were not.

An excerpt from a letter from Reed Sprinkel, Major, RAFR (Retired Air Force Reserve) follows:

> Dear Dr. Brown:
>
> As a B-24 Bomb Squadron, Lead Pilot of the 484th Bomb Group, stationed in Torrento, Italy, 15th Air Force, I and my crew were very aware of the Tuskegee Combat flight squadrons that would provide us "cover" during our B-24 flights into the enemy target area of Northern Italy, Austria, and other missions and then 'pick us up' on our return flights home.
>
> These Tuskegee combat pilots were highly skilled and precision fighter pilots. When they were 'covering us' from enemy fighters, they would bring their aircraft 'in tight.' We could see the faces of the pilots. We were extremely proud of these airmen, in the air and when we would see them in Foggia, Italy, when they must have been on R & R from their home base in Italy. We could identify them apart from other airmen because their uniforms were 'freshly pressed' with iron creases in their shirts and/or pants. Their high black boots (not G.I.) were polished giving a special shine. They all had a true 'military' bearing.
>
> Should you see any other airmen or pilots of the Tuskegee Air Group, please let them know that a 90 year old retired B-24 combat pilot still remembers their precision in flying their P-51Cs in formation, covering our Group on our combat missions.
>
> Thanks for 'bringing me home' many times and today I can express my true gratitude for their flying skills and possibly allowing me and my crew to talk and write about them 67 years later.

The son of a B-24 pilot, Steve Langley, wrote to let me and other Tuskegee Airmen know that the legacy of their achievements was continuing into future generations:

> I would personally like to thank the heroes of the Red Tails. They hold a special place in my family. They flew cover for my dad. He flew B-24s

Figure 20. Colonel B. O. Davis, "By Request." Courtesy of the Air Force Historical Research Agency.

with the 15th Air Force. He always told me as long as he had Red Tails, he knew he was a lot safer. . . . Thank you for keeping him safe. . . . My son went to the USAF BMT (Basic Military Training). . . . His squadron mascot was the mustang. At first I assumed it was the wild horse. After finally seeing a photo of the unit mascot, I realized that it was a tribute to the Red Tails. . . . so I told my son that the Red Tails continued to fly cover for him as they had for his grandfather.

Perhaps the most enduring symbol of the respect felt by the bombers for the Tuskegee Airmen was the phrase "By Request" painted on Commander Davis's plane.

II

DECEMBER 1944

When I arrived at Ramitelli in late 1944, many of the older, experienced German pilots had already been killed in action. Germany did, however, still have one big surprise and that was the introduction of two new fighters late in the war. One was the Messerschmitt 262 (Me 262), an operational twin-jet engine fighter aircraft, and the Me 163, a single rocket-engine fighter aircraft that was flying but never became a fully operational fighter. These two new aircraft used technology that was far more advanced than any aircraft the Allies were flying.

The Me 262 was a formidable challenger in the air. It was the latest and the best. Although the United States had jets, none were developed to the extent that they functioned as a critical force in the war. Colonel Davis later wrote in his autobiography: "If Hitler had concentrated on building and manning these jet fighters, he could have effectively stopped our bombing operations. The jets were a frightening development, and their advantage over our prop planes could have been overwhelming."[1]

When Me 262s attacked the bombers, they came in well above the B-17s, which cruised at around 29,000 to 30,000 feet. The Me 262s dove down into the bombers' stream, going extremely fast, constantly shooting, at the first B-17 to the last. They would usually make one, or at most, two passes.

December 9, 1944

We had grown accustomed to the enemy fighters' non-engaging behavior, their flying around without attacking, but on December 9, 1944, their behavior changed.

Our fighter group was providing cover for the bombers when we were jumped by nearly a dozen Me 262s. I was in the lead flight with the squadron commander, Major Campbell.

In formation flying, four planes make up a "flight," the flight leader with his wingman and the element leader and his wingman. If the four planes ever engaged in combat, they separated into pairs for greater maneuverability. On this mission, I was the element leader and Daniel Rich, class of 44-D, was my wingman, the guy who watched my back if enemy fighters were coming in. We were in the same squadron overseas, but had never flown in the same flight until this day.

As the Me 262s approached the formation of bombers and fighters, Major Campbell said: "These guys are coming in." We didn't hesitate to drop our wing tanks. Campbell said, "I'm going to grab the first one. You grab the second one." As they came in, Campbell timed his turn so that he could dive on the first one. When the planes came within a reasonable range, we knew, because of their speed, that we would have them in our gun sights for only three or four seconds. We either got a shot off or they would be past us and we would have lost the opportunity.

The second guy started his run into the bomber formation, and as he crossed in front of us, Rich and I timed our turn to get in one burst of our guns. Instead of flying through the bomber formation, the 262 performed what had been a favorite maneuver of the slower Me 109 and Fw 190: He immediately rolled over and pulled the nose down, performing a Split S, and we followed him.

Suddenly, I found myself chasing an Me 262—something I should not have been doing. I should have broken off, I should have given up the pursuit, but at twenty years of age and with the exuberance of youth—my eagerness led me to make judgments that I would not have had I been older or more experienced. Daniel Rich and I dove with the Me 262 straight down from 32,000 feet, shooting all the way. Our speed reached nearly 440 miles per hour. The German plane was quickly out of range; we were too far behind to hit him. There was no real chance that we could catch an Me 262 in a P-51. We were just hoping to get in a lucky shot. After all, he was still in our gun sights. So we went straight down from 32,000 to 22,000, the planes screaming all the way. I still got him a little bit in my sight and I am hollering at my wingman, "Shoot, we might get in a lucky shot." Well, we stayed with him . . . and we stayed with him.

He could have easily separated himself from us if he had leveled out and flown straight. With its two big thrusting engines, the Me 262 could reach a maximum speed of 500 miles per hour, whether it was flying straight and level or going straight down. The P-51 did not have the power to reach its own aerodynamic maximum speed in straight and level flight, but going straight down, it was helped by gravity to reach a higher speed, more than 400 miles per hour, still slower than the 262. So when the Me 262 rolled over and went straight down, his separation speed was less than it would have been if he had just flown straight and level. This allowed Rich and me to keep him in our sights a bit longer, even though he was distancing himself from us.

The Me 262 leveled off at 1,000 feet. We were skimming over the treetops in pursuit. As we chased the Me 262, he led us over a flak trap. Suddenly everything erupted below—every gun imaginable—short-range guns, pistols, Uzis—they were all firing at us. I assumed I was hit. I didn't know how bad Rich's plane was.

We both rapidly climbed out, but got separated in the clouds. My radio was out, and Rich, as he told me later, was screaming at me, giving me a heading to get back to home base. We could always call the "homer," a device that would give us a heading to go back home. The homer's radio waves worked well into Germany, but my radio was dead. I knew that I was in Northern Italy and in friendly territory. I assumed that I had been hit because I was losing fuel. Here I was at 25,000 feet, now with a dead engine due to fuel exhaustion, and this thing is dropping like a rock.

I've told many young kids that the worst thing you can do is to give a fighter pilot too much time to think, because he is used to reacting. He's been trained, in most circumstances, to respond fast enough and soon enough to save himself and the aircraft. But here I was with a whole lotta time on my hands.

I began to talk to myself: "Now what are you going to do, Harold? . . . You going to bail out? . . . You going to use the parachute? . . . I don't know . . . I got lots of time . . . I'll worry about it later." I am just going down, down, down.

I began looking for a place to crash land, when, at about 9,000 feet, I spotted an abandoned airstrip below. "Good news," I thought to myself. "I got it made! I'll come in and land there and then call the nearest base and ask them to send up a fuel truck. I'll refuel and be home in an hour."

The bad news was that there was a ditch that divided the strip into two sections of 2,000 feet each. The Germans had put a big ditch in the center, which

I couldn't initially tell from the altitude at which I was flying. Sometimes it's difficult sticking it on a 5,000-foot runway and here I have 2,000 feet to work with. I had no engine, so it was all judgment.

"I can do it, no sweat!" I said to myself. You can do anything when you are twenty years old. At least you think you can.

So I came in. On final approach, I was still dropping like a rock. I was really hot. With no engine, the plane was coming down at a speed 20 to 30 miles per hour faster than the "first stall warning." I had to keep the speed up by keeping the nose down. It was still slower than cruising speed but had to be fast enough not to stall.

At the same time, however, the airspeed had to be dissipated before I could land. Once I lost the engine, I was essentially gliding. When I was ready to land, I had to slow the plane up. All the while, my mind was bouncing back and forth: "I think I'll land in the first 2,000 . . . nope—too hot. I'll land on the second . . . nope . . . on the first . . . nope . . . on the second." Now this was occurring in microseconds, because I was falling so fast. So I finally decided to put it down on the first half of the runway.

I landed wheels up (a belly landing) but skidded into the ditch. I went into the ditch going pretty fast, so much so that the airplane came up on its nose. The fuselage of the plane teetered for a while and then it broke to the side. I was afraid that it might flip totally over, but it dropped back on its belly. I had jettisoned the canopy before the crash, just in case I might be trapped with residual fuel left to burn. I jumped out, the plane now resting on its belly.

The plane was heavily damaged, but I was not hurt. I dusted my uniform off and walked away from it. As I frequently remarked later in life, using an old saying: "Any landing you can walk away from is a good landing."

An Italian farmer who was close by and saw the crash gave me a ride in his buggy, taking me to the main road. I thumbed a ride on a 6-by-6 military truck to the nearest base, about forty miles south of where I had gone down. At the base, I let them know about the plane I had "parked" up the road, since it had guns on it. I also asked them to keep the gun cameras and send them back to the group.

On the base, I called in to Major Bill Campbell back at Ramitelli. At that point, all the home base knew was that Rich and I had been reported missing in action. Major Campbell asked where I was and what had happened. He finally asked: "Lieutenant Brown, why didn't you break it off? He had to be so small in your gun sight. He must have been no more than a dot."

I jokingly told him to blame it on the "exuberance of youth," but I said to myself: "There was no way I was going to break it off when I was that close to a victory," but I couldn't tell him that.

Campbell replied: "'What do you mean, 'the exuberance of youth'?" He went through the ceiling. Oh, did he chew me out. He cut loose and called me every name you could imagine. He asked me just exactly how long it was going to take me to get back to base.

I hitchhiked my way to Naples, where we went for R and R. It was on the way back to base. I waited there for a couple of days until the regular truck from Ramitelli showed up. Six days later I arrived back at my home base. Rich made it to the nearest base with little fuel remaining. He was able to fly back to our home base the next day.

The "Narrative Mission Report" for December 9 from the *History for December, 1944, 332nd Fighter Group* summarized my adventure in the sky in direct terms: "64 P-51s took off from Ramitelli at 0946 hours. 7 returned early (5 mech., 2 escort). Lt. Rich and Lt. Brown last heard calling "Highfield" at 1400 hours. Place unknown. Sorties: 54."

In layperson's terms, this report indicates that my fellow pilots and I took off at 9:46 A.M. and that five airplanes had mechanical failures—an illustration of why we always sweated engine problems. Rich and I were last heard at 2:00 P.M. trying to contact the homer, the radio that could give us a bearing to our home base. It was not clear where we were. Finally the report said that a total of fifty-four single planes flew the mission (sorties).

WHITE BOMBERS AT RAMITELLI

Initially the white bomber pilots in the war had no idea who was flying the Red Tail planes. However, in December 1944, we had very bad weather and a few bomber pilots had to land on occasion at our airfield with emergencies. They would spend the night and their observation typically was: "You mean to tell us you guys are flying those Red Tails? We didn't even know you were flying in the war."

On one day in particular, December 30, nearly twenty B-24s had to land on our field. "Suddenly," as Colonel Davis later recalled, "we had more than 200 white visitors scattered throughout our camp, living, eating, and sleeping as best they could under the severely crowded circumstances."[2] The weather was so bad that they couldn't get out for several days. All we had were our tents for four or five people. We just made room for our guests. Colonel Davis later reflected: "Such a mixing of the races would never have been allowed to occur in the United States. . . . They [the B-24 pilots] enjoyed their stay and learned that, in matters of humanity, we were not any different from them."[3]

Through this visit, the bomber crews really found out who the Red Tails were. Word got out in a hurry from that time on. "Hey, do you know who's flying those Red Tails?" That's how they knew who we were. It got to the point at which the bombers were requesting us.

A Review of 1944: "A Definite Milestone Has Been Passed"

As a whole, December 1944 was relatively uneventful and a time for all of us airmen to reflect on achievements of the past year. It was a particularly gratifying time for our leader, Colonel Davis, who wrote the following to the officers and enlisted men of the group, as noted in the *History for December, 1944, 332nd Fighter Group*:

> A definite milestone has been passed in our history. . . . When we embarked for foreign service, we were completely untried. . . . Since that day the Group has taken on the many varied assignments given it and carried them out with distinction and success. . . . I cannot fail to mention the all-important fact that your achievements have been recognized. Unofficially you are known by an untold number of bomber crews as the Red Tails who can be depended upon and whose appearance means certain protection from enemy fighters. The bomber crews have told others about your accomplishments, and your good reputation has preceded you into many parts where you may think you are unknown. . . . The Commanding General of our Fighter Command has stated that we are doing a good job and that he will so inform the Air Force Commander. Thus, the official report of our operation is a creditable one.

The *History for December* went on to share that Colonel Davis, who had completed a tour in the States, had returned on Christmas Eve. "His granting of interviews on Christmas Day to officers and enlisted men was a great boost to morale." Overall, "the first Christmas overseas for most of the personnel was one to be remembered, and certainly, one enjoyed."

Even with the celebratory mood that concluded the month of December, there were always tragedies that were part of service during a war. I lost two classmates that last month of the year. The report indicated that among the various losses in December, one included "a freak mid-air collision that resulted in the deaths of 2nd Lt. Earl B. Highbaugh and F/O James C. Ramsey of the 302nd, while on a transitional flight during the month." Highbaugh and Ramsey were not even on a mission. They were flying locally and somehow they ran into each other. No one ever knew what happened, but we had to move on. Death was a fact of life. These men were my friends, but I just accepted it. That's the way it was.

THE WAR IN OTHER PARTS OF EUROPE

While we were grounded for a significant part of December, the rest of the war marched on relentlessly. During this month, the Battle of the Bulge, which "became the largest battle in American military history," was waged.[4] The Allies did not believe that the enemy, reeling from earlier losses, could wage an offensive, especially in the winter months. Yet Hitler staked the future of the Reich on this one last attempt at victory. The offensive, begun in mid-December, lasted longer than a month and involved more than a million men.[5] In the end "roughly one in ten U.S. combat casualties during World War II occurred in the Bulge, where 600,000 GIs had fought."[6]

Those of us at Ramitelli had little idea of what was going on at the Battle of the Bulge, other than what we read in the *Stars and Stripes*. It may have been Hitler's last stand, but we didn't know that. For us, it was just one more battle. It was only in retrospect that we learned of the great loss of life in that bloodiest of battles.

12

JANUARY TO FEBRUARY 1945

THE WEATHER IN THE MONTH OF JANUARY 1945, the worst operational month in the history of the Fifteenth Air Force, continued to slow operations down.[1] The "Personnel Narrative" of the *History for January, 1945, 332nd Fighter Group* indicated: "Frequent rains, snow flurries and freezing temperatures were instrumental in curtailing operations." Not infrequently after the intelligence officer had rendered his message to us, the briefings terminated with a succinct "Stand Down." The "Special Accounts" section of the *History* further noted: "While generally a cold dark grey murkiness prevailed during most of the month, the Red Tails did find opportunity to register eleven missions against the enemy. Diversified missions and targets included Photo Reconnaissance escort and bomber escort missions to communications and oil targets at Vienna, Munich, Praha, Stuttgart, Regensburg, and Linz. The Luftwaffe, with seemingly no reluctance, continued to relinquish its rights to the air."

The news of the war certainly was improving. The *History for January* also stated: "With the German counter offensive completely stopped on the Western Front and the momentous Russian advance from the East, morale has taken an upward trend. . . . One could hear nothing but words of praise for the magnificent Red Army."

By February 1945, the nature of the war in the air had begun to change. The "Special Accounts" of the *History for February, 1945, 332nd Fighter Group* noted: "With strategic attacks reducing the enemies' oil production to a minimum, motor transportation has been greatly curtailed, and thus, rail traffic has boomed in a desperate attempt to supply a once arrogant and lawless army operation on many fronts. Determined that this vital avenue of escape would not be left unguarded, our pilots were ordered to strafe rail traffic in the areas bounded by Munich, Ingolstadt, Linz, and Salzburg."

As the weather improved, the number of missions increased as well. I flew around fifteen missions in February. I was also promoted to first lieutenant.

"Please Come and Identify Your Brother"

Equally important during February, I would reconnect with my brother. I had scarcely even thought of him until one of the most memorable experiences of the war occurred for both of us. I had not seen or written to Bubba since June 1942 when he went into the service. At that time I had been happy to see him go.

In February 1945, Bubba decided that he would try to reach me. I was stationed near Foggia, Italy, and Bubba was in Northern Italy close to the Po Valley. Bubba's battalion provided ammunition to the soldiers as they pushed forward through Italy. That February he got a leave and began the trek to my air base. He was on a 6-by-6 military truck when he was involved in a severe accident. As Bubba recalled the experience, "I was the last guy of ten to board the truck and was riding near the tailgate. As we went across a one-lane, muddy bridge over a river, the truck fish-tailed, hit the guard rail, and tipped over into the river. As the last one on board, I was the first to fall off, and the truck pinned me under it in the river." There were a total of twelve guys aboard the carrier, two in the front and ten in the back. Bubba later shared: "Four guys got killed, four guys were scared to death and four of us got severely injured." Apparently attempts had been made to repair the bridge after the Germans had destroyed it, but the repairs weren't enough.

Luck played a role in Bubba's survival, as it did not for some of his comrades. A steel rod from the truck went into Bubba's back, barely missing his spine, but the water was so cold that he didn't bleed as he would have under normal circumstances. He took gravel and rocks, and propped them under his head to keep his head above water. This kept him from drowning. Some of the guys did, indeed, drown. Others were injured. One man had his private parts smashed. Bubba remembered this man trying to urinate but not being able to do so. A rescue truck finally came the next morning and pulled the overturned truck off the men.

When Bubba woke up in the hospital, he was absolutely amazed to find that it was desegregated. Hospitals, it turned out, "were the only places in the

Army where segregation was not practiced." Even though he was badly injured, that time in the hospital seemed "normal" to him, since he was finally "on equal standing with people of various skin shades."

While at the hospital, Bubba told the staff to call his brother, Harold, who was in the 332nd Fighter Group at Ramitelli. I remember the shock of receiving that call. I was told that a Staff Sergeant Brown was in the hospital, and I was asked to come over and "identify" him. I don't know why the caller used that word, but I thought Bubba was dead. I immediately went to Wendell Lucas, the squadron operations officer and a close personal friend, to borrow his jeep to go see Bubba.

Wendell Lucas was one of the older guys who had taken Bob Williams, George Iles, Wendell Hockaday, and me under his wing. Lucas had graduated from Howard University and was already a first lieutenant when he applied for flight training. He had taught us younger men to drink scotch and urged us to become "Kappa" men when we went on to college. I went overseas with Lucas. He and I were both replacement pilots for the 99th. After the war, I never saw Lucas again. He left the military immediately and went to medical school at Howard and became an oncologist. He became one of the many Tuskegee Airmen who went on to successful careers after the war.

It only took me five or six minutes to reach the hospital, since it was adjacent to the airfield. After not speaking for several years, my brother and I were now minutes from each other. When I arrived, I couldn't believe my eyes. Bubba looked like hell. Every inch of his body was bruised. I could tell that it was he, but he was a mess. A real mess! His first request was that I brush his teeth. Having lain in that muddy creek for hours, he was desperate to have a clean mouth. I had to take a washcloth to get the toothpaste out of his mouth. I left Bubba and told him I would return to see him after I came back from a rest and recuperation trip to Naples for seven days.

A Promise Made but Not Kept

After a pilot had flown ten to twelve missions, he would be granted a week of rest and recuperation. There was no set time for this to occur, primarily because of the shortage of pilots. In December and January, the weather was so bad that we didn't fly much. There was little need for R and R. That February, however, after flying fifteen straight missions, I was ready for some R and R by the beginning of March. During the week that a pilot had off, he would go to a big hotel in Naples, Italy, which served as our rest center. There were bars and a great nightlife. The hotel was on the bay and I could see Mount Vesuvius from the hotel windows.

On one occasion I visited Pompeii and saw some of the ruins of the old city, including the ruts in the roads where the chariots had gone to the houses of prostitution. I also saw signs that had been prominently posted on poles; one was a "flying cock," a large penis with wings. Stores also sold pictures of women in various sexual positions, pictures that had been posted above the doors of the houses of ill repute. I felt like I was witnessing the "last days of Pompeii." At twenty years of age, this was quite a sight to see.

On the day of my return from R and R, I saw Bubba and promised that I would see him again after flying a mission the next morning. That was a promise I would not keep.

The next day Bubba could hear the planes from my mission coming in right over his head in the hospital. When Wendell Lucas, still in his flying clothes, came wandering into the hospital, Bubba knew something was wrong and the first thing he said was: "Is he alive or dead?" Wendell told him that I had bailed out of my damaged aircraft, that they had watched me all the way down in my parachute, and that I was alive when I hit the ground . . . or at least I appeared to be.

That was the last time that Bubba and I saw each other before being reunited back in Minneapolis in June 1945. Bubba's journey back to the States was arduous, to say the least. The original hospital to which he was taken was makeshift, a little dinky place with a dirt floor. The staff couldn't even X-ray his wounds. Eventually he was taken to Naples, where he stayed for three additional weeks before being shipped to Algeria, then on to the Canary Islands, and ultimately to Bangor, Maine. The hospital in Bangor served as a staging area where the wounded were segregated. Bubba was quick to point out that "segregation in the hospital meant that you were segregated according to injuries."

Finally, Bubba was flown with others by C-47 transport on a direct flight to Bushnell Hospital in Brigham City, Utah, a hospital that specialized in treating those with severe injuries such as amputees and those with brain injuries. Bubba had a paralyzed right arm, whose use he would eventually regain. He stayed at that Utah hospital for nearly four months.

The expression "Band of Brothers" describes the closeness that developed among the wounded in the hospital. After all, "There was always someone worse off than you were," Bubba recalled. One kid from Kentucky had a piece of shrapnel in his head. "They cut a big incision in his scalp, and they peeled it down and took a lot of the bone out. He had a big concave spot on his head where we could see his brain pulsating," Bubba shared.

The desire to go home became overwhelming. The wounded soldiers practiced singing a song for several days and then descended as a group on Captain Booth's office. The captain said not to let them in, because he knew they were just trying to get home. Their song went something like this: "Wanna go home, but it ain't no use. Captain Booth won't turn us loose. We've got the Bushnell Blues." Finally, after hearing the song multiple times, the captain jokingly said: "Just send those dumb sons of bitches home!"

When he arrived in Minneapolis, Bubba first went to Fort Snelling and had his bandages changed. He said that the doctor was startled when he took his shirt off and saw the size of the wound in his back and the size of the bandage. "It looked like six Kotex napkins—it was huge." From that point on, Bubba could go home almost every weekend. When he left the hospital for good, he stripped his bed and put the blankets and sheets in the barracks bag. Once our mother, Allie, got hold of them, those blankets and sheets made pajamas for both him and dad.

I had sixty days of leave when I arrived home and Bubba had ninety days. From this point on, we—the brothers who had had no contact—became best friends. In 2012, as part of the memorial service for my brother, I shared the following in my eulogy: "A strange thing happened that summer of 1945. I really can't explain it. I can only tell what happened. Bubba and I greeted each other like lifelong friends. The five-year difference, which had earlier hindered our relationship, had simply vanished. We palled around like Siamese twins—we were inseparable. This lasted two months of that summer and then I had to depart for my next assignment. I realized then that Bubba had become my dearest and best friend; he remained so for the rest of his life."

13

MARCH 1945

I HAVE FREQUENTLY BEEN ASKED WHAT WAS memorable about my thirtieth, and last, mission. I typically respond: "I survived."

Most of my missions were as a bomber escort, but occasionally I picked up a high-priority strafing mission. On these, our focus was to fly low and shoot as many bullets as it took to take out a target. Often the missions were to seek out road and rail traffic, and disrupt and destroy them. Sometimes our targets were locomotives pulling up to a hundred cars loaded with war materials such as trucks, tankers, munitions, and fuel.

During my time overseas, I was on five separate strafing missions and almost always one or more of us got hit by enemy fire. We usually all got back to the base, but most of us arrived back with holes in our aircraft. Although it was exciting, strafing was also the most dangerous kind of flying we were asked to do. Even though these missions were significantly more dangerous than others I undertook, I was no more cautious than usual. When I saw a ground target, it was balls out. I swept right in on them. It actually became fun going in on a target. I would start shooting close to the tail end of the train, at the caboose, and then just walk right up the train, shooting all the way up to the locomotive. If I shot something that had an explosive on it, the car would blow, and I would say, "Good deal!" When I got up to the locomotive engine and continued to fire for an extra three or four seconds, the engine would blow up. With that, I'd peel up off the target. I didn't give anything else a thought. I was just having a ball.

These flights were more dangerous than others because I was flying very low and more and more people were able to shoot back at me using whatever weapon was handy. On missions where it was strictly strafing, I got hit *every* time. I would come back without even knowing I'd been hit. When I returned from my first strafing mission, the crew chief said: "You've got a hole." Way back in the elevator on the tail, there was a little hole from small-arms fire. It was difficult, however, for ground fire to bring a plane down. I would be coming in at nearly three hundred miles an hour and a man with a rifle wasn't likely to hit me. If he did, he would have to hit something very, very vital within the engine to bring me down. Nonetheless, strafing missions were much riskier because everybody and anybody was shooting at me.

A single strafing mission could do significant damage to enemy resources. According to the March "Narrative Mission Report," on the day I was shot down, twenty-one planes took off and by the end of the day, the record of damage was: 18 locomotives either destroyed or damaged; 136 box cars either destroyed or damaged; 37 flat cars damaged; 8 oil cars damaged; 7 motor transports on flat cars damaged; 3 railroad stations damaged; 2 railroad buildings damaged; 1 power station damaged; and 1 warehouse left burning.

On bomber missions, in contrast to strafing, fighter pilots couldn't leave the bombers and go off on our own seeking targets. On occasion, however, a flight from a squadron would be able to seek "targets of opportunity" on the way home, once the bombers were secure. The problem with seeking railroad-ground targets after completing a bomber escort duty run was that the Germans knew the exact time we were returning from a bomber mission. In anticipation of such air attacks on their troop and supply trains, they could use the numerous tunnels in the Alps to hide the trains until the fighters were gone.

It Was Going to Be a Field Day

On March 14, 1945, the day of my thirtieth mission, the Fifteenth Air Force wanted to run a special mission against high-density rail traffic connecting the cities of Bruck, Leoben, and Steyr near Linz, Austria. The tracks ran for nearly one hundred miles southward from Linz. In addition to the rail lines, there were several marshaling yards (railroad yards used to separate railroad cars on to one of several tracks). It was a very, very heavily traveled area. The Fifteenth Air Force wanted it wiped out. The 332nd was given the mission, and the 99th was selected to fly it.

This mission was not part of a bomber run, so the Germans could not predict when we would be returning—adding an element of surprise for which the Germans could not prepare. Major Campbell was the squadron leader of our twenty-one airplanes. I was part of the lead flight and was Major Campbell's wingman. Wendell Lucas was the element leader.

Our airfields weren't set up for night flying, so we took off just as the sun was starting to come up. We arrived at the southernmost point of the one-hundred-mile stretch and headed north toward Linz, Austria. The steam from the locomotive engines in the distance indicated a high level of rail traffic. "Oh, man alive—look what we just found," Commander Bill Campbell said. We had put up every plane we had, and we had caught them out in the open. It was going to be a field day.

As the squadron headed north along the rail corridor, every twenty miles we dropped off a flight of four. Each flight was responsible for destroying all the rail traffic found in that area. For the next hour, there was a constant flow of chatter from all the separate flights, describing the destruction of rail traffic: "Here's one over here!" "Boy, I just got one" "Did you see that locomotive blow up?" Our guys were just shooting up the place. It seemed like each time we pulled the trigger, we blew up a target.

Our 99th fighters would blow up the locomotive and then make a couple of sweeps of the box cars, thirty or forty in a string and all loaded, until they blew up. We had a really good day of destroying locomotives and boxcars. The drop-off pattern had continued until Major Campbell and I reached a point just south of Linz, where we turned around and began to head back down the valley.

We were collecting flights as we returned south. The other pilots had been circling, waiting for us, and so in turn they now joined the growing group. Most of them were out of ammunition and there was not much left to be done, until Major Campbell looked down and saw a huge locomotive. "Hey," he said, "somebody missed one down there."

"It's Always the Last One"

In later years when I thought about that moment, I often remarked: "It's always the last one. That's the one that always gets you, the very last one. It always happens that way, every time." At the time Campbell told me: "Let's run down and wipe this one out." As the two of us dove toward the target with Campbell in the lead, I could see little trails of smoke coming over his wing from his guns as he fired. Finally, he ran out of ammunition so I told him to get out of the way, that I had a few bullets left.

As he peeled away, I dove in. I can still see that locomotive today. It was huge with a double set of drivers on it. It had a big, big engine and a long string of boxcars. I thought to myself: "A locomotive that size has to be hauling everything!" So I went in, focusing on the locomotive. I carried six .50 caliber guns, and each time a bullet struck the locomotive, it would sparkle. It was clear I was hitting my target because the engine sparkled like a Christmas tree.

But the locomotive wouldn't blow, so I kept driving in on the target. Suddenly, the first boxcar behind the engine dropped its sides and two multi-barrel Pom Pom guns began to fire at me. Immediately, another boxcar, a little farther back, dropped its sides and its guns began to fire. That was a total of four guns, each with four barrels, or sixteen barrels, *all* shooting 20 or 40 millimeter shots at *me!*

Close to every fifth bullet was a tracer, a bright bullet, showing the shooters where their bullets were going. The glow of the tracers looked like red golf balls coming right at me. As I saw this, I said to myself, "Harold, what have you gotten yourself into? You are in deep, deep trouble." I concluded that if I pulled up, I would be a sitting duck, showing the gunners below the whole profile of my airplane and becoming a perfect target. My only choice was to continue to drive into the targeted engine, pass over it, and then keep the plane on deck at tree-top level long enough until I was far enough out to break off and get out of there. I kept saying to himself: "Come on, blow up. Blow up. Blow up. You gotta blow up!"

I got my wish. Just as I passed right over the engine, there was a *huge* explosion. When the engine blew, everything blew, including the boxcars that had the guns in them. Timing is everything! If it had blown three seconds, or even two seconds, before, I might have had time to pull up and get away from the major force and debris of the explosion, but it went off just as I passed over it.

I felt the airplane rock and roll. I came out of it upside down on my back, so I rolled it back over and began to climb. All I could think about at that moment was: "Wait till I get back to the base and the guys see these pictures! Just wait until we begin to review these pictures. These are going be the most beautiful camera pictures that the guys will ever see." Our planes carried a camera in the wing to record everything we had been shooting; mine had been recording pictures the whole time as I passed through the explosion.

The three members of my flight began to circle me. They were calling and waving wildly. They could see that I was trailing black smoke, something I was not aware of until then. I was soon to discover my problem: All the debris that came up when the locomotive engine exploded had hit my airplane, knocking out the oil line and fatally damaging the engine. About this time, the instruments started going crazy. The oil pressure was heading to zero and the oil temperature was pegged right to the maximum. Years later after the war when we were all back at Tuskegee, the guys told me that they had said to each other, "Poor Brown, he's had it."

I had sufficient airspeed when I was hit with the debris to climb to about 1,000 feet and I headed due east, hoping to get out of German territory and to the Russian lines. I thought: "If this thing can just keeping running for maybe fifteen or twenty minutes, I can get pretty close to the Russian lines and I just might get out of this." Within a minute or two, however, the liquid coolant from that Merlin engine came blowing out against the windshield. Once I had lost that coolant, I knew the engine might run thirty or forty seconds, but then it would freeze up and I'd experience total engine failure.

At 1,000 feet with no power, a frozen engine, and the propeller windmilling, it was clear to me. "This is the end of the road. Now I need to start thinking about getting out of the airplane." The first thing a pilot thinks about is his own safety, and I had few choices. It was clear that there was no place to crash land. I was in the foothills of the Alps with snow deep on the ground.

Everything was happening so fast that I reacted automatically—based on my extensive training. I'd gone over this a thousand times in my mind. I knew what I had to do. Get out of the plane and get the chute open. I jettisoned my canopy, pulled the plane up, rolled the plane over, released my seat belt, kicked the stick forward, which popped the nose up, and I just dropped out of the plane. Once clear of the airplane, I pulled the D-ring and felt the shock of the chute opening, and finally saw the beauty of a fully opened parachute.

I thought to myself with a big sigh of relief: "Well, at least I have a good chute so the first part is okay."

I was concerned about a "good" chute because we had heard that a few of the parachute riggers in one of the fighter groups had pulled the silk out of some of the chutes, sold it, and re-stuffed the chutes with a substitute. Silk was highly prized and sold for a high price. I don't know whether that had actually happened, but my fear of a faulty chute was certainly on my mind right before I jumped.

The guys were circling me as I was coming down. I can still see Campbell sitting in that plane as I was coming down, waving at me. So the guys, seeing my chute fully deployed, broke off, and headed for home base. This was the first and last time that I ever pulled the cord and parachuted out of a plane. I have often remarked over the years: "I would *never* be a skydiver. To jump out of a good flying airplane makes no sense to me at all. No indeed."

After the guys departed for home, a most interesting thing happened. Once I was alone, it got deathly quiet. There was just a little whisper of the wind in the chute. I could hear the sound of the airplanes dying out in the distance. At that moment, I was so lonely. I thought: "Man. I'm up here all by myself. Not a soul I can turn to. What has happened to me?'

In a notebook that I carried with me at that time, I later noted that I had bailed out between Bruck and Steyr. Military records reported: "1st Lt Harold H. Brown of the 99FS was reported lost with his P-51C at 1115 hours east of Bruck, Austria, after being damaged during a strafing attack."[1]

For their heroic actions on this day, five members of the 332nd Fighter Group and its 99th Fighter Squadron each earned a Distinguished Flying Cross, which is awarded for heroism or extraordinary achievement in aerial flight.[2] I was not among those who received this recognition, which was certainly disappointing, but the recommendation for the DFC had to go up the chain of command to the group commander. It was easy to recommend and award the DFC if a pilot had shot down enemy aircraft. It was more difficult to determine if a pilot had flown a "heroic" or "extraordinary" flight. Group Commander B. O. Davis was very conservative in this regard. I am not aware of anyone in our group being given the DFC after being shot down, as I had been, or being given it posthumously. I don't even know if Major Campbell had submitted my name for consideration. In the end, what I had done was not regarded as sufficient to be awarded a DFC. I was disappointed, but that was that.

ENEMY TERRITORY

After I bailed out, I floated for about two minutes and the ground was coming up. I don't know what the rate of descent was when that chute opened, but boy, I was dropping fast. I wasn't that high when I bailed out, and then, boom, I hit the ground. I landed on the side of a hill in the snow, up to my knees. The "Narrative Mission Report" for the 332nd on March 14, 1945, described my landing as follows: "Pilot bailed out at 1115 hours at 4738N – 1439E, was last seen about to land in the snow halfway up a mountain. Cause unknown."

After landing in the snow, I began to gather my wits about me. I grabbed my little escape pack, which contained a map, a compass, and a few other things. I pulled up the chute and grabbed hold of it, and started tromping through the snow to get to a small nearby wooded area. As I got close to it and there was still no one around me, I thought: "If there's some way I can just evade the enemy, head east, and make some decent time without being picked up, I might just be able to get to the Russian lines in seven or eight days."

However, I had not gone more than a half an hour before a couple of civilian skiers came up over the hill. I could see them sling off their rifles and they both took dead aim at me. I realized that I had to act quickly and throw away my .45 caliber handgun. I had been told that it wouldn't help me anyway, and I'd be better off not having a weapon on me if I was captured. I never really understood why pilots were given a weapon. What were we going do with it anyway?

The skiers told me in gestures that I was going with them. They got me to a road and within a half hour they had marched me back to Hieflau, a small Austrian village in one of the target areas. Well, I was scared as hell. The fear was pretty much coming from the unknown, not knowing what was going to happen. I didn't speak the language. By the time we reached the town, there was a cursing and ranting mob of people staring at me. I began to have a few thoughts about the briefings the intelligence officer had repeatedly given us: "Whatever you do, get as far away from the target area as possible, because people there are upset and angry." The civilians were the ones suffering from the shrapnel and bullets flying around. Even though the pilots had not been shooting at civilians, the bullets could easily have ricocheted, randomly striking people in the towns and villages.

A mob of over twenty-five very, very angry people had gathered in the town. They were screaming at me. Although I couldn't speak or understand German and I didn't know what they were specifically saying, I clearly understood the signs they were making: pointing their fingers as if they were guns or making a gesture to indicate a noose of a rope. A number of the villagers had ski poles and were jabbing at me, saying, "Boom. Boom. Boom." It was clear what they had on their mind. As far as I could tell, they were arguing among themselves about how they were going to kill me. It was clear that they finally decided to hang me. They took me to a perfect hanging tree, with a nice low branch, and they had a rope. I can still visualize that tree today. I knew at that moment that I was going to die.

It is very interesting what goes through a person's mind in such dire circumstances. First, it was hard for me to accept that this was happening to me. I kept telling myself that it just couldn't be true. Then the realization hit me: "There is a war going on. Here you are and you are the enemy. You just got caught. What do you think is going to happen to you?" I continued to think: "This is absolutely crazy to be in this situation. Here I am only twenty years old, and me of all people, with this face, being here in Germany. This is the last place I need to be, in the middle of a war."

I was probably in a state of shock. I kept asking myself: "What are you going to do? You've got to do something. What are you going to do, Harold?" But I had no answers. I just assumed that I was going to die. I couldn't see an alternative. I finally decided that I would go kicking and fighting as they put the noose around my neck.

As I learned discussing such matters with others after the war, my reaction at being captured, that of surprise, even shock, was fairly typical among prisoners. Historian David Rolf, writing about POWs, explains, "Every man who was captured went through a traumatic ordeal. . . . The only common feeling was one of surprise that he should be 'in the bag' at all. Overwhelmingly, men report, they thought of being maimed or even killed. But taken prisoner?"[3] That was the farthest thought from their minds.

I cannot recall exactly how long it took to get to the village, but from the time they picked me up until they got me back to the village could have been forty or fifty minutes. It didn't take long for a larger angry mob to form. It was likely that the villagers had seen my airplane when it came off the locomotive target and saw that it was smoking. That probably alerted them to the possibility of my bailing out or of my crashing.

While caught up in my own thoughts, I had not been paying attention to what was now going on around me. Then I noticed what appeared to be a local constable, dressed in riding breeches and boots and carrying a rifle, moving toward us, speaking to the mob in German. There was a very rapid discussion with the skiers who had caught me. It went on for a few seconds and then those two guys dropped their guns and backed off into the mob. The constable moved toward me and then I felt his hand on my shoulder as he snatched me backward and stepped in front of me. I could hear him hit the bolt on his rifle. I suddenly realized that the constable was going to help me.

The constable now began to speak loudly to the villagers. It was apparent that they did not want to listen. He screamed at the villagers, and the villagers screamed back at him. Years later, reflecting on this experience, I thought: "He was a constable there. He knew every one of those people. They were probably his friends, and here he was, holding them off with his rifle."

The two of us backed up almost a quarter of a mile into the middle of the village, the crowd following close behind. He continued to hold the gun on the crowd. We arrived at a pub. The constable kicked the door open and ran out all the people. I can still see those steins that they poured the beer into from the tap. The mob outside continued to scream and curse.

The constable and I moved the heavy furniture, the big oak tables and heavy chairs, in order to barricade ourselves in. The crowd broke out the windows, but they couldn't get in because there were bars on them. It was already late afternoon and the sun was going down. It was mid-March and cold outside. The crowd began to disperse. We stayed in the barricaded pub until about midnight, when it had grown quiet. We assumed most of the villagers had gone home. The constable and I went out the back door and walked about two to three miles to another small village. The constable made a phone call and within four hours two soldiers came to pick me up.

As the soldiers took me away, I saw the constable for the last time. He had saved my life. If he had wanted to hurt me, all he had to do was turn his back and just let the mob do what it wanted. I was the enemy, but I wasn't *his* enemy at that time. As the district constable, I was his responsibility.

Apparently my treatment as a recently downed airman was fairly typical of pilots during the war. Historian Thomas Saylor, who interviewed many POWs, wrote: "Airmen everywhere could expect better handling from those in uniform. Indeed, there are numerous accounts of military or policemen protecting captured airmen from mistreatment or death at the hands of enraged civilians."[4] In the end, I regretted that I had never sought this man out to thank him for saving my life.

LIFE AS A POW

The soldiers and I got into a truck and were transported about ten miles to a small jail, where I was kept for three days. Most of the time I was scared as hell. I didn't know what was going to happen. I didn't know the language. Every time the guards walked up to the cell, I wondered: "What are they going to do to me now? Are they going to kill me?"

During the course of the day I was given a small portion of bread and something that looked like a weak soup. That happened a couple of times a day. Other than that, I just sat there. I think that was the most unsettling thing of all, because from minute to minute I never knew what was going to happen. I kept playing this unknown factor over and over in my mind.

A few days after arriving, I heard bombers going over in a raid and I thought: "I might just have company before long. Someone is going to get shot down." The number of American POWs in Germany was close to 93,000; of this total, nearly 33,000 were airmen, with the majority being crew members of heavy bombers.[5]

I was indeed correct about that sound, and my prediction proved to be true. A bomber had been shot down. By 10:00 P.M. that evening, the Austrians had rounded up all eleven members of a B-24 crew and brought them to the jail. They were wild-eyed and half frightened to death. Many were as young as I. I could imagine how I must have looked after I had bailed out and been transported here.

I thought: "I've had three days to be frightened to death, and now I am the old guy."

The guards divided the new prisoners up into four cells, three or four to a cell. It was here, in this small Austrian jail cell, that I experienced integration for the first time. The crewmates who were placed with me in my cell naturally wanted to know who I was. When they were brought in, they looked around curiously. When they saw me, I could see that they wondered: "Who in the world is this guy?" I could see the suspicion in their eyes.

I had my jacket on, and wings on my jacket, but here I was a black guy and I guess a lot of folks still hadn't heard we were flying airplanes. I figured that this crew was part of the Fifteenth, based on location, since the Eighth would not be in that area.

One of them finally asked if I was an American. I told him, "Yes, I'm an American."

"You're a pilot?" he asked.

"Yeah, I got wings, just like you've got wings. Same kind of wings, you know. I was shot down, too." I added: "I'm also a member of the Fifteenth Air Force. I probably escorted you at some earlier time."

Once their suspicion was gone, the bomber crew pelted me with questions: "What are they going to do with us? What's going to happen to us? How long have you been here? Where are we going next?"

I could only answer, "I've been here three days. I have no idea, guys. The only difference between you and me is that I've been here for three days and you're newcomers. That's the only difference."

One frightened young man approached me and said: "I'm scared to death. I'm Jewish." To try to lighten the situation, I told him: "All you've got to do is to keep your mouth shut and nobody will ever know you're Jewish. You got it made. Look at me. I can't hide. They know what I am." Everyone got a laugh out of this. It was meant to be a joke, but it was still a fact.

As I was to learn later, the threat to prisoners of Jewish origin was real. In February 1945, shortly before this bomber crew was shot down, one of the most notorious examples of abuse occurred when Jewish and Jewish-looking prisoners were transported from the IX-B Bad Orb POW camp to the concentration camp at Berga; many of these men suffered abuse and died.[6] I also found out later that "In many places the airmen's dog tags, stamped with information that included their religion and name, were scrutinized. If the tag showed the letter 'H' (for Hebrew) or if an airman had a German-sounding name, he was usually handed over to the Gestapo but often he would be murdered on the spot."[7]

The Trip to Nuremberg

After a couple of days in the small jail near Linz, we began the trip by truck to Nuremberg, the location of the interrogation center for aircrews in Southern Germany. It took nine days of traveling to get the twelve of us there.

Because we were POWs, the two guards who were always with us picked up any vehicle—an old bus, train, whatever could be found—to get us to the destination. More than once we were dropped off with our guards and placed aboard a local bus with civilians. Another time we were transported in a cart as we went from one village to another on our trip to Nuremberg.

We had a fair number of guards who were members of the German Air Force. Back in those days, our Army generally looked on the Air Corps guys as the "goof-offs." I found the men of the German Air Force to be "just as lax" as the men in the US Army Air Corps. The Wehrmacht, the regular German Army, was all *military*. These men were regimented and were fighting for their lives daily. They were well trained and rigorous in their behavior, because their lives were at stake every day.

Most of the men in both the German and US Armies or Air Forces were certainly qualified to do their jobs, but the men in the Air Force did not have the military bearing and were far less regimented. In the Air Force, there was a relatively loose military structure. The mechanics, communications people, and armament people were all skilled. They were great at their jobs, but they weren't great soldiers. They never did a lot of marching the way the regular Army did. They just went to work and did their jobs. The mechanics would go to the flight line and work on the airplanes well into the night to keep them flying, but they just lived a different life from infantrymen.

It turned out that the German Air Force was the exact same way. The

German Air Force guards were loose and we could talk, even BS, with them. I thought: "Things really don't change all that much. Here I am in Germany with foreign troops, and it's the same way that it is back in the States."

One of the most terrifying moments of my captivity, however, was when we were on a train containing both boxcars for carrying munitions and other military goods, and passenger cars. We looked out and saw a flight of P-51s. I thought with some relief: "Oh, it's our guys!" But it quickly dawned on me that these planes were getting ready to strafe *this* train. Now I knew what it felt like to be on the other side of an attack.

Everyone on the train dropped to the floor. We could hear the bullets go raking over the boxcars—tearing them up. We could hear our airplanes coming in and there was no place to run, no place to hide. We were just out there with our bare behinds, hoping that we didn't get hit with a bullet with all those guns firing. I don't recall if it was an engine with ten cars, twelve cars, fifteen cars, or more. At the time it felt like there was only *one* car, the car that I was in. It seemed as if all the bullets were being directed toward that one car. I know that wasn't the case, but that's what it felt like.

It was the most terrifying experience I had ever been through, to see these guys coming down, strafing our train. All of us—guards, civilians, prisoners—were panicked. We ducked into little corners, hid under the seats, and went anywhere we could find in the passenger portion of the train, hoping the guy driving the train could get into the tunnel before the whole train blew up. In my mind I was telling that engineer: "Full throttle, Go! Go!" The windows were being blown out as the sound of "PATATATATAT" continued. All I could think was: "Jesus Christ, don't tell me I'm facing a meatball rap, that I might be killed accidentally by my own guys."

Fortunately, the engineer was doing everything he could to get to a nearby tunnel and it didn't take long to reach it. Once inside, we were all right. That was the big thing. As we pilots knew, whenever the trains were attacked, they would run for a tunnel. Once the train had reached safety, the P-51s broke off the attack and went on about their business. Amazingly, no one in our car was injured.

WELS AERODROME

As we made our way to Nuremberg, we arrived at Wels Aerodrome, the huge German air base in Wels, Austria. This gigantic airfield was well known to all of our pilots because it had a couple hundred fighter planes, and whenever we flew close to it, we could expect Wels planes to come up after us.

As we came in by truck, we passed revetment areas, barricades made of sandbags designed to provide shelter against bombing fragments or strafing attacks for the Me 262s being housed there. As we were driven across the airfield, all I saw were those Me 262s. They were beautiful. There were three or four airplanes in each revetment area. As the winding road passed through the base, there were revetments on each side, one after another. There were times when we were only a few feet from the planes. At one point I pounded on top of the truck, telling the driver that I had to get off the truck. He responded: "*Nein, nein, nein,*" but I wanted to get a closer look at those beautiful airplanes, so I jumped off. The guard immediately aimed his rifle right at me, which convinced me that I should hop right back on that truck. I guess jumping off wasn't too smart on my part, but I just wanted to see those beautiful airplanes.

When we arrived at the Wels Aerodrome jail, we were put in a small cell where we stayed for a couple of days. At one point in our stay a German captain, really sharply dressed, wearing breeches and boots, came into the jail. He wore pilot wings and spoke perfect English. He asked: "Any fighter pilots in the crowd?"

"Yeah, I'm a fighter pilot," I answered.

He said, "Yes! I know about you guys. You're the black outfit." He called us *Schwarze Vogelmenschen* (Black Birdmen), the name that the German Luftwaffe used to describe the pilots of the 332nd.

The captain was also a fighter pilot. He told me that he flew the Me 109 (a German Messerschmitt single-engine fighter) and the Focke–Wulf 190 (also a single-engine fighter). Earlier, in our training, we had been told to be very, very careful of what we said if we were captured so as not to give up any secret military information, but I wasn't suspicious in this case. The war was beginning to wind down, and there appeared to be very little risk in discussing airplanes with this pilot. We were having an almost normal conversation for pilots, just as if I had met any other pilot for the first time.

"Hey, how are you doing?" "What airplane do you fly?" "I fly such and such." "Have you ever seen such and such?" It was not an interrogation. We all knew that the war wasn't going to last much longer—three months, six months, a year maybe at the outside.

I was surprised at his perfect English. The captain told me: "I was trained in England and went to Oxford University." He had spent a good part of his life there and said that he hoped to go back either to England or to America after the war. After his schooling, he had come back to Germany and had wound up in the military.

The captain asked me: "Have you had any encounters with German aircraft? Have you ever run into an Me 109?"

I told him that while I had seen them, I had never engaged one, but the pilots who had didn't think much of them. They thought the 109 was slow. A pilot could turn one reasonably well, but it was slow. The captain agreed.

The captain then asked, "What about the Focke–Wulf?"

I responded, "The speed of the Focke–Wulfs was comparable, but the 51s were still able to outturn the Focke–Wulf."

The captain was not quite willing to concede that point. "Well, I've been in a few dogfights, and I just don't know about that."

I told the captain that I had even chased a Me 262.

He said, "An Me 262? How can you chase an Me 262?"

I responded, "Well, we came in at about thirty thousand and peeled down on him. As long as he was going straight down, we were staying with him."

The captain said, "Well, yes, that's about right. But what happened when you leveled off?"

"Well, there was a difference then," I said.

I always believed that Hitler made a mistake by not mass-producing the Me 262. If he had been willing to put more of them up in the sky, he might have been able to keep fighting longer, but Hitler apparently believed that any plane that couldn't drop a bomb was useless.

As my conversation with the captain came to an end, I was surprised to realize that we were just batting it back and forth, talking about airplanes, pretty much like any two old fighter pilots would do. After a half hour, the captain asked us if we were hungry, if we had eaten.

I told him, "We haven't eaten for the last three or four days."

The captain left and came back with four loaves of bread, each roughly eight inches long and four inches across. He also brought in a big bowl of strawberry jam. I can still see that bowl of jam. I could not believe my eyes. Where in the world would he get jam, and such a big bowl of it? The captain also brought in a chunk of baloney, roughly twelve inches long and six inches in diameter.

The captain told us, speaking in English so that the guards could not understand: "You notice how the guards are looking at you? Now, you are eating better than they eat. I'm going to sit here and you just eat as much as you can, because when I leave, they're going take what's left."

My fellow prisoners and I just ate as much as we could. Almost wiped it all out. That was the first meal we'd had in a while. When the captain left, there was a small chunk of meat there. As he walked out, a soldier came over and picked up the small chunk of meat that was left, the jam, and what was left of the bread. It happened just as the captain had said.

Just before he left, the captain gave us some parting advice: "The war's not going to last much longer. Don't do anything stupid, don't try to escape, and don't give them any reason to shoot you. The worst that can happen to you is that you wind up in a prison camp, and all you've got to do is just sweat it out, because the war just isn't going to last much longer." With that, he wished us good luck and left.

14

NUREMBERG

After leaving the Wels Aerodrome jail, we were taken by train to Nuremberg. At the train station, the eleven other POWs and I had one of our greatest scares. The station was large, with rubble all around. As we were standing around waiting for transportation to the Interrogation Center, up walked an SS officer.

One of the guys said, "Oh my God, this guy's SS."

The officer had a patch on his coat lapel showing that little symbol, the double lightning bolts, which represented the initials SS and the terror they inspired.

Looking sharp as a tack, he walked up and said something to our guards, who had popped to attention as he approached. He was obviously talking about us, pointing to us while speaking German. He seemed to be asking questions about us, like "Who are these people, who are they?"

The guards indicated that we were airmen who had been shot down. At one point, he stopped talking and walked over to us. We kept our heads down and no one said a word. He walked around us. Then one of the guys looked up and the SS officer spit right in his face—right in his face and no one said a damn word! I just knew he was going to do it to me. I said to myself: "He can spit all he wants but he will get no response from me." He continued to walk around our small group, murmuring things under his breath. By the tone of his voice and the expression on his face, I could tell that his words were all ugly and directed at us. After he walked around us a final time, he said a few more words to the guards and then walked off.

In retrospect, there was probably nothing preventing that guy from pulling out his gun and just shooting one of us. No one would have said a word. The guards would not have stopped him. If the civilians had seen it, most of them would have said, "*Gut, gut* [good, good]." We had all heard of the Gestapo, the German Secret Police, and the SS—about what mean people they were—and all we could think was, "Jiminy, am I going to have to face this guy? If this yo-yo gets pissed off for no reason, none whatsoever, he could pull out his gun and blow off my head." We just didn't know what the hell was going on and what would happen next. Once again, that whole unknown factor got to us. Not a comfortable position to be in at all.

The temperament of SS officers was well known. They were very nasty people, and they shot anyone they felt like shooting. Even the German Army soldiers, the Wehrmacht, were afraid of them. It may be most easy to understand the difference between the Wehrmacht and the SS by understanding their names. *Wehrmacht* means "defense force" in German, while SS (*Schutzstaffel*) roughly translates as "protection squadron," as in the protection of Adolph Hitler and the Nazi Party ideology. The SS troopers would die for Adolph Hitler, and they committed unspeakable acts of terror and brutality in his name. This was an elite group of what I would call a big bunch of murderers.

INTERROGATION CENTER

The primary reason we had to go all the way to Nuremberg to be interrogated was that the Germans were in full retreat from the Americans. The Americans were making fast gains during this point in the war. They had landed in Normandy in June 1944 and were rapidly moving across Europe, pushing the Germans back toward their homeland. The original *Dulag Luft*, the abbreviated German name given to the transit POW camps for Air Force prisoners, had been in Frankfurt. The word *Dulag* signifies "transit camp," and *Luft* means "air" in German. The purpose of these camps was interrogation before the prisoners were transferred to "*Stalags*" or permanent camps. A *Stalag Luft* was a prison camp for captured Allied airmen. *Stalag Luft* camps were identified by roman numerals and often by the nearest city or town. There were seven camps for airmen.[1]

We were interrogated in Nuremberg. Captured airmen were interrogated in more depth than the other men in the military, primarily because we spent most of our time in friendly territory and knew what was going on by having access to newspapers and real-time briefings. Soldiers out in the field, on the frontline, did not have such opportunities or information. They were just fighting day-to-day, and didn't know what was going on in a broad sense, about the war. They were rarely assigned back to a safe place behind the lines, where they could hear the news and get a bigger picture of the war and its progress.

THE MAJOR

A major in the German Army was my interrogator on my first day in Nuremberg. He was wearing a freshly pressed military uniform with breeches and sparkling boots. I was in a ragged flight suit, and had not shaved, combed my hair, or bathed since my plane had crashed.

The major spoke perfect English, having gone to school in England just like the captain I had met at Wels Aerodrome. When he first began to speak, I thought: "His English is better than mine."

The major began by asking simple questions, such as, "At what altitude do you fly your missions?" I thought to myself: "The major has seen airplanes flying over hundreds of times and his question seems trivial."

The major then asked me, "Would you be able to distinguish a red cross on the roof of a house?"

I thought to myself and remembered, "Old Pitts said not to get into extended conversations with these guys; just give them your name, rank, and serial number. So I kept saying, "Harold H. Brown, First Lieutenant, AO830783."

The major continued to ask me if I could distinguish a red cross.

I thought to myself: "From 30,000 feet, I could hardly distinguish a small building much less the writing on it," but I said nothing. I could only surmise that a Red Cross building had been bombed and that the major was trying to determine if a pilot could have seen the red cross from the air.

The major continued with questions and shifted to low-level missions, asking if we were flying any of those. He also asked if I had encountered any civilians and, if so, how had I been treated. I repeated my name, rank, and serial number.

Finally, the major kind of smiled at me, and said: "Yeah, I know, Harold, your name, rank, and serial number. I know all about how they train you guys."

He then told me, "I'm going to send you back to your cell and then I'm going to bring you back in here tomorrow morning. You are going to tell me everything I want to know or else I'm going to turn you over to the civilians."

The major further emphasized, "You came here and you shot up the place, so I'm going to turn you over to the civilians out there."

Well, that will strike fear in the bravest man's heart. The civilians were the ones who were really suffering from all of the bombings and strafings. The casualty rates were probably higher among the civilians than among the German Army itself. With those kinds of threats, I was given good reason to stay up that night wondering: "Is this guy serious or not? What do I know? What can I tell him? If it comes to saying something, or being thrown out there to the civilians," I thought, "what are some things I could say, but at the same time not say anything?"

The next morning was pretty. The sun was shining as the guards came to pick me up and take me back to the major's office.

The major's first question surprised me. "You hungry, Lieutenant Brown?" he said.

I responded: "Well, yes."

The next question surprised me even more: "How'd you like a nice orange?"

He gave me a great big, juicy orange, one that I can remember to this day. I thought to myself: "Hey, this is great, you know. Piece of fruit. Oh, boy."

So I'm munching on the orange and the major says: "You think about what I said yesterday?"

I responded with a simple "Yes."

The major continued to press me, "Are you ready now to talk to me?"

I responded, "Name, rank, and serial number, sir. Nothing else."

The major's next statement surprised me even more: "Matter of fact, I probably know more than you know, Lieutenant Brown. I don't believe that there's anything you can tell me that I don't know. Come back in my office. I want to show you something."

I went with the major and on his desk I saw five bright blue binders with white-colored lettering on their covers. One said, "The 332nd Fighter Group." The other four volumes were the Squadrons of the 332nd: "The 99th," "The 100th," "The 301st," and "The 302nd."

The major asked me: "You recognize those names, those numbers, right, Lieutenant?"

I said, "No." That was probably one of the few times that I kind of smirked.

The major continued, "Oh, come on. Let's stop playing games. You know perfectly well that's the 332nd Fighter Group, and you know that we know that there is only one group of *Schwarze Vogelmenschen* in this war."

The major added, "We know that you were trained at Tuskegee. We can tell your graduation date, and we can tell exactly when you departed from Newport, Virginia, the Port of America."

I sat in shocked silence for a moment, but then thought to myself: "When you stop and think about it, all that the major knew was in the newspapers. All he had to do was go buy a newspaper to get all that information. But still . . . it was very impressive. Very impressive."

I was still playing the game with the major when he stated: "You were in the 99th Fighter Squadron," and my response was: "Oh?"

The major continued: "You want to know how I know?"

I responded: "*Nein*," or "No," one of the few German words I knew.

The major declared: "Your airplane's number was A-32. You were in the 99th Fighter Squadron. I know it from your tail number. You were shot down in A-32, and only the 99th Squadron has the A suffix."

The intelligence officers had told all of us pilots to never look surprised when interrogated, to never give anything away with our facial expressions, but at this moment, I feared that I had given myself away. I knew this guy was watching my face, saying to himself, "I saw that expression change!" Yet I was determined not to admit anything.

The major continued, "I know the squadron you were in, and as young as you are, I would guess that you probably haven't been over here more than six, seven, or eight months. So you probably graduated, oh, back probably in March, April, or May, in one of those classes. And that would have been, in May, Class 44-E. April would have been 44-D, but that's probably close enough." I just looked at him, and tried to not appear surprised, because my class was, in fact, 44-E.

The major then said, "Let's talk about the 99th." He pulled out one of the great big books. At first I was amazed. There he had the pilots, the guys with victories, and the guys who had gone home on rotation. I reassured myself, however, that the major had read all of that in the newspaper and that was all there was to it.

The major continued, "Now I'm going to tell you something you don't know. It was awful nice of old Captain Pitts, who is your intelligence officer, to give you all of those intelligence briefings. He's the one that tells you to give nothing but your name, rank, and serial number. Of course, it is certainly easy for an intelligence officer to say this since he isn't flying a mission. He's sitting back there, nice and safe in his little tent, back there in Ramitelli, where you fly out of."

The major then told me: "I've got news for you. Captain Pitts was just promoted to major. Now, I know you don't know that, but this happened after you were shot down. He's now Major Pitts."

The major shared other information as well. He started thumbing through cutouts of articles in papers. He told me about a couple of the American pilots who had shot down three or four German planes. He talked specifically about Captain Toppins, who had four victories and was in the 99th, and Charles Hall, who was also in the 99th. The major mentioned how much he had looked forward to interrogating these pilots about their victories.

At this point, the major asked me if I had any questions and told me: "I can answer more questions than anything you can probably ask. I know all about your outfit. Ask me anything you want."

I maintained my silence except to say, "No, sir." And that was the end of that.

The major told me that sometime during the afternoon, I would be taken to a POW camp on the south side of Nuremberg. "I am sending you back to the camp. I am through with you."

Then he became quite friendly. In fact, he gave me advice that was very similar to that which the captain at Wels Aerodrome had given: "When you get in prison camp, don't try to escape and don't give the guards any reason to shoot you. The war isn't going to go on much longer, and there isn't any doubt that it's just a matter of time before the German Army is going to have to surrender. Good luck."

I said goodbye to the major and he said goodbye as well, and that was the end of the conversation or interrogation.

Nazi Propaganda and Violence

On the way back to my cell, I encountered another Tuskegee Airman, Lincoln T. Hudson, who was in 44-F, the class immediately after mine. Civilians had beaten Hudson almost beyond recognition. When I saw him, he was just a mess, a mass of bruises. His face in particular was just terrible and even his hands were all bloody.

When I first saw him, I was startled. "Lincoln?" I asked.

And Lincoln, equally surprised to see someone he knew, said: "Harold?"

I said, "Yeah. What the hell happened to you?"

Lincoln's lips were thick and swollen. He could barely talk and was just mumbling most of his words. He told me that he had gone down in the target area and had been picked up by civilians. A couple of soldiers had come and taken him from them, but when a larger group of civilians had shown up, the soldiers had simply turned him over to the crowd. "They weren't going to stick their necks out for me," he shared.

The civilians literally beat the hell out of him. "They were kicking me, stomping me. All I did was just lie there and pretend I was half dead. I was almost unconscious anyway so it was easy to do. I just laid there until the civilians got tired. Then the two soldiers came back and grabbed me by the arms and got me on my feet."

Lincoln, who had gone down due to engine trouble on March 23,[2] had been transported down from northeast of Vienna to Nuremberg, where I encountered him. It seemed ironic that we had ended up in the same place. Lincoln's experience with the civilians was certainly an interesting contrast to mine. First, he hadn't had a uniformed person intervening on his behalf as I had. Second, his more traumatic experience may have also been partly due to where he crashed. "The likelihood of violence, even lynch justice, being directed toward downed airmen was highest in and around urban areas, the primary targets of bombing attacks."[3]

Compared to Lincoln, I had lucked out again. It was not until many years later, in the summer of 2013, that I learned just how lucky I was. During that summer, we were visited by two Austrian historians who were doing research for the University of Graz and for the Austrian Ministry of Defense. They were investigating war crimes in Austria and Hungary, including ones related to the Tuskegee Airmen.

In particular, the historians were investigating the death of Walter Manning, Class of 44-D, someone I had known quite well. Manning had crashed on April 1, 1945.[4] He had been reported as MIA in military records since his plane had never returned. Through research, the historians were able to document that Manning, "a prisoner of war at the Linz–Hörsching air base, was publicly hanged by a mob that included members of the Luftwaffe in the early hours of April 4, 1945."[5]

The historians were able to link the violence against American pilots, but especially against the Tuskegee Airmen, to the propaganda against the black pilots that had appeared in German newspapers. The historians shared: "Skin color was a crucial factor in how the men were treated. It had become known in the Alps and the Danube region that the U.S. Army Air Force, which practiced racial segregation, had a separate formation of African American men. These were the so-called 'Tuskegee' airmen, who flew in the 332nd Fighter

Group. According to Nazi propaganda, these men were not only 'terror flyers,' they also fell under a Nazi racist enemy stereotype."[6]

While I was in Germany, I had seen a big poster of a Red Tail airplane in a dive. I can still see that poster vividly in my mind. The Red Tail plane looked just like our fighters, and there could be no doubt that this was what the picture was depicting. The plane was strafing a mother with her child in her arms. In the cockpit of the plane, there appeared the head of a great big gorilla with a hairy face and with goggles on. A tail is coming out of the cockpit. The pilot shoots at the woman as she huddles, trying to protect her child. The caption under the picture said: *Mörder von Frauen und Kindern* (Killer of Women and Children). The portrayal of black men murdering German children apparently was an effective tool of the Nazi propaganda of the day. It was designed to incite the civilians to violence, and unfortunately, in the case of Walter Manning, it had worked only too well.

THE MISSION TO BERLIN

Very shortly after Lincoln had gone down in his plane and about the time I was reaching Nuremberg, another drama was playing itself out for the Tuskegee Airmen.

On March 24, 1945, the Red Tails participated in the very famous mission to Berlin. This is generally considered to be the most important mission of the Tuskegee Airmen. The 332nd Fighter Group earned its only Distinguished Unit Citation of World War II for bravery during this mission. It was a point of great pride for all the Tuskegee Airmen, including me, and was later featured in the 2012 movie *Red Tails*.

I would likely have been on this mission had I not already been a POW.

The trip to Berlin was the only one the Fifteenth Air Force made of that distance—1,600 miles round trip. For the fighter pilots, it would have been an eight-and-a-half-hour trip. It was my impression that the leaders of the Fifteenth Air Force wanted to bomb the German capital just to be able to say that they had done it. The Fifteenth had never attacked the German capital before; this was an assignment that was usually covered by the Eighth Air Force. Flight crews "dreaded the most viciously defended city in Europe," known to some bomber pilots as Big B. It was a likely target since it "housed not only the [German] regime but 5 percent of Germany's *Volk*."[7]

The specific target in Berlin on March 24 was the "Daimler–Benz tank assembly plant, which produced armored vehicles resisting the advances of the

Allied armies.[8] The tank plant was expected to be heavily defended by anti-aircraft artillery and by the best German pilots, who would be flying Me 262s. In preparation for this mission, "the Fifteenth Air Force assigned no less than five of its seven fighter groups to escort the bombers."[9] Each fighter group had an assignment. The 332nd Fighter Group "was assigned to provide close escort for the 5th Bombardment Wing on penetration to the target."[10]

"The aerial dogfights" of this encounter "were incredibly intense. The Germans launched as many as 30 jet Me 262s against the bombers."[11] "Eight of the Mustang pilots each shot down an enemy airplane that day."[12] The Tuskegee Airmen of the 332nd claimed three of those victories and was the only one of the five fighter groups to earn the Distinguished Unit Citation (DUC) for the mission.[13] A very victorious day for the Tuskegee Airmen, indeed!

Stalag XIII-D

After my encounter with Lincoln T. Hudson at Nuremberg, we were all put on a truck and taken about seven miles south of Nuremberg to the huge POW camp, Stalag XIII-D. There was barbed wire all around the outside of the enormous camp, and within the larger camp were smaller compounds of about two hundred men each. Every compound was also encircled with barbed wire. I was interned there for about a week and a half.

As the other prisoners and I walked up to the POW camp, we could see the prisoners inside peering out from behind the fence. They were a motley bunch—unshaven, wearing the same clothes they had been captured in. When new prisoners were brought in, the POWs inside would move to the fence and look for anyone they knew. We could hear them say: "Hey, prisoners coming in. Anyone we know in there?" Then they began to holler: "Anybody from the 56th Fighter Group? Anybody from the 88th Bomb Wing?" Occasionally one of the incoming prisoners would shout back: "Yes, I'm from the 88th." It was almost like a homecoming.

Just by chance, as I looked at the faces at the fence, I saw another Tuskegee Airman, my classmate and one of my dearest friends, George Iles. Of all the luck, George was here. We were together throughout the war from that point on. George was twenty-five while I was just twenty, a big age difference. He was married and more experienced in life than I. Iles was also really smart. After the war, when there no longer was a need for as many men in the Army Air Corps, many of the guys, including myself, applied for the regular army. If a guy was "regular army," he could make a career of it. If he was only a "reserve officer," he served at the pleasure of the military and could be eliminated at any time. Iles was one of the very few to be selected and offered a regular commission. He made full colonel in the field of intelligence and had several missions behind enemy lines in Vietnam.

George had been shot down on February 25, 1945, and had been reported "missing at 1245 hours (12:45 PM) over Augsburg, Germany, after being hit by antiaircraft artillery fire."[14] The February "Narrative Mission Report" for the 332nd further notes that Iles "was heard over R/T to state that he was on a course of 250 degrees headed towards Switzerland (plane coolant hit by flak)." We thought that he had made it to Switzerland, but in reality his plane was badly damaged. He crash-landed right before the border. If a pilot got to Switzerland, he had it made. The Swiss, being neutral, would keep a POW there, but in a nice hotel. They would not give him up, but wouldn't let him go either. Iles would have been the "guest of the Swiss" and could have lived the good life for the rest of the war.

Instead, Iles and I were in a German prison camp. Within each compound, there were usually small groups of ten or twelve men who had something in common. As it turned out, I wound up in the same compound with George. Since George had been there a few weeks, he had already become associated with a small group. He introduced me: "Hey, this is my classmate. We were in the same outfit, the 99th, flying together. And I was shot down two weeks before he was." We were the only ones in there from the same outfit. Flew together. Trained together. Went overseas together.

I asked Iles: "What happened? I thought you were making it to Switzerland."

He said, "Harold, that airplane quit on me. I thought I had Switzerland made, but I crash-landed it. I jumped out and I am running like crazy, because I saw these German soldiers and they were running after me! I could see the Swiss border, but the Germans chasing me fired a couple of shots over my head. I knew I'd never make it and that they would blow me away if I kept running. So that's when I stopped and that's how they caught me."

I was able to deliver some great news to Iles: "Hey, Iles, you're now a first lieutenant. The orders came out after you were shot down. We were on the same orders and promoted at the same time."

Iles said: "I am? Well, that's great. Now all I have to do is to find some silver bars to replace these gold ones."

Not all of our classmates were as lucky as George. On the same day, February 25, 1945, that George was reported missing after being hit by antiaircraft artillery fire, Wendell W. Hockaday was reported missing "at 1225 over Uttendorf, Austria, after suffering damage during a strafing attack."[15] The "Narrative Mission Report" of the 332nd for that date further notes: "Lt. Hockaday was last seen at 10,000 feet near Uttendorf (plane disabled by concussion from exploding locomotive)." Years later, Wendell Lucas, a pilot who was also on that mission, told me that part of Hockaday's left wing had hit the locomotive while he was strafing the train. He was still flying, but he couldn't gain any altitude and had to get over the Alps to get home. Two of the aircraft stayed with him.

Lucas flew up in front and checked the height of the mountain to see if Hockaday could get over it. He told him that it wasn't possible to clear the mountains. Apparently there were some clouds and the other two pilots lost sight of Hockaday. They did not know if he had hit a mountain or if he bailed out. They never heard from him again. The Austrian historians who visited our home indicated that Hockaday had tried to bail out but lost control of the aircraft. He reportedly died in a crash not far from Salzburg.

SAME DAMN BOAT

The prison camp was quite similar to the portrayal of such camps in the movies. It looked almost exactly like the camp on the 1960s television program *Hogan's Heroes*, which was also called Stalag 13.

When a pilot was shot down, the most dangerous period was getting from where he was shot down to a POW camp. If anything bad was going to happen, it was going to happen during that time. Once a guy got into a prison camp, he was relatively safe. Yes, he was locked up. He didn't eat regularly, but at least he was safe. No one was going to walk in and shoot him unless he did something stupid to give the guards an excuse. Prison camps were not concentration camps. It was not the most pleasant of conditions, but at least a prisoner could survive within the camp.

I have often been asked if I ever thought about, or even tried, to escape. The answer is "No." The camp was well organized by the senior American officers who were present and they repeatedly warned against escape attempts.

We slept on three-layer bunks made of wooden slats. The first thing that happened each morning when we got up was a head count. Shortly thereafter, in an hour or so, the guards brought in food. It was always the same: a loaf of bread and this so-called soup. That was it. The guards didn't require us to work. There was no slave labor, none of that stuff. We were just there for the duration. Waiting.

We could walk out of our barracks and around the building. Within our little compound's barbed wire fence area there were stalls where guys could at least get water on their faces. But that was it. No bathing, no nothing. The whole time I was there I wore the same clothes I had on when I was captured. That was the least of my concerns; I was just trying to survive.

I often joke that when I was a prisoner of war, I experienced integration for the first time. I had to be shot down to become integrated. There were Englishmen, Americans, Australians, and Canadians in our compound. No one person was treated any better or worse than the next person. There was no segregation in the POW camps. Some of us were officers and some were enlisted members of flight crews. We became very friendly with a number of the guys in there. We were all in the same damn boat, living the same way, day in and day out.

One of the most memorable experiences at the POW camp was watching the British bomb Nuremberg at night. There were numerous British pilots at the camp and they all went outside at night to see the lights. The British flew their missions primarily at night and never got into massive daylight bombing raids the way the Americans did. The British had identified several towns for saturation bombing as payback for what had been done to London. These towns were to be completely, totally obliterated, and it was done systematically, night after night. Just bombed it out, square, by square, by square. Nothing was to be left standing. Nothing. Nuremberg was one of the cities designated for this saturation bombing.

On one evening before the bombing began, a British pilot explained what was going to happen. "First, the Pathfinders, airplanes with full crews and full navigation systems, are going to come in and locate the targets for the bombers. Because there is almost complete darkness, the Pathfinders will begin dropping flares to line up their targets."

As we watched, soon flares were dropping all over the place. Then here came the bombers. They weren't flying in big mass formations, but were almost bombing like single airplanes operating independently. From the ground we couldn't see them coming in, nor could we know when they released their bombs. We could, however, hear the "boom, bloom, bloom" of bombs exploding as they struck their targets. We suddenly realized that if the bombers got too close to the camp, some of that damn shrapnel, which could fly for miles, could hit us.

15

THE MARCH TO MOOSBURG

GEORGE AND I WERE PART OF A MUCH larger human drama when we were ordered to evacuate our POW camp at Nuremberg. By the mid-1940s, the Allies had driven the German forces back to their country's prewar borders. The POW camps suddenly came within range of the fighting. The German High Command decided to evacuate the outlying prison camps rather than allow them to be liberated by the advancing Allied forces. The decision to empty the camps created enormous problems for the Germans, because tens of thousands of Allied POWs had to be moved. Germany's transportation system was collapsing, which meant the men had to walk. There was little shelter and food along the way.

I had been at the Nuremberg camp for only a week and a half when the other prisoners and I were told that the Americans were getting close. All the prisoners had to be evacuated—all 10,000 of us. We had to walk almost eighty miles from Nuremberg to Moosburg, Germany. Moosburg is about thirty miles north of Munich. The trip would take about two weeks. The journey began with a walk through Nuremberg. The Allies had left virtually nothing standing. All we saw were just some framework and steel girders. The town was just rubble.

One terrifying moment occurred just as we were getting out of Nuremberg. We looked up and saw the Eighth Air Force coming to bomb Nuremberg. At first, we thought: "Oh, great."

As the airplanes dropped their bomb loads and began turning off their bomb run, their flight path was coming right over us. Some of the POWs, who were bombardiers themselves, said: "Oh, my God. If a bomb is hung up, them damn dumb bombardiers are going to kick it out."

It was not unusual for a bomb to hang up in the bomb bay. When that happened, the bombardier would go back and literally kick it until it fell out of the plane. The bombers certainly were not taking a live bomb home. As we watched from below, we had visions of what it would mean if a bomb were kicked out over us. That was a real "sweat session." It was certain death if it fell on us. Fortunately we made it out of Nuremberg without incident.

ON THE ROAD

We were quite a mob as a group walking together, a string of 10,000 men, walking in groups of about two hundred. We walked two or three abreast, so the line stretched out for quite some distance. The pattern was to walk for fifty minutes and rest for ten.

I preferred the walking each day to being cooped up in the prison camp behind barbed wire. It was really quite nice being out on the road. At least it gave us something to do. Then there were those ten-minute stretches when we would halt and generally just sit around on the ground. In a short while we would hear, *"Raus! Raus!"* ("Up and out! Up and out!") We would get up and start walking again. We walked from daylight until wherever we were supposed to go before it was dark.

At the end of the day we were usually out in the countryside. The guards— just a couple for each group of two to three hundred prisoners—would put us on or near a farm, where we were to set up camp. Within seventy or eighty yards there would be another two hundred of us with a guard or two around. That was much nicer, living out under the stars instead of being in the POW camp. We slept for the night on the ground. We all had been given a blanket when we left camp. Iles had two or three changes of socks that he had scrounged from someplace. He gave me a pair of wool socks and said, "At least you can change your socks." I was still wearing what I had on when I had been shot down. In one instance we ended up in a church and slept there. It was a rainy night so we thought that was a good deal. Men simply picked a spot and slept on the floor.

The men on the march had one overpowering concern "that dominated thoughts and conversations": food!—or rather, the lack of it. "With the economy in shambles by spring 1945, the Germans simply were unable to supply the wandering columns of prisoners crisscrossing the countryside. Men searched frantically for anything edible."[1]

Many of the POWs didn't smoke, and since I had a baby face and looked about fifteen years old, they gave me all the cigarettes they had received in Red Cross parcels and I used them to barter for food. I would go up to a farmhouse door, knock on it, and beg for potatoes in exchange for cigarettes. The guards did not bother us about this, so I became the trader. Even decades later, I can remember the little bit of German that I had used to barter for food at that time. *"Haben Sie Kartoffeln für Zigaretten?"* (Do you have potatoes for cigarettes?) or *"Haben Sie Brot für Zigaretten?"* (Do you have bread for cigarettes?) I was reasonably successful on many occasions getting three or four potatoes, or a loaf of bread. Other times they would just say, *"Nein, nein, nein."* (No, no, no).

On one occasion, George Iles and I decided to put our knowledge of Southern cooking to work. Many people, particularly Northerners, don't know anything about greens. We had picked up a very small piece of meat, along with some potatoes. We then camped near a little farm where we saw all these dandelions. We picked a mess of greens, pulling the dandelion heads off and cleaning them the best that we could. We had little cans that we used for cooking utensils, and went up to the farmhouse to get some water. We were cooking greens! We threw in those few potatoes and the small slices of meat and there we had it: the flavor.

I can only compare the experience of cooking those greens, potatoes and meat to a cartoon I had seen where there is a little wisp of smoke in which the cartoon character kind of floats. He looks like he is floating in air. That little aroma was like that wisp of smoke. The other POWs started coming over to us, wondering: "What's that? What are Brown and Iles cooking?" They then saw the dandelion greens and asked: "What are those? Weeds?" Once George and I had convinced them that the smell was more important than the sight of the greens and that greens were "damn healthy for you," the guys started picking their own dandelions and then tried to simply throw the whole mess of dandelions into their pots. When their results were just awful, we had to explain that they had to cut the dandelion flower from the stem and then carefully clean the greens.

All in all, we lived well while we were walking. It didn't matter where I was, there were good people everywhere, just like the captain at Wels Aerodrome. Another instance of kindness occurred when I knocked on the door of the home of an old German woman who was just as sweet as she could be. She had to be at least eighty years old, perhaps ninety, and stood just about four feet tall. I began to ask her in my broken German whether she would be interested in trading. I asked for potatoes and onions in exchange for cigarettes or chocolate. The old lady looked at me, smiled, then walked right up to me and began to talk to me in German. I'm certain the questions she was asking were about me personally.

"Who are you? Where are you from?" I was probably the first person of color that she had ever seen.

She touched my face gently, and just as gently touched my hand. Then she rubbed it. "Is that a color or is that dirt?" she must have been thinking.

She left for a few moments and, using a hand motion, told me to wait. It was clear from the hand motions that she was going to get something for me. She came back with a bag of potatoes and gave me five or six big ones. She also gave me a couple of onions and a chunk of pork. Now that was eating. That was first class.

I offered her cigarettes but she said: "*Nein, nein, nein.*" She would not take anything and just smiled at me. I said, "Thank you, thank you, thank you." She waved at me as I left. It certainly gives a person a different perspective when experiencing encounters like that.

ON TO MOOSBURG

During my days as a POW, I carried a small black notebook in which I recorded some of the dates and several of the cities that we passed through on the way to Moosburg. It shows that I bailed out on March 14, that we reached Nuremberg by March 25, that our forced march to Moosburg began around April 4, and that we reached Moosburg around April 18.

After the war, I tried to find the towns and villages mentioned in my notebook on a map of Germany. My spellings do not always match the German spellings of today and some towns (perhaps villages) are not even included on current maps, yet enough of them still exist that our path, as we were moved south toward Moosburg, was clear.

The list of cities and towns also indicated the days that food parcels were delivered to our camp by truck convoys from the International Red Cross. This was the most critical part of any week. At that point we were living on what we received in those parcels, and were seeing them only every seven to ten days. The Germans had no food either so they took their share, too. The parcels, stamped RED CROSS, were in a box that was about 14 by 14 inches

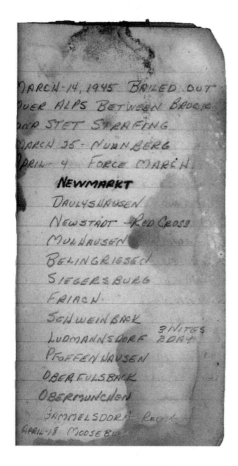

Figure 21. The journey to Moosburg.

and 6 inches deep. Besides chocolate and cigarettes, the parcels contained tins of all kinds of food, from ham and eggs to stews to something resembling Spam. The military, in those days, ate everything in rationed portions, and the Red Cross parcels were no exception.

In every prison camp, the highest-ranking officers among the POWs, primarily colonels, would be put in charge of the prisoners. As word got out that we were going to be put on a forced march, some of the camp commanders had told us to save whatever food we might have, since it wasn't clear when we would get more food parcels.

The officers also stressed not trying to escape. "Look, this war's going to end soon. Don't go crazy and try to escape. Where are you going to escape to? Where are you going to run to? Don't take the chance. If you're thinking about it, forget it."

On the march we often shared a can of whatever we were eating that day to make the parcel last longer. If we were very, very careful and if we could pal up with someone, we could really stretch those food parcels. There was probably enough food for one person in a parcel for a couple of days, but that could be wiped out very easily. Two partners, instead of both opening up a tin, opened one tin and shared it. Other times we took the powdered milk, the chocolates, and other food and mixed them all together into a great big ball, which then hardened. At least that was something to munch on.

The Germans also gave us one loaf of black bread each day for every seven airmen. The bread looked like a brick and was very, very coarse but I came to love it. The Germans stacked the bread like bricks and then covered it with a big canvas to keep the weather off it. We were also told that because there was such a shortage of flour, the Germans were stretching it by adding fine sawdust.

We constructed makeshift knives out of tins. We *Kriegies* (shortened form of the German word *Kriegsgefangenen*, or war prisoners) threw nothing away. We were pack rats and kept everything. With various parts they collected, some of the guys even made radios.

When we got our little loaf of bread, the cutter, a duty that rotated daily among the seven of us, would measure very precisely and mark the pieces off. All seven of us would look at it, and if we all said we were satisfied that the pieces were equal, only then would the cutter very carefully cut the bread, making sure that each was a nice straight cut. Each of us took our slice, making sure we got all of the crumbs that went along with it.

If I have one memory of those days on the march, it was that we were always hungry. We talked constantly about what we would eat when we got home.

A section of my small notebook was devoted to what I most wanted to eat. I entitled it: "Foods I Must Eat."

Many of the foods on my list were ones I had grown up eating in Minneapolis. The entry for "Corn beef/beer" reminded me of the meat made in the Jewish community in Minneapolis. It was best eaten with rye bread and a beer. Chow mein was a special treat that my mother bought for the family once or twice a month. It was the food that I dreamed of most while a POW. I could just taste those crispy noodles—those chunks of chicken—those button mushrooms.

While we were walking on the trip from Nuremberg down to Moosburg, the Germans would occasionally bring out a big pot of what they called soup, but was mostly water. Sometimes it appeared to contain a few vegetables. We

Food I MUST EAT
1. BREAKFAST
   a. Glass of Orange Juice
   (b) Bowl of Strawberries + Cream
   c. Waffles
   D. HAM
   (e) MAPLE Syrup
   (F) Glass of cold Milk
2. DINNER
   (a) SIRLOIN STEAK Covered
      with Mushrooms
   (b) French Fried Potatoes
   (c) Biscuits / Butter
   (D) lemon Pie w/ICE cream

) Milk
   SUPPER
   a) Fried Chicken
   b) Peas / Carrots
   3) Hot Rolls / Butter
   4) Cake / Ice Cream
) MILK
   Fruit ALL OVER The House
   Ice Box Kept Full of Beer
   OTHER THINGS
   Coney Island
   Malted Milk
   BANANA Splits
   HAMBURGERS
   CHOW MEIN
   BAR B CUE BEEF / RIBS
   Hot Dogs

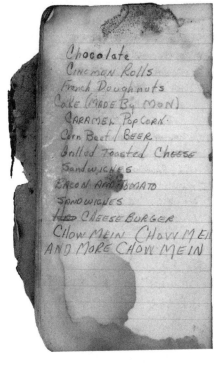

Chocolate
CINNAMON Rolls
French Doughnuts
Cake (MADE BY MOM)
CARAMEL PopCorn
Corn Beef / BEER
Grilled Toasted CHEESE
Sandwiches
BACON AND TOMATO
SANDWICHES
CHEESEBURGER
CHOW MEIN CHOW MEIN
AND MORE CHOW MEIN

Figure 22. "Foods I Must Eat."

Figure 23. "Foods I Must Eat," continued.

might even see a sliver of something that looked like a celery stalk in the water. Our guys became really inventive. The little tins that they kept became bowls and cups. Each POW got one scoop of soup, regardless of the size of bowl.

One day the soup came in and the guys were saying, "Hey, there are some nice beans in the soup." The guys quickly lined up. Well, when we looked a little closer at the beans, after they had been cooked, they were loaded with weevils. So there were weevils floating around in the soup along with the beans. The beans and maybe a few kernels of corn would break open and a weevil would be inside.

I have always been fairly particular about what I eat, but not then. I looked at George Iles and asked him if he planned to eat that stuff. Iles said: "Harold, I'm hungry." I was hungry as heck so we both ate our bowls of weevil soup. At first we tried to move the weevils out of the way, but finally gave up and just ate it as it was served. Some of the guys couldn't handle it, but we went back for seconds. We told them: "Hey. It's been cooked. We got meat! It's a little protein. It's not going to hurt us."

While George and I may have had cast iron stomachs and even went back for seconds, many in our group become sick with diarrhea from that day's meal. The next day we saw little dots of white all over the hillside—the remnants of the tissues the Red Cross had provided in the survival packs.

THE JOURNEY CONTINUES

As we were walking in Germany on April 12, 1945, we got word that Franklin Delano Roosevelt had died. At first we thought it was a hoax, but some of the British *Kriegies* had made radios out of practically nothing and picked up a news update from the BBC. We knew that he had been extremely ill and weren't all that surprised by the news.

Most of the walking was uneventful. There was a group up in front of us and one as far behind us as we could see. There were a lot of curious people standing on the streets as we came by. "Look at all those prisoners. And the guards." There was never an incident with the civilians. Nothing.

The only truly bad incident we had on this march was when we got strafed and several of the men were killed. We were about halfway through the march and were near a little marshaling yard where there was a lot of railroad traffic. Suddenly we saw a flight of P-47s (the Thunderbolt, an American single-engine fighter plane). "Hey, 47s! Yes. They're probably going to hit that marshaling yard."

Then we saw the planes peel off and dive and we realized that they were coming in toward us. Everyone said: "Oh, no!" and we all started running. Our groups were stretched out both within the town and beyond, and those that hadn't even entered the village yet. Those of us in the village just started running. The guards dropped their rifles and their packs. We all dropped everything we had and were just *running*. We didn't know where to run; we were just running. A small company of us, including Iles and me, got behind this big woodpile. A couple of German guards joined us. There were about seven or eight of us all huddled together.

While I knew that the plane that came in on us was not aiming at me directly, it felt like it was coming right at me, cutting lose all eight of its .50 caliber guns. This experience was as terrifying as the time I was on the train that was strafed. Maybe worse. After a few bursts of fire, the plane suddenly broke off.

Then there was more panic. The guys were saying, "Is anybody hit?' Is anyone hurt?" This was going on around us. We were all just looking at each other. "I'm okay." "I'm fine." "Are you guys okay over there?" And then somebody says, "Uh-oh. Somebody was hit. Down here!"

Word got back to us that six or seven guys were hit and were dead. Then we heard that someone from another group was hit. The news slowly came filtering back. It was sheer panic among the several hundred people of our group. There were also a number of wounded. I'm not even sure what happened to them. The guards wasted very little time, indicating that anyone who wasn't hurt should start marching. They immediately marched us out of that place and right back on the road again.

Later we learned that the P-47 pilots had been briefed that if they saw long strings of people, they should be very careful because these groups of people could be POWs. The pilots were told that there was a lot of prisoner movement going on. The first or second plane had fired before he had actually seen the POWs; the ricocheting bullets had killed any number of men.

All we could think about as the march began again was: "What a meatball rap. To be killed this close to the end of the war in a freak accident."

On April 18, 1945, we arrived at Moosburg, Stalag Luft VII-A. Because there were so many of us, prisoners continued to arrive for a few days. There were tens of thousands of us at Moosburg. It was very crowded. In fact, it was only after we were liberated, and the fences had been knocked down, that I began milling around and realized that there were a number of other Tuskegee pilots also interned there.

16

LIBERATION

GENERAL GEORGE S. PATTON'S 14TH ARMORED DIVISION liberated us on April 29, 1945. We knew Patton was getting close. The night before he arrived, we could hear the tanks rumbling in the distance. Early the next morning, the guards all pulled out. They got in their formations, and simply marched off and left the camp unattended. Our guys even waved at a number of them. We had almost gotten friendly with them.

The guards had barely gotten out before we saw a couple of lead tanks, with Patton following in his jeep. The other tanks were following him. Then Patton came roaring in. He was a big man, about six feet, two inches tall, a real warrior, a real soldier. Patton knew that there was a big prison camp in Moosburg and he loved publicity, so when he came into the camp, his jeep was spotless. Somewhere out there along those dirty roads his staff had managed to find enough water to clean and shine that jeep. He was in tan breeches and knee-high cavalry boots, and wore two pistols on his sides. His suit looked like it was just freshly pressed and he had those four stars across his helmet.

Patton's attention to his appearance was well known. One story that was widely circulated about Patton was his response to a reporter who was interviewing him.

The reporter asked, "Why do you wear those pearl-handled guns?"

Patton's response was: "The only people who carry pearl-handled guns are pimps in New Orleans. These are ivory and don't you ever forget it."

Patton talked to us for about five minutes. He had the filthiest mouth of any man I have ever heard in my life. Every other word was a curse word. He stood on the hood of the jeep and told all the troops: "I am on my way to Berlin, and when I get there, I'm going to find that paper-hanging son of a bitch and I'm going to hang him by his balls." I have sometimes been asked why Patton called Hitler a paperhanger.

There is no substantive evidence that Hitler ever actually was a paperhanger. We do know, however, that he perceived himself to be an artistic genius who "scorned the notion of working to earn one's daily bread."[1] He sold a few paintings but was, according to his biographer, Ian Kershaw, a failed artist. Patton's suggestion that he was a manual laborer was certainly intended to denigrate the Führer and his message.

The crowd of many thousands was hollering and screaming, saying, "Yeah, Patton." He was standing up there just loving it. After five minutes, he told us that he was on his way and that we were liberated. "You'll soon be going home. Good luck to you."

As Patton was leaving, he told us that the kitchen was right behind us and we were going to get a good meal. Those guys with mobile kitchens came in and set up with amazing speed. They were popping those food cans open, all those great big cans of C-rations, and they were cooking them up. What a great meal!

When Patton came into the camp, he had knocked down a big portion of the fence with his tanks, but then he left with all of his tank battalions. The big problem was that there were now many thousands of POWs set free. We could not just be allowed to roam the countryside. After all, there was still a war going on. As this realization became clear to the American forces, all of us POWs were gathered up. We had American soldiers standing around trying to keep us from straying too far.

We were told: "Hey, guys, don't go too far, because there are still enemy troops in this general area. One of you could get hurt. We've got to get you out of here and into France to a processing station."

The fence to the prison camp was repaired to keep better control of the POWs, but we were still allowed to go out and walk around. We stayed in the prison camp another three or four days.

On one of those days, while Iles and I were walking around, we ran into a few GIs who had come in after Patton. They said, "Hey, another platoon up here has just caught four SS troopers. We don't take these guys as prisoners. Do you want to shoot them?"

We said, "No, we don't want to shoot them."

They said, "Well, hell, we don't take these lousy bastards as prisoners after all the dirty stuff they've done. They probably would have shot you." And they probably would have. I'd already had one incident with an SS guy who scared the hell out of me.

But we said, "Well, thanks, but no thanks."

We left them and shortly thereafter we heard some shots. I said to George, "Let's just keep walking." We were officers and would be expected to behave as such. We certainly couldn't condone killing enemy prisoners, even if they were SS.

I told George: "I don't even want to know what's happening. I don't want to have to tell a lie." I assumed that they could have been shooting at rabbits or something, but I doubt that.

SS troopers were known to murder POWs in cold blood. In one incident, known by Allied officers and soldiers alike as the Massacre at Malmedy, more than one hundred GIs had attempted to surrender but were gunned down by their captors. Those remaining were executed by SS with their pistols. The few GIs who had survived by playing dead reported back what had happened and word spread from foxhole to foxhole. Formal decrees in at least two regiments were to no longer take SS men as prisoners.[2] Patton also had told his staff that no SS prisoners were to be taken alive.[3]

As our experience had shown, our MPs were finding little clusters of SS men and likely shooting them. Officially, none of that ever happened, but I think it was happening more often than we would like to think. When we came back home, it was *never* mentioned. We were never interrogated about such things. Thomas Saylor, a historian who interviewed me and many other POWS, told me that shooting German prisoners was "one of those things that is very much not in the accounts of World War II." However, he said, "We've heard in interviews more than once of Americans shooting captured Germans."[4]

THE FALL OF THE REICH, APRIL 29–30, 1945

While we were jubilant in our prison camp at being liberated, we were largely unaware of all the other activity going on very near to us in and around Germany.

On April 29, 1945, around the time we were being liberated, US soldiers arrived at the concentration camp at Dachau, near Munich, where "31,000 inmates from forty-one nations remained behind the electrified fence. Another 13,000 had died in the previous four months, mostly from typhus and starvation."[5] The horrified troops discovered "2,310 decomposing corpses, some naked, some in tattered blue-and-white camp livery."[6] The camp was just a short distance from our POW camp. Some of my fellow POWs went to visit the camp after liberation. I had no interest in seeing the degradation that went on there.

Munich, known as a "Führer City," because it was regarded as the "Capital of the Movement" and the "Capital of German Art," was attacked by four American divisions on April 29 and had fallen by April 30.[7] Munich was about an hour away from our camp by vehicle. Several hundred miles north in Berlin, it had become clear that the Soviets would take the city and any of its occupants as hostages. The Führer, who had recently wed his mistress, Eva Braun, committed suicide with her on April 30, 1945, as they heard the rumble of artillery only a short distance away.[8] On April 29, emissaries of Germany capitulated unconditionally, and by May 7, 1945, Germany had surrendered.[9] For the first time in almost six years, there was peace in Europe.

While all of this activity was going on in other parts of Germany—both near and far—we POWs were mostly dreaming of getting back to the good old USA. We were largely oblivious of the great events that were occurring around us.

17

GOING HOME

A FEW DAYS AFTER OUR LIBERATION BY PATTON and his troops, we departed Moosburg and were transported by truck to an airfield near Straubing, where we boarded C-47s (cargo planes). There were umpteen transports out of there, but only one landing strip. We were flown to one of the big processing stations, Camp Lucky Strike, near Le Havre, France, on the coast of Normandy. Several camps at that time were named after popular cigarettes of the day. The camps were originally named after cigarettes "for two reasons. First, and primarily, was for security. Referring to the camps without an indication of their geographical location went a long way to ensuring that the enemy would not know precisely where they were. . . . Secondly, there was a subtle psychological reason, the premise being that the troops heading into battle wouldn't mind staying at a place where cigarettes must be plentiful," especially before they were departing for combat.[1]

In reality, Lucky Strike was a huge military base. When we got there, the first thing we were asked to do was to take off all of our clothes and throw them in a pile. For nearly all of us, that's all we had worn since we were captured. For me, it had been nearly seven weeks. We were full of lice and you name it. I had a pair of Australian black boots that were absolutely gorgeous and I had to give them up. Oh, I wanted to keep those boots so badly, but nevertheless, I got naked, left all my clothes behind, and enjoyed the first hot shower I'd had since I was shot down. I can still remember that hot water, and as I soaped up, I thought, "Damn this feels good!" Then the authorities sprayed us with whatever was in those sprayers—they called it delousing.

Next, we put on a clean uniform. The authorities asked me: "What size are you?"

I told them, "I was a 32 before, but I'm thinner now." So they gave me a uniform that fit and a few bucks, and we just waited for transport home. It was just a matter of waiting until the ships arrived.

As POWS, we were given one of the highest priorities to get back home, but we still had to wait. Most of our guys were just going crazy. The authorities had a tough time keeping us in one place, yet no one wanted to miss his ship home.

The briefing was: "Don't go running around the countryside, because if you do and you miss your ship, you will go to the bottom of the line." So Iles and I just hung around, but after three or four days we decided to go to Paris. Each day we thought we'd go, there would be a rumor that a whole contingent of ships was arriving in Le Havre. This happened throughout all of May and it was almost six weeks before our names finally came up on the list. We never did get to Paris and only visited a few nearby villages.

I was a slim five feet, eight and one-half inches and weighed only 129 pounds when I went into the service, so I didn't have much weight to lose. By the time of the liberation, I could count my ribs. Figure 24 is one of the few available photos of me when I had just returned to the States, at age twenty.

During all the time that I was overseas I was seldom in contact with my parents back in Minnesota. They had received one telegram sent on April 2, 1945, telling them in a "BATTLE CASUALTY REPORT" that their son was "MISSING IN ACTION OVER AUSTRIA SINCE 14 MAR 45." I think that the military waited for a period of time, just to make sure that a soldier who was missing did not show up, before sending the first telegram.

My parents had received another telegram telling them that Bubba was "WOUNDED IN ACTION."

Finally, they received a telegram sent on May 15, 1945, telling them that I had been "RETURNED TO MILITARY CONTROL." In the remarks section of the telegram, it was noted: "HQ 3rd U.S. ARMY. *AMER. POW LIBERATED FROM MOOSBURG CAMP. ADDRESS—605 OLSON HIGHWAY, MINNE-APOLIS, MINN."

One can only imagine the agony our parents felt, just waiting to hear news about each of their sons. They obviously knew that each had been in extreme and potentially fatal danger. It's hard to imagine the joy they must have felt to find that both of us were alive and coming home!

Back in the United States

Our ship left on June 12 and landed in Newport News, Virginia, on June 20, 1945, a journey of a mere eight days. It was a cruiser that had been turned into a troop carrier. It was a crowded ship, but much nicer than the Liberty ship that had carried us to Northern Africa.

After our cruiser docked and I was ashore, I was processed immediately at Camp Patrick Henry, Virginia, a big port of reentry. After I was given a ticket, some money, and a few more clothes, I was on my way home. Within two days of arriving back in the United States, I was riding a train headed for Fort Snelling in Minneapolis. There were eight of us traveling together. When we got to Chicago, we changed trains and were on the Hiawatha passenger train. It took just four hundred minutes to go from Chicago to Minneapolis.

We didn't have any sort of psychological assessment or treatment when we returned, not at Lucky Strike or at Fort Snelling. It could have occurred at any part of the process, because medical people did look us over, but they were looking at us physically. "Okay, you lost a few pounds, but otherwise you're fine." If someone had been a POW for a year or two, they might have been assessed more closely. My imprisonment was more of an inconvenience than anything else. I had the war made. I spent just about a month and a half as a POW.

I have often been asked what it was like coming home to America. I was twenty years of age, and nothing had changed with respect to race relations. It was still the 1940s. The military didn't integrate until 1948. Before that formal move, it was still a segregated Air Force. In 1946, when I first went to Lockbourne Air Force Base in Ohio, I learned that there had been a big protest about a year or so before in Columbus against the theaters where African Americans had to sit in the balconies, affectionately called "Negro Heaven." The African Americans simply wanted to sit wherever they pleased. So segregation continued to exist, even in Columbus, Ohio. It was almost another twenty years before Congress passed the Civil Rights Act.

Once we had arrived at Fort Snelling, the seven other POWs and I, all from Minnesota, were lined up and were told that we were going to receive the Purple Heart. I thought: "Oh, shoot. I wasn't wounded or anything. Just got a few scratches landing and getting out of the plane." There was laughing and giggling. The guy came down the line and gave us each a Purple Heart and asked us to sign a document. He said, "A copy of your orders will catch up with you." The orders, which proved that I had actually won the award, never arrived. I set the award aside. In later years, I wrote to Fort Snelling and was told that

Figure 24. Just home from
the war, June 1945.

there ought to be a record someplace, but the orders still never arrived. Such
an award doesn't mean anything without appropriate documentation. I put it
in its case and there it remained.

After the ceremony, I got in a cab and asked to be taken to 605 Olson Highway. I arrived home on June 22, not old enough to vote and not able to go
legally into a bar. I was occasionally asked if I thought I might be headed to
the Pacific since the war was still going on over there, but I didn't give that
a second thought. After all, the military was still segregated, and I would be
heading only where our Tuskegee group was assigned.

Sixty Days in Minneapolis

Going home was quite an experience. First, I had been gone for almost three
years. Bubba was also home for a ninety-day leave. I had seen him briefly only
on two occasions during the war: the morning after his accident and seven

Figure 25. Just home from the war, with Bubba.

days later, after I returned from R and R in Naples. Then I was shot down the next day. So, here we were both at home after both coming so close to death. We were extremely happy, particularly for Mom and Dad, who had to wait out the war not knowing if either one of us would make it home alive.

Our parents never asked either of us what our experience was like in the war. They never asked and we never told them. I don't know if they didn't ask because perhaps they thought, "He doesn't want to talk about it," or "He'll tell us when he feels like telling us about it." Our parents really didn't intrude into our personal lives, and it would have been entirely out of character for them to probe. We weren't a very vocal family. It wasn't that it caused me any pain or discomfort to talk about my experiences. I just didn't see any reason to do so.

Strange as it seems, Bubba and I, who were anything but close to being friends before the war, instantly embraced each other and all the bad years immediately vanished. We were immediately the best of friends. The first few weeks we just adjusted to being home. We spent much time renewing old friendships, especially with those who were home from the war like us. We went to multiple parties that included far too much consumption of alcohol.

After a few weeks of continuously going out, we seriously reduced our partying routine and settled down to a saner and quieter routine with some of our closest friends. With so much "leave time," it was easy to relax, enjoy Mom and Dad, and just enjoy the moments. Out in public, we were almost treated like little gods. It was even that way before, when I had just finished flying school. To have gone overseas to fight the war and come back wearing ribbons on our chest—that made us heroes in the eyes of the hometown folks.

I have often been asked if I had any idea at that time, when I had just returned from the war, what my legacy as a Tuskegee Airman would be. The answer is "No." After all, I started the process of entering the military at seventeen and came home at twenty. A legacy was the last thing on my mind. I never thought for one second that I was doing something wonderful, that our successes would have the impact that they did. Only years later I realized our actions impacted what eventually happened back here.

As my sixty days of leave approached its end, I was becoming a little bored and began looking forward to military life on active duty during peacetime. A whole new life experience was about to start, and I had just turned twenty-one on August 19, two weeks before I would again leave home. Of course, Dad and Mom, especially Mom, hated to see me leave, but this was my chosen career and both wished me well. I promised to come home as regularly as possible and I departed for Atlantic City at the end of August, just in time to catch the Miss America Pageant.

PART III

THE POSTWAR YEARS

THERE I WAS, AN ELEVEN-YEAR-OLD SCHOOLKID, playing with paper airplanes and dreaming of flying. I knew that, if given a chance, I'd be a great pilot. As I built model planes, I could just see myself becoming a hero, a hot rock pilot. I kept believing that all the problems related to blacks and flying would be resolved.

I had experienced my childhood dream. I had learned to fly in a simple stick and rudder biplane, had graduated to more powerful trainers, and had finally gotten my hands on a magnificent piece of machinery, the P-51 Mustang. Suddenly, the war was over. Did this mean the dream was over?

18

TO STAY OR NOT TO STAY

AS TUSKEGEE AIRMEN, WE HAD A CHOICE to remain in military service when we returned to the United States after our overseas assignment. Many, including several close personal friends, immediately went back into civilian life and on to successful careers in a wide range of fields—from physicians to engineers to educators. Coleman Young even became mayor of Detroit.

Very, very few Tuskegee Airmen were able to make a career out of working for a commercial airline. It took a number of years after the war before the door to commercial flying was open to blacks.

I decided to stay in the military. My goal all along had been to be a military pilot.

For the next twenty years, I was given responsibility early, including command positions, as I moved up the ranks. It is unlikely that I could have gotten the training, the advancement, or the overall personal growth I achieved other than in the Air Force. It is also important to remember that the Civil Rights Act wasn't passed until 1964, almost a decade and a half after the integration of the military.

I was also highly motivated. I was determined I was not going to be second best. I have always had a set of goals for myself, and once I achieved them, I established another set. I was, and am, goal-driven. The military has a very clearly defined hierarchy of rank, so my plan was always to be moving up. To set my next goal, I compared myself to the next guy who outranked me. There were very few instances where I saw that guy doing his job better than I could do it.

ATLANTIC CITY

At the end of August 1945 when I had completed my leave in Minneapolis, I spent two weeks in Atlantic City. The US Army Air Force had arranged for exclusive places for those of us returning from combat to pick up our new assignments. It felt to me like "the icing on the cake." The accommodations were first class, almost like a rest and recuperation hotel. There were big, fine resort hotels in Atlantic City, in Los Angeles, and in Miami. The hotel in Atlantic City was located right on the Boardwalk. At these resorts we were treated like kings.

On my first night in Atlantic City, I went over to the black side of town, where I ended up in a bar called the Square D. Even though the Square D was huge and crowded, I ran into a bunch of enlisted men from the 99th who had just gotten back from overseas. While we were exchanging greetings, I looked up and saw the manager of the Square D coming toward us, and I recognized him. He had been my tent mate down in Biloxi but had been washed out when we were retested.

When we saw each other, it was a big reunion—definitely party time. The manager said: "Okay, Harold, you and the Tuskegee Airmen, go over there. I want you six guys to each select three women you want to stay in the bar." So we did as we were told. The manager put everybody else in the bar out, and closed and locked the door. Then he said, "The drinks are on the house." Sometime around 4:30 or 5:00 A.M., I got a cab and struggled back to the hotel to hit the sack.

There was also a big nightclub show in town called the "Atlantic City Follies." When I walked through the door, the guy who owned it said, "Tuskegee Airman, the drinks are on the house." Later on in the evening, the owner brought over the singers and the chorus line, a bunch of high kickers, telling them, "Now you are going to meet a real hero. A Tuskegee fighter pilot." Oh, my God! Here I was, surrounded by women, all of them talking at once. The drinks were free and we were having a great time. There was one chorus girl who was a real cutie pie. I had just had my twenty-first birthday on August 19; I think she was twenty-three. We hit it off, and I spent most of the time lollygagging with her.

One of the featured singers at the Follies was Marva Louis, the wife of Joe Louis. When I met her, she said, "Hey, we are going to be down in Montgomery, Alabama." She gave me the date, sometime in November or December. In those days the shows went on the road from city to city, only stopping a few days at each new location. I promised Marva and the others that I would be sure to meet them in Montgomery.

The two weeks in Atlantic City ended much too soon, but after two weeks of drinking more than I should have, I was eager to receive my orders for my new assignment.

COMING HOME

There were only two primary locations available to the black men who had chosen to remain in the US Army Air Force in 1945: Tuskegee and Godman Field at Fort Knox, Kentucky. I was not surprised to learn that I was heading to Tuskegee Army Air Field as an instructor pilot. I traveled by rail. During the trip, sitting in the car behind the locomotive, and enduring all the other inconveniences, I was reminded that nothing had changed; segregation was still the norm of the day.

Because all black pilots were trained at the same base and most of us either knew or had heard of all the pilots who had fought in the European theater, this was almost like coming home. When I arrived, many of my friends were excited and shocked to see me, because they did not know I had survived and or that I had been a POW. This was like a big reunion with my best friends.

All the pilots that I knew who had decided to stay in the military were down in Tuskegee as flight instructors. This included Colonel McGee, who was Captain McGee at that time. During his career, McGee flew 409 combat missions in World War II, Korea, and Vietnam.[1] McGee was a twin-engine instructor. I became a single-engine instrument instructor, along with two of my classmates, Bob Williams and Thomas Jefferson.

It seemed a bit odd returning to Tuskegee as a flight instructor. The cadets looked upon us with respect and awe. We were now the old, experienced pilots who would teach the younger cadets who aspired to be like us, and most of us were barely into our twenties.

There were several photos taken of me when I first returned, some with other pilots and friends. In Figure 26, I am in front of the AT-6 in which I was instructing younger pilots.

One of my best friends at Tuskegee was Lowell Steward. Figure 27 is a photo of us back at Tuskegee.

Lowell was older than the rest of us. He had been a basketball star at Santa Barbara State College in California and had entered flight training with a college degree. Lowell had been in an earlier class, had flown over one hundred

Figure 26. Back at Tuskegee in front of an AT-6.

Figure 27. Back at Tuskegee with Lowell Steward.

Figure 28. Back at Tuskegee with Thomas Jefferson (left) and an unidentified airman.

missions, and had earned a Distinguished Flying Cross. He had returned to the States before most of the rest of us. I first met him after coming back from overseas.

Figure 28 captures me with one of my closest friends, Thomas Jefferson, sitting on the wing.

Thomas was my roommate in Primary and a close friend. He was a small, quiet kid from Chicago who had flown as part of a four-ship reconnaissance mission to protect a P-38 on the last mission of the 332nd Fighter Group. On that mission he got two victories. The thing that I remember most about

Thomas, however, was the day he jumped up from his bed when he heard reveille and immediately fainted. For the rest of my life, I always took a few seconds on the edge of the bed before getting up.

Thomas Jefferson, Lowell Steward, Bob Williams, and I became a team of four friends. Bob had been in Lowell's squadron overseas, so he and Lowell were already good friends. While we were instructors at Tuskegee, we flew to Chicago regularly on the weekends. After we had completed flight instruction on Friday afternoons, the four of us would take off around 6:00 P.M. We would fly to Nashville, refuel, and then fly on to Chicago, arriving around 10:00 P.M. Lowell was a good friend of a manager of the Pershing Hotel on 64th and Cottage Grove; such hotels were called "black hotels." The Pershing had a big ballroom, a lounge, and a nightclub. Lowell would call his friend as soon as we arrived and he always seemed to find a room for us Tuskegee guys. Since Thomas was a Chicago native, he introduced Bob, Lowell, and me to the town. Late on Sunday afternoons we would head back so the planes we were flying would be ready for training the next morning.

UNDER THE HOOD

At Tuskegee, I was instructing cadets on Advanced Instruments, as were Thomas Jefferson and Bob Williams. The focus of this training was to fly exclusively by observing the instruments within the cockpit, without the advantage of any visible sight of the ground or the horizon. Before any of us could teach Advanced Instruments, we had to go through the training program ourselves. We had to spend flight time "underneath the hood." This involved pulling a gray canvas material across the interior of the cockpit canopy, which completely limited our vision outside the cockpit.

In October 1945, this training led to my third and last crash in an airplane, a midair collision. I had already survived two of the worst accidents that could happen to a pilot: a crash landing and a bailout from a crippled aircraft. Adding the midair collision makes me, I believe, the only Tuskegee Airman to survive the three worst accidents that can occur in a plane.

On this day I was the one flying under the hood in a T-6. Captain Clarence Dart, who had also been overseas in the 99th, was in the front seat on this very hazy day acting as the safety pilot. He could see out to keep us clear of other traffic in the area, since there were no air traffic controllers keeping the traffic separated. I was flying blind, practicing navigating and flying final approach by radio beams.

While Clarence and I were airborne, another instructor was also in the air providing instruction to a cadet. Neither Clarence nor the other instructor saw each other until the last minute. It was just pure luck that Dart, seeing the traffic, abruptly snatched the stick and forced our plane up, and the instructor in the other plane dumped his stick forward, forcing his nose down. Had both safety pilots reacted the same way, it would have been a head-on crash. The left wing of our plane hit the tail of the other plane and cut it off. That plane went into a spin and the pilots could not control it, so they bailed out.

As soon as Dart made such a violent maneuver with our plane, I knew what had happened. I came out from under the hood and was ready to jump, and Clarence said: "It's okay! It's okay." He was hollering at me over the wind, while I was pointing at that great big gaping hole in the wing. It looked to me as if it had almost cut through the main spar, which meant that nothing but the skin was holding that wing on. I had visions of the whole wing collapsing and the plane spinning out of control. I yelled: "Dart, it's nothing but skin, and we don't know how much of the spar is left. If that gash extends through the spar and the wing fails at low altitude while we are landing, we've had it. We will be too low to bail out."

Clarence continued to assure me that it was okay, so we stayed with the plane and landed it, but we sweated it out coming in on final. We taxied down the runway and that wing went slow-w-ly lower and lower. It was almost dragging by the time we brought the airplane to a halt.

No one was really at fault. I was right on the radio beam, right where I should have been. I was heading for the so-called cone of silence, which was directly over the beacon. In those days, we just had a radio station with four beams on it, and there were a number of others flying instruments up there that day. Separation of our aircraft was maintained by flying specific altitudes. Depending upon our heading, we would fly even altitudes (2,000 feet, 4,000 feet), or if on the opposite heading, we would fly odd altitudes (1,000 feet, 3,000 feet). The airplanes on the other two legs flew even plus 500 (2,500) or odd plus 500 (3,500), so there should always be a 500-foot separation between us, if we should all arrive at the cone at the same time.

To determine what had actually happened, a board of inquiry was convened. I knew that I was on the right altitude, but the other pilot said: "Well, we might have been off, but we weren't off any more than just a hundred feet."

I said, "Well, then, you guys were wrong, and you guys should have changed your altitude." It was a tricky situation but someone had to be held responsible. The board chose to give Clarence a $300 fine, and that was the end of it.

Years later, when I saw Clarence at conventions, I would tell him: "I let you talk me into staying in that airplane. I had to be the biggest dummy that ever lived! How could I ever have done it?"

Clarence responded: "I got you down safely, didn't I?"

"Yes, you SOB, yeah, and you took ten years off my life!" I jokingly answered.

End of an Era

When I returned to Tuskegee to serve as an instructor pilot, I helped train the last class of pilots to graduate from Tuskegee in March 1946. A total of 992 pilots had been trained at Tuskegee Army Air Field (673 single-engine, 252 twin-engine, 51 liaison, 11 service, and 5 Haitian).[2] In June 1946, Tuskegee began the process of shutting down. The war was over and there simply wasn't a need for pilots. It was sad to see it go with so many great memories, but at the same time, we were all looking forward to the future.

There were only two options available for the pilots remaining at Tuskegee: Either go to Lockbourne Air Force Base in Columbus, Ohio, the site of the 477th Composite Group, or leave the service. The 477th offered black men the opportunity to fly B-25s and P-47s.

Many of the pilots, however, left the US Army Air Force altogether. Lowell Steward, for example, went back to California and became one of the first successful African American real estate brokers in L.A. County. Bob Williams also ended up in California as a businessman and part-time actor. He would go on to coproduce *The Tuskegee Airmen*, the 1995 movie that was based on Bob's memories of his military career.

B. O. Davis, in his autobiography, explained what it meant when he and the other black military men heard of the bombing of Hiroshima and Nagasaki: "It was apparent that the Pacific war was soon to be over and our lives were to be radically changed once again. Most of our people were suddenly asking themselves how soon they could expect to get out of uniform and move back into a civilian life that only a few days before had seemed far in the future. Nobody had any way of knowing what the postwar Air Force would do with its black veterans."[3] Davis assumed command of the 477th Bombardment Group at Godman Field, in Kentucky, in June 1945.[4] The 477th became a composite group, consisting of the 99th Fighter Squadron and two B-25 squadrons. The group remained at Godman while a search for a suitable base was conducted.

Eventually, "despite the loud objections of the *Citizen,* one of Columbus's two major newspapers," the group was relocated to Lockbourne in March 1946. Davis recalled: "The move to Lockbourne constituted a milestone in the struggle of blacks to gain an equal footing in the armed services. For the first time, blacks were to administer an AAF base in the continental United States without the immediate supervision of white officers. Many doubted our ability to develop a successful operation, but in spite of chronic personnel shortages, Lockbourne became one of the best bases in the Air Force."[5] Eventually, in 1947, the 477th Composite Group was inactivated and the 332nd Fighter Group was activated again, in its place, with fighters only.

Initially, the attitudes of people in Columbus were no different from those in the South. Davis wrote: "In the late 1940s, Columbus was still a segregated city with racial divisions, customs, and practices similar to those in the Deep South. Some of the men's and women's clothing and shoe stores preferred not to have black customers, no black needing a haircut dared to walk into a white barber shop, and the YMCA and YWCA maintained separate white and black facilities. In general, the attitude of whites towards blacks, while not actively hostile, was definitely cool."[6]

Over time, the people of Columbus, who had first objected to having a black base even eight miles out of town, began to regard Lockbourne as their base. Davis wrote, "Lockbourne became understood as a major asset in the minds of all Columbus's residents, whites as well as blacks. Undoubtedly, the base's payroll contributed to the changing attitudes."[7]

19

THE FUTURE UNFOLDS

Before I left for Lockbourne, an opportunity for additional training became available. The Officer in Charge (OIC) over Instrument Instruction at Tuskegee, Captain Hood, asked me if I would be interested in attending the Central Instrument Instructor School (CIIS) at Barksdale Air Force Base in Bossier City, across the river from Shreveport, Louisiana. I eagerly accepted the offer. It was a top school in the Air Force. Only a select few were fortunate to be chosen. Captain Hood selected me out of a group of about fifteen instructors. The school made us outstanding instrument pilots, and qualified us to be "instrument check pilots" (pilots who checked the skills of other pilots and passed or failed them).

Across the whole spectrum of black pilots, there were only five chosen to go through the CIIS: Daniel Chappie James, Charles McGee, Weldon Groves, Rolin Bynum, and me. McGee was a captain while the rest of us were first lieutenants. It was at the CIIS that I first became acquainted with Chappie James and we became good buddies. I was known as Little Hoss, and Chappie was known as Big Hoss, primarily because of the contrast in our physical size. While we were in training, we visited the black side of Shreveport together and made numerous friends.

When we first arrived on base, the five of us were invited to the commander's office. He extended a welcome to us, told us that we were welcome to go anywhere on base and that he hoped we would have a good experience. This was 1946 when integration was still two years from reality. Not all of our group felt welcome at all places on base. On one occasion, Chappie went to the swimming pool at the Officers' Club. It was the middle of summer and very hot. Numerous white officers and their families were there. To this day, I can still see Chappie in his red trunks, all full 6 feet 4 inches and 250 pounds of him, climb on that diving board, do a belly flop, and make a huge splash. I kidded Chappie after that and told him: "Your big splash splashed all of the white folks right out of that pool." Indeed, the white people fled the pool the minute he entered it.

At Barksdale, there was a black service squadron on the other side of the field. A couple of soldiers were badly beaten when they were in town. The base commander asked us, and McGee as the ranking officer in particular, to come in and to offer our advice for protecting black servicemen. He didn't want to restrict them to base, nor did he want them injured. One of us suggested that he extend the hours on base and let the servicemen invite visitors to the base for dances and other activities. As officers, we were also invited to talk to the servicemen to help raise morale and to encourage them to think of a better future ahead.

After graduation from our two-month stay at CIIS, I returned to Tuskegee in August 1946, only long enough to get my belongings and my orders to go to Lockbourne, where I was stationed for three years. While I was there, I flew the P-47N, the Thunderbolt that had been designed to escort B-29s on long missions.

Vertigo

The highly publicized crash and death of John F. Kennedy Jr. and his companions in 1999 brought a lot of attention to the subject of vertigo in flying, yet it was a fairly common experience for pilots new to nighttime and instrument flying. At Lockbourne, we had a vertigo experience that nearly resulted in the death of a young pilot.

Lieutenant Harvey was leading our flight of four to get in some night flying. We took off on what was a reasonably nice day, but with a lot of clouds. We were skimming around clouds just before nightfall. We had a good formation and everything was going along fine. Visibility was excellent and we could clearly distinguish the horizon with the stars above it and the ground below. As it became darker, the horizon appeared to touch the ground and the earth was no longer distinguishable—it all blended together. Stars that were low on the horizon appeared to touch the ground. On a clear night like this, a pilot can become confused about where the horizon stops and where the ground begins. It is essential when this occurs that the pilot reorient himself by checking his instruments and trusting them, not relying on his senses. This is especially true when there are no lights on the ground to assist him. This was exactly the case as the formation was killing an hour or so before landing and was out of sight of any city or ground lighting.

Suddenly Lieutenant Butler said: "Harvey, why are we upside down?"

I knew immediately what the issue was with Lieutenant Butler. I was the instrument check pilot for the squadron by virtue of being an instrument flight instructor at Tuskegee and having successfully completed the Air Force's CIIS. This was a clear case of vertigo.

Harvey said: "No, no, Butler, you are okay."

Butler replied: "No, no, I know that I'm upside down."

I told Harvey: "Just let me talk to him."

I began: "Butler, look down to your right side. Do you see a light down there?"

"Yeah, I see a light, but I'm upside down."

I told him again: "No, you aren't upside down."

I then told Harvey, "Don't do anything. Just keep flying straight and level. If you start turning, Butler will think you're upside down and make all the opposite moves. Just fly straight and level." That's the way it went. We'd begin to convince him and then he'd panic. We could hear the fear in his voice.

I said to myself: "Oh my God, if he panics too much, he's going to jump out of his airplane." We were concerned that he was going to jump and the plane would crash, perhaps into an urban area below.

This went on for a good five or six minutes. He'd say: "Damn it, I'm upside down." Time was running out. If he didn't jump, he was going to "right" the plane and really be upside down. Either way, it was bad news.

Fortunately there was a big city just outside Columbus coming up. I told Harvey to fly straight for it. As soon as Butler saw the lights from the city below, he was okay. While the experience of flying with vertigo was not an everyday occurrence, it happened often enough that we were very cautious and stuck close to inexperienced pilots flying at night or in cloudy conditions.

INTEGRATION OF THE MILITARY

In 1947, an independent US Air Force was created. In 1948, President Truman, by Executive Order 9981, mandated the desegregation of the armed services, but they were not integrated immediately. It had become clear to the military that segregation was inefficient and uneconomical. That aside, desegregation of the military occurred almost a decade before schools were desegregated in the 1954 Supreme Court decision and almost twenty years before the Civil Rights Movement forced desegregation in public accommodations and guaranteed voting rights. Integration of the military was a first, pivotal step in integration for the nation as a whole.

The Air Force was the swiftest of the armed forces to integrate in approximately ten months, while the Army and Navy took two years to "begin even token efforts at integration."[1] Commander Davis reflected later with pride that the 332nd Fighter Group's record in the war contributed to the relatively quick integration of the Air Force: "It became my fixed belief that the Air Force had led the way in integrating the armed forces because of the basic professionalism in air operations that had been demonstrated by black units during World War II, moving the cause of integration forward to a much earlier date than could have been achieved otherwise."[2]

With integration, some of our pilots initially felt ambivalent about being parted from the group that they had come to know so well. Chuck Dryden, who thought of Lockbourne as Camelot, had no doubt that he and the others at Lockbourne would perform well professionally, but he noted: "I was not really ready to be desegregated. I was not ready to leave the supportive cocoon in which I had been nurtured for those eight years. Desegregation meant that I was going to be in the inhospitable White world without the . . . kind of close support that had been welded during those eight years that we Black Eagles had been together. Now we were about to become Lonely Eagles scattered to the far corners of the globe."[3]

I personally was not particularly concerned with the thought of integration, except that I would be separated from many of my dearest friends. I strongly believed that I would adapt easily to my new assignment. I feel certain that this was a reflection of being born and growing up in Minneapolis. Many of my friends were raised in far different circumstances in the South, so they had a different set of concerns. I embraced integration as the only way for blacks to advance to higher rank and to enjoy a full career in the US Air Force. As long as we were segregated, all the available slots for promotion were filled. Someone would have to leave the military, either voluntarily or by dying, for one of us to advance. Most of the concern felt by others vanished when the men, including Dryden, received the assignments that they had requested.

Figure 29 shows part of the 99th Fighter Squadron, 332nd Fighter Group, in December 1948 at Lockbourne.

Figure 29. The 99th Fighter Squadron, Lockbourne. I am the fourth from the left in the second row.

With the coming of integration, I had decisions to make about my career if I intended to remain in the Air Force. George Iles, who was the training officer at Lockbourne in the 99th, told me that I was nothing but a high school graduate and that the only thing I knew how to do was push a throttle. He told me that if I expected to stay in the military, I would have to do more than fly an airplane. He suggested that I think about going to one of the military schools. I wasn't even sure what they were, but George said that the hottest thing going was airborne electronics, the radar systems that were on aircraft. Iles asked me if I liked math. When I responded with a yes, Iles said that airborne electronics might be a good fit for me. The program was eleven months long, which was all right with me. Iles submitted my name for that school. Once again, just like during the war, George was watching out for me. Iles had applied for and been accepted for the regular army, one of the very few to be accepted. His future was made.

In 1948, shortly after Iles had coached me, I was scheduled to meet with the board headed by Commander Davis to determine what I wanted to do in the military. All the pilots at the base were asked what they saw as their future career. Some of the guys had not even thought about that. I told the board that I'd like to go to Airborne Electronics School at Keesler Air Force Base and was given that assignment. In June and July, we began to leave Lockbourne. Several of my friends ended up as part of the 49th Fighter Group in Japan, flying F-80s in Korea. However, from time to time there were big reductions in force and some of the guys who had only wanted to fly were the first to go.

The successful integration of blacks into the Air Force came as no surprise to Commander Davis. He wrote: "The large number of black units in the Air Force—more than 100 in June 1949—was reduced to nine by the end of December 1950. By that time, 95 percent of the black airmen in the Air Force were serving in integrated units."[4] The guys had gone to the four winds and were serving in positions throughout the Air Force.

ONE OTHER DECISION

Lockbourne was the first permanent assignment for the Tuskegee Airmen in the North. It was quite different from our base in Alabama, where our social life was highly restricted. I cannot remember a single nice restaurant or bar in Tuskegee. Columbus, Ohio, offered a variety of social activities and supported a large population of black Americans. In fact, in March 1948, I met my future wife, Maxine Gilmore, at one such social event. For the first time, our lives as Tuskegee Airmen were complete. The big joke was that all of the single guys at Lockbourne married girls in Columbus. Max and I began to talk about marriage when the integration of the base became a reality. There was much uncertainty about where my next assignment might be.

Upon learning that I would be stationed at Keesler Air Force Base, Max and I married in July 1949. In August 1949, she informed me that she was expecting our first child, Karen, who was born in the winter of 1950. Because there was no suitable housing at Keesler, Max stayed in Columbus. I saw her only once during the eleven months I was gone.

Two Different Kinds of Heroes

It was one of my greatest privileges to know two of the highest-ranking Tuskegee Airmen: Chappie James and B. O. Davis. Their careers led to both becoming four-star generals. As individuals, these two men had little in common, and their paths to success were entirely different. B. O. Davis was the consummate military man, disciplined and focused. He had survived four years of the silent treatment at West Point. He brought this disciplined approach to his time overseas. He always made it clear that there was a job to be done and that the pilots were responsible for guarding the bombers and not to be seeking fame by chasing German fighters. He was a hard-nosed leader who believed deeply in the ability of black men to achieve their highest goals.

Chappie, in contrast, enjoyed life to its fullest. He was always in the limelight. He helped form a jazz band that became a traveling show for the Ninth Air Force. Chappie was gregarious, and after a few drinks, he would jump up, grab that microphone, and start singing. This behavior was in stark contrast to the man who served as his commander at Lockbourne, B. O. Davis. Chappie was a pilot's pilot and greatly admired for his skills in the air. He was known as a "hot rock," a really good and fearless pilot.

Most of the Tuskegee airmen assumed that B. O. Davis, rather than Chappie, would be the first black man to become a four-star general. He had been the 1936 West Point graduate who had provided the leadership for the 99th Fighter Squadron and the 332nd Fighter Group in World War II. Most of those who followed Davis credited him with preparing them for the integration of the armed services. B. O.'s recognition, however, was not to come until many years after he commanded troops. He retired from active military service in 1970 and was made a four-star general in 1998. Senator John McCain sponsored a bill that brought Davis out of retirement for one day. He was promoted to a four-star general and then went back into retirement.

B. O. would never, ever stoop so low as to complain in public about Chappie becoming a four-star general before him. That would clearly have been below B. O., but it must have pained him deeply. Here he was *the* man. He was the

Figure 30. Electronic officer training class, 1950.

first three-star black general. He got his third star before Chappie got his first. Then Chappie moved up quickly until he finally outranked B. O. That must have been a pretty bitter pill to swallow.

RETURNING TO BILOXI

I left Lockbourne in August 1949 to go to Keesler Air Force Base in Biloxi for eleven months of training as an airborne electronics officer. This was my first experience in the integrated military. I was the only black officer in the class; however, I was well received and soon became close friends with several classmates. The course was long and rigorous—six hours per day, Monday to Friday. We spent much time together in after-class study sessions. In addition to classwork, the half of us who were pilots flew the B-25 to maintain requirements for flight proficiency. I was also placed on orders as an instrument instructor and check pilot on this new base since I was a graduate of the Central Instrument Instructor School. This recognition of my flying skills was very satisfying and proved to me that I was being treated fairly based on my skills and background. Figure 30 is a photo of our class.

While I may have felt that I was being treated equally on base, off base was another matter. Biloxi was one of two cities to which I never wanted to return, the other being Linz, Austria, where I had been shot down. Even though the military had been integrated, the racist traditions of the South were still well entrenched. I recall a particularly ugly moment that drove this home for me. I had a good friend named Beck who had a couple of joints located across the railroad tracks in town—little raggedy places, each with beer, booze, and a jukebox.

Beck had recently purchased a new white Buick convertible for himself. One weekend we were going to Jackson in his new car. On the way, we stopped at a traffic light in a little town along the route. Two or three young white kids said: "Look at that pretty car and look who's driving it. Bunch of niggas." They walked up and spit all over the car. We didn't say a word. Beck said: "Harold, keep your mouth shut, just keep it shut." When the light changed, we drove off.

20

THE KOREAN WAR

AFTER FINISHING ELECTRONICS TRAINING, I was assigned to the Far East
Air Materiel Command (FEAMCOM) at Tachikawa Air Base in Japan. It was
July 1950, just as the Korean War was beginning.

When I arrived in Japan, I met with Colonel Unruh, the Maintenance
Group CO, who informed me that I was welcome to be on the base, but stated:
"You are the first black officer to be assigned to our base. I do not believe in
integration. I accept you, but you will have to prove yourself to me."

I thanked him for his honesty and told him I would like to meet with him
in another year to see if I had changed his mind. As it turned out, within two
years the colonel recommended four captains for promotion to major "below
the zone" (they had not yet met the minimum years in grade to move up to
major) but who had demonstrated outstanding service. I was one of those recommended for promotion. Even though I was not selected for the promotion,
I was pleased that I had been able to change the colonel's perception of my
abilities as an officer, no matter what my color.

THE FAR EAST AIR MATERIEL COMMAND (FEAMCOM)

FEAMCOM provided support for the Korean War effort in several ways.
FEAMCOM was responsible for the highest level of maintenance for radar
systems and aircraft in the Far East during the Korean War. It was also a big
depot that processed equipment and supplies to all the Air Force bases in the
Far East. In fact, it was so large and disorganized that on one occasion, when

Figure 31. File photo of me at twenty-six years of age.

we couldn't find a CPS-5 Ground Radar System in one of the warehouses, we began a search with thirty airmen to find it. Eventually, we found all 586 boxes, of various sizes, from which the system was assembled.

My first assignment at FEAMCOM was officer in charge (OIC) of airborne radar. I had two hundred Japanese employees and fifteen skilled enlisted men who were in charge of various parts of the shop. The shop completed overhauls and repair of airborne radar systems from bases all over the Far East.

As the Korean War progressed and the need for ground radar rapidly increased, I was reassigned to the ground radar system shop. This shop had six hundred Japanese technicians and about thirty American enlisted men in charge of various work teams. There were three officers assigned to the shop. The officers' duties included taking teams of three to four enlisted men to bases in Japan and Korea for installing, replacing, and performing maintenance on radar systems.

There were times, when installing radar systems in Korea, that we were warned by the military police about advancing North Korean troops. The military police were good at giving us advance notice when the enemy was getting close to our position. We would stop work, load up our equipment, and get out of the area. It was often the case that, within a few days, the Americans would regain control of the area and we would return to complete the job.

However, there was one time when the military police warned us that the enemy was moving very rapidly and we had to leave immediately or run the risk of being caught. We left all our equipment and radar in place, jumped in our jeeps, and ran for our lives. As we headed south, we heard gunfire from both sides. In about a week we returned and found the radar and our equipment exactly as we had left it. Apparently the North Korean troops failed to recognize the value of the equipment and had left it intact. We had experienced a close call, but learned a valuable lesson. When the military police said "Go," we went, without asking questions.

BECOMING JET QUALIFIED

The ground radar shop was located in a large building just across the street from the flight-testing hangar. Planes that had been in for major repairs had to be flight-tested before they could be sent back into service. The officer in charge of flight-testing was Major Kelly. After settling into my job in ground radar, I introduced myself to Major Kelly and inquired if he needed any help. I knew Kelly was by himself and could probably use the help. It would also get me back into fighters.

I told Kelly about all of my flying experience in fighters, which included combat flying in the P-51, and three years of flying in the P-47N from 1946 to 1949 at Lockbourne. He was quite impressed and asked if I would do all the P-51 flight-testing. That would free him up to flight-test all the jet fighters. The arrangement worked well for both of us and we became good friends.

Kelly also offered to let me be the first to fly a T-33 (two-seat jet trainer) when one came in. The T-33 looked a lot like an F-80, but it had two seats to allow for training. The whole idea of jets was revolutionary. They caught everybody's eye. When the T-33 arrived, Kelly called me to let me know that after minor maintenance problems were fixed, he and I would fly it. I read the flight manual the night before and was ready the next morning. On that day, I was in the front seat of the T-33, with Kelly in the backseat. The takeoff was uneventful and we climbed to 20,000 feet. We went through a series of maneuvers, like barrel rolls, slow rolls, loops, etc., for about twenty minutes.

Then we entered the traffic pattern to shoot a couple of landings. We were over Tokyo Bay and Kelly says, "Let's get this down in a hurry," so he rolled it over and pulled the nose down in what's called a Split S, extended the dive brake, and we came screaming over Tokyo Bay at about 500 feet. Kelly popped into the traffic pattern at about 1,000 feet and made the first "touch and go" landing at Tachikawa Air Base.

He told me: "This is a very clean, sleek airplane. The only way you slow it is to brake it. You don't have a big prop up there to slow you down." I made the next full stop landing. We taxied in, climbed out of the plane, and he declared me a fully qualified jet pilot. We had flown all of forty minutes.

The very next day, I was to have an experience that I would not soon forget. Kelly called me at the office and said: "I have an F-80 ready for test flight—do you want to fly it?" The answer was: "Yes! Of course." I was a hot rock pilot and was always ready to go. I put on my new flight helmet and twenty minutes later I was strapped in the plane, ready to start the engine. I fired it up and taxied out to the runway. "Man, I'm a jet pilot," I thought to myself. I held the brakes, ran it up to full throttle, and went screaming down the runway.

I took off, climbed to 30,000 feet, went level, then suddenly heard a loud noise, like a 500-pound bomb going off. I felt this rush of wind around me and then there was quiet. I was temporarily blinded. Initially, I thought that the engine had blown up. I pulled up the two handles of the ejection seat, and was prepared to punch out. But before I did, I took a careful look around the aircraft, checking all my instruments, and noticed that the sliding portion of the canopy above my head was missing. I had experienced an explosive decompression! On this aircraft the windshield was fixed, but the canopy could be slid back to open, and forward to connect it with the windshield. All the movable parts of the canopy had blown off, but the windshield was still in place.

The pressure in my cockpit was instantly lost and I immediately went from sea level to 30,000 feet. Anything that was not nailed down was sucked out of the plane. Even my goggles had been blown off my face. Luckily I had my helmet strapped on or it would have blown off, too. All pressure in my cockpit was lost and I had to depend on the oxygen mask that was strapped to my helmet to survive.

I called Kelly on the radio and explained what had happened. He laughed and asked me if I had had the hell scared out of me. I said, "Yes." He then asked if the plane was okay and I told him that it was handling as sloppy as could be. That was when I looked at the exterior of the aircraft and found that when the canopy blew off, it had cut off the rudder near the fuselage. I told Kelly: "I don't have a rudder."

Kelly replied: "No big deal. Duck your head up behind the windshield, drop the dive brake, and come on down." The airplane was still flyable, just sloppy in the turns without a rudder. I could do a turn but only while doing a little skidding. I came down from altitude and entered the traffic pattern for landing. All the fire trucks were out in case they were needed.

I told Kelly: "This is going to be a long final approach so that I'll have plenty of time to line up, since I'm skidding all over the sky."

No sweat. It was a good landing. I pulled off the landing strip on to a taxi strip and shut the engine down. Kelly was right there to greet me and said: "It sure took the rudder off smooth."

He then looked at me rather strangely, and said, "Harold, take off your flight helmet."

I did and saw a two-inch gap running from the front to the back of my helmet. A corner of the canopy had ripped through my helmet when it flew off. Fortunately, the webbing inside the helmet provided about two inches of space between my head and the helmet. That two inches saved my head from being split open from my forehead to the back of my head. I kept that helmet on my desk for months. I was one lucky man. Some greater power was certainly taking care of me that day.

The canopy flying off was just a mechanical failure. It was rare, but known to happen occasionally in the F-80. A friend and engineer who was in the Air Force once remarked that there were a lot of pilot funerals in the 1950s when the Air Force was just figuring out how to fly jets. He said that there was a lot of modifying in the models themselves. They just weren't perfected in those days.

Flight Deliveries

Part of the Air Materiel Command's regular duty was to deliver critical parts to keep airplanes flying and the radar working. I flew into the three big South Korean bases: K 2 down in Taegu, K 9 at Pusan, and K 16 located in Seoul. I typically flew C-47s with high-priority parts.

I had a green card instrument rating, which meant that I had a lot of flying time in weather and was proficient in flying in difficult weather. Otherwise, I would have had a white card that would have required me to go to Operations to have my flight plan signed off. That green card allowed me to be my own clearing authority. This worked well for me, because flying between Japan and Korea meant I sometimes had very bad weather at the departure base, en route, or at the destination. I was able to sign my own flight clearance and go. I flew in some of the worst weather conditions imaginable. Icing was quite common at the altitude we flew the C-47.

That C-47 was a big clumsy thing; we called it a "gooney bird," but it was very stable. It was a beautiful airplane to fly when making landings in minimal weather conditions.

Typically, after leaving Korea and arriving at the beacon located on Oshima, a small island in the Sea of Japan, I would turn on to my final approach into Tachikawa Air Base. I would shoot a Ground Control Approach (GCA) into Tachikawa. On this approach procedure, the GCA operator would provide me with course corrections and altitude. He would say, for example, "Go left two degrees; now down five degrees; steady on that course; now down five degrees." The operator had my exact position on radar, and without my being able to see a thing, he would guide me down to land, sometimes with a ceiling of only 200 feet and with a quarter mile of forward visibility. In very bad weather, with low ceilings, one of them would talk to me until I had touched down. It was just a routine flight. We did it all the time.

STRAP IT ON MY BACK AND FLY

I had been getting flight time in the C-47 going over to Korea when I heard about a temporary duty assignment in flight-test maintenance at Kisarazu, where Major Sellers was the officer in charge (OIC). He was the only pilot on location and the only one current in all the fighters. He was known to be difficult to work with and to be a hardnose, but I can get along with anyone and volunteered for a temporary duty of sixty days. I saw this as a tremendous opportunity. Not only was there an opportunity to fly all the fighter aircraft for the Air Force, but I would also be flight-testing light aircraft for the Army.

The jet fighters arrived in Yokohama from the United States via aircraft carriers. They were offloaded with a big crane and put on barges to be ferried across Tokyo Bay and taken to Kisarazu, a substation of the Far East Air Materiel Command. We had only a small contingent of men down there, but they were the sharpest guys that we had. They would take the aircraft, put them in an assembly line, and hook up all of their systems, getting them ready for flight-testing. It took just about seven days from the time a plane started on the assembly line until it was ready for flight-testing.

When the assembly crews were done, the planes were ready to go down to the flight line where the ground crew "tabbed" the engines; they would run them up so that the throttle and the RPMs were in perfect sync. After the engines were tabbed, the planes were ready for flight-testing. It was necessary to flight-test each plane before we signed off on it and turned it over to the unit that was to receive it. The planes did not always check out perfectly. There were times when I would start the engine and couldn't get full power, or I'd start taxiing out and some of the indicator lights were not functioning correctly. Even with that, our assembly crews did a great job assembling those planes.

After flight-testing, we would call in ferry pilots to fly them over to Korea. We had all the Air Force jets: the F-80s, F-84s, F-86s, and F-94s. We also supplied the same level of service for the Army aircraft, the L-5s, L-16s, L-17s, L-19s, and L-20s. I flew all of them and flight-tested them all. I became "current" or proficient in over twelve aircraft, making me one of the few pilots in the Air Force, white or black, who had the opportunity to be current in so many aircraft at the same time.

There was no special training involved in learning how to fly the different types of aircraft. I would just strap it to my back and fly it. It was an airplane. I was a flight-test pilot. Pilots fly airplanes. Get in. Read the manual. Fly it a few times and then I was an expert in it.

The F-86 was my favorite jet aircraft, while the P-51 remained my favorite aircraft with a reciprocating engine (piston engine). The F-86 was sweet; its overall performance was better than any other aircraft I had flown. It was faster and more maneuverable—it just did everything better than the others.

Man! That Guy Could Fly

Commander Francis "Gabby" Gabreski was one of the top American fighter aces (a pilot shooting down at least five enemy planes) during World War II. His fighter group was known for its success in the P-47; in fact, it wouldn't give up the P-47 for the P-51 when that aircraft became available during the war. I met Colonel Gabreski at Kisarazu while we were preparing his F-86s for service in Korea. Each plane had to be flight-tested before we could release it to him.

As soon as two or three aircraft had been tested, members of his fighter group would take them out. They would not fly across the water, even though it was the most direct route. That would suck up too much fuel, unless the pilot had ferry tanks. It was also the first time that the plane had been flown since flight-testing. The general rule was that the pilots would fly down the coast from base to base, in case there was an emergency. They'd fly all the way south and then cross over to Pusan and then up to Seoul. If a pilot were to get low on fuel, there would be any number of bases where he could land, refuel, and continue on to Seoul.

One of Gabreski's first questions for me was: "How much time do you have in the F-86?"

I chuckled and said: "You don't want to know."

Then I told him about my background in flight-testing and he said: "You've got a pretty neat job flying all these jets."

"Best job I've ever had," I said, and smiled.

Gabreski also wanted to know how long I'd fly a plane to test it. I told him 30 to 35 minutes, "just to make sure the damn thing will fly."

When I got back from my next test flight, I told him that it was his plane and he could do anything he wanted with it. I signed it over to him, refueled it, and he jumped in for some thirty minutes of fun in the sky. The entire time he was in the air, he was buzzing the field and doing every kind of imaginable aerobatics. He'd come screaming across the runway—100 feet off the ground—roll it over, and fly inverted all the way down the runway. He'd pop the nose up and roll it out. All the guys working in the hangar assembly areas stopped to watch Gabreski wring that plane out. He eventually landed, got out of it, and told me it was in good shape.

There were a few times in my younger years when I rolled an airplane all the way down the runway a few hundred feet off the ground, but I could never compare my aerobatics to the great Colonel Gabreski.

TIME TO MOVE ON

I ended up staying in Kisarazu for almost nine months. It was the best flying experience I had in the Air Force. I also got to know the mayor of Kisarazu quite well. The United States was a big employer of his citizens. I went to parties with hot baths, low tables filled with food, and the geishas to serve us. I used various reasons for staying in Kisarazu, but my commanding officer eventually told me that it was necessary to return within three days. Reluctantly, I did so.

After returning to Tachikawa, my wife, Maxine, came to Japan, in April 1952, and stayed until December. I had to be overseas eighteen months before dependents could join me. Maxine brought our daughter, Karen, with her. Max became pregnant while in Japan, which meant I couldn't finish my last year of service there. I had to get her to a permanent base, because her travel would soon be restricted. I was reassigned to Ellington Air Force Base in Texas (25 miles east of Houston). She was six months pregnant when we left Japan. We were back in the United States by December 1952 and Denise was born the following February.

At Ellington I was reassigned as an electronics instructor in the Air Force's Navigation School. My job was to teach electronics to navigator/bombardier flying cadets. This six months of training had been integrated into the curriculum because of the significant number of training missions on the B-47 that had been aborted due to problems in the navigator's radar system. The navigator/bombardier was a member of a three-person team, including a pilot and copilot, who flew the B-47. The cost of aborting a nine-hour training mission shortly after takeoff was extremely expensive in terms of lost training. In many cases, the problem in the radar system could have been repaired in flight by the navigator, if only he had an understanding of its electronics. Hence, electronics was added to the curriculum. After I was an instructor for several months, I was named Chief of Basic Electronics and had some twenty instructors working for me.

DENISE

During the time in Houston, another story developed, the story of my daughter Denise. Maxine and I noticed that our younger daughter, Denise, born in early 1953, wasn't crawling or doing any of the things that our older daughter, Karen, had done.

We mentioned it to the pediatrician, and after an examination, he said he didn't like the way her head was growing. He made an appointment for us with a civilian neurosurgeon in downtown Houston. When we visited the neurosurgeon, Denise and I couldn't sit in the white waiting room. There was a little cubbyhole off to the side where we waited.

The neurosurgeon immediately said that we had a real problem. He began explaining what "water on the brain" or "hydrocephalus" was. It was obvious that it was serious. There are three ventricles on the back of the head through which the spinal fluid goes down the spine and comes back up. They are supposed to circulate the fluid through the spine. The doctor told us that there was likely a blockage that was preventing the natural flow of the spinal fluid. He arranged for us to go to a neurosurgeon in San Antonio, where there was a huge regional military hospital with a large neurosurgery department.

I took Denise, who was about six months old, to San Antonio while Max stayed home with Karen. The doctor confirmed that it was hydrocephalus. He told me that the only option was to go inside the backside of the skull and put in a polyethylene shunt that would bypass the blockage and allow the fluid to circulate. In the meantime, however, when the fluid had no place to go, it would continue to force the head to expand, causing brain damage. That was what made the condition so horrible. The doctor warned us that Denise would not live for more than five years. In fact, the shunt might only last three or four years. At best, the operation would only be a short-term fix. She would grow and after three or four years, this growth would cause the tube to become detached. It might be possible to reattach it once, but no more than that. The operation was just too delicate. I told him, "Let's do the operation now and we will worry about the other later."

At that point, he gave me the following advice: "Put her in a home for children. Go home and get your wife drunk. Get her pregnant, and have another child."

I said: "No, no, no way am I going to put her in a home."

He said: "Okay, but you do know what you are up against."

I took Denise for the surgery early one morning a few weeks later, while Max stayed home with Karen. I remember so well the two big burly six-foot nurses' aides—military guys—who took this little bundle, this six-month-old baby, on this long table into the operating room. The operation lasted from 8:00 A.M. until 1:00 P.M. When she came out, she was all bandaged up. She had done well, but she needed to stay in the hospital a week to ten days to make sure the tube was working correctly. She was finally released; we had no instructions on what to do with her when we got home. We just had to take care of her needs as best we could.

Denise had already had trouble crawling before the surgery because her head was getting bigger and bigger. We put her on the floor on a blanket and she would move just a bit. That went on for almost three years. It was very noticeable that her head was getting larger and larger, which we were told would happen. She grew to a little over three feet tall.

The shunt was only working so well. At best, it wasn't that efficient. When the spinal fluid was not circulating well, the fluid would collect in the five-inch-by-one-inch channel that had been cut in her head. A knot would develop—a bump a little smaller than the size of my fist, right in the back of her head. There were times she had what we called a "pressure attack." Sometimes the bump was nice and soft but other times, when the fluid collected, it got hard as a rock. When that happened, she became only partially conscious—somewhat like a coma. She would just lie there listlessly, with a few moans, but mostly she just slept with a periodic groan. The softest part of our heads is the brain, so all that pressure was being forced on her brain.

Her condition progressed just exactly as the doctor had predicted. Whenever she had an attack, something in her brain was destroyed and she lost that function. She lost control first of one hand, and then the other. Then she could no longer move her fingers. She couldn't sit up, had no control of her legs, and was completely helpless. She had to be fed and was in diapers her entire life.

In order to accommodate the big bump while her head continued to grow, I bought a big sheet of foam rubber and cut it into a square. I'd layer it and then cut a hole in it for the bump. The bump fit into the hole so at least she was comfortable. She could only lie one way since she had lain that way for so long and her muscles were so tight. We often held her in our arms, just to give her a break.

When Denise was about four and a half, I read in the *Reader's Digest* that a machinist whose daughter had already had one operation for hydrocephalus was told that she could have only one more. He asked a neurosurgeon what kind of device would need to be implanted to improve his daughter's functioning. It had to be small and pressure-sensitive so the valve would open and let the fluid bypass the obstruction and then close when the pressure was gone. The machinist began to work in his basement and developed a small valve. He and the doctor tried it, and it worked fairly well.

I approached Dr. Sayers, a neurosurgeon at Children's Hospital, with what I'd read about this new valve, the first mechanical shunt, and asked if we could get one for Denise. He told me that I would not like what he had to say: "These men are making these valves one at a time. They are not being mass-produced yet. One day they will be, but not yet. There are only a few of these valves being turned out a month. I would love to give Denise one, but she has had so much brain damage already. I'm saving every valve I can get for a newborn child without the brain damage."

I could understand what he was saying on a rational level, but on a personal level, as he had indicated, that was not what I wanted to hear. The doctor asked me if I knew what he was faced with, and of course, I said that I did. When I went home and told Max, she took the other view, believing that Denise had as much right to a valve as any other child. Max never accepted that our daughter was too seriously damaged to warrant using this mechanical value.

Within five years, the valve had been refined to the point that it was almost 99 percent perfect. By then the valves were being mass-produced and they became the standard for hydrocephalus. There were no more polyethylene tubes. Today, if a child is born with hydrocephalus, it does not end up with an enlarged head. A valve is put in and the child can grow up perfectly well. Unfortunately, Denise lived in an earlier time.

As she got older, at around eight, she became quite alert to everything around her. She started to develop an awareness of her world and started to communicate. She could say a few words, and slowly her vocabulary began to grow. It was as if there was this whole compensation going on that was totally uncontrolled by any external force. I got her a wheelchair so that she could be propped up and look around and so we could take her out for walks. We would wheel her up to the dining room table for dinner. If Max began to feed her, she would cry out: "No, no. Daddy, will you feed me?" I fed her the evening meals and Max fed her during the day.

Throughout the day, we'd lay her on the couch and turn on the television. Her verbal skills began to improve so much that she knew all of the children's and regular programs and even the times that they came on. *As the World Turns* was one of her favorites and she knew it came on at one o'clock. She was even beginning to learn the alphabet.

When Denise turned twelve, we were able to get a tutor for her. We had asked for assistance before from the school system, but were denied. The board believed that there was nothing the school system could do for her. I approached the school board again and asked if she could be provided with some tutoring. This time she got a tutor, a very patient woman named Mrs. Kosar, who spent about three hours a day with Denise, two days a week. She and Denise became the very best of friends. She colored birds with Denise and helped her learn their names. When Mrs. Kosar came, Denise insisted on wearing her prettiest dress. Mrs. Kosar came to our home for almost three years, until it was determined that no additional progress could be made.

Oddly enough, after her thirteenth birthday, Denise had no new pressure attacks. The lump slowly reduced to a nice soft spot. Her verbal skills improved even more. The blockage was gone, but the brain damage had been done. By this time, I had retired from the military and was teaching at Columbus Technical Institute (later Columbus State Community College). Denise knew when

I was coming home. When she heard the car come up, she'd tell her mother: "Here comes Daddy." When I came into the house, I'd ask her how she was doing and she'd say: "I'm doing just fine. How are you doing, dear old Dad?"

I might tell her that I'd had a rough day so she'd say: "Sit down here and tell me all about it. I want to know what happened." On weekends, I would often sit on the floor with Denise and grade papers. I had stacks of lab reports that would take hours to grade. I was also taking a couple of courses toward my master's and doctorate degrees, so I sat there and did a lot of writing. On Saturdays, in particular, Denise and I often "went to the opera." I had finished off our basement and had a complete hi-fi system with fancy speakers. We would listen to *Madame Butterfly, La Traviata, The Barber of Seville,* and many other wonderful operas. We spent the better part of the day that way.

During the last week of October in 1970, Denise caught a very bad cold and was admitted to Children's Hospital on a Friday. Max and I took turns staying with her, Max during the day and I during the night. On the Sunday that she died, I had arrived at around 5:00 P.M. Max and her mother had just left. At that point, Denise was not responding to anything. Mostly, I just sat there with her.

After about a half an hour, all of a sudden, she started gasping for air. I grabbed her out of the bed and shouted for the doctors, telling them, "She can't breathe." A couple of doctors came in with a nurse. They took her and pushed me out of the room. They were with her about fifteen minutes and came out and said: "Harold, we couldn't save her. We are sorry but she died."

I had not been at the hospital for more than an hour. As I drove slowly home, I thought to myself: "This is going to get difficult. Max is going to wonder why I'm home." When she saw me, Max said: "What are you doing here? Denise is dead, isn't she?" I don't think that Max ever totally recovered from the loss of Denise. I know that I will remember that experience until the day I die. Denise was seventeen years, eight months, and eight days old when she left us on November 1, 1970. For years, even after our divorce, Max and I shared in placing a cemetery blanket on Denise's grave each December.

21

STRATEGIC AIR COMMAND

DURING THE YEARS THAT DENISE WAS GROWING UP, there were several major shifts in my career. One of those included my movement into the Strategic Air Command (SAC), our primary deterrent to the Union of Soviet Socialist Republics (USSR) after World War II. Our relationship with the Soviets at that time was called the Cold War.

I was assigned to SAC in 1955 as a result of a personnel project called "Blue Flame." Blue Flame was a response to SAC's need for pilots. So . . . here I was, sittin' in this nice and easy, comfortable job in the Air Training Command in Houston, with flying skills that more than fit the requirements of project Blue Flame. I was a senior pilot, with single- and multi-engine flying hours, jet qualified, and a green card instrument rating (the highest rating possible for instruments), a perfect fit for reassignment to SAC.

No one really wanted to go into SAC. The big joke was that there were two kinds of people in the Air Force: those in SAC and those who had yet to be assigned to SAC. SAC was rough duty; it maintained a steady state of combat readiness. We were always playing war and it was reflected in everything we did. The training flights were long and required us to practice all the skills we would need to complete a mission anyplace in the world, should there be a war. When we were not flying, we were on "Alert Duty" or working on some phase of our "war mission."

The Strategic Air Command was established in 1946, shortly after World War II ended and shortly before a separate US Air Force was formally established. In 1948, General Curtis LeMay took over command of SAC. As the

Commander in Chief of SAC (CINCSAC), General LeMay was one of the brightest men in the Air Force. He was a battle-tested, hard-nosed, no-nonsense disciplinarian. SAC was a reflection of General LeMay and was structured according to his specifications.

LeMay and the other US generals had not trusted the Soviet Union since the end of World War II, when Berlin had been divided into occupation zones. That was essentially when the Cold War began. Under the leadership of General LeMay, the entire SAC was built for one thing—to protect the West against the Soviet Union.

SAC Operations

When I was assigned to SAC, it consisted of three numbered Air Forces: the Eighth, located in the northeast; the Second, covering the central portions of the country; and the Fifteenth, covering the Western United States. CINCSAC headquarters was located in Omaha, Nebraska. The operational control of SAC was through a network of command posts beginning with CINCSAC and flowing through the numbered air forces to various bomb groups located at bases throughout the country.

My first step in joining SAC was to become qualified as an aircraft commander. I had to be triple-rated (pilot, navigator, bombardier) to fly the six-engine B-47. I was assigned to Navigator/Bombardier School and was sent to James Connally Air Force Base in Waco, Texas, for six months. Upon completion, in October 1956, I was assigned to the 801st Air Division, 91st Strategic Reconnaissance Group, at Lockbourne Air Force Base in Columbus, Ohio.

My training to become an aircraft commander for the B-47 also required me to take a two-week survival training course at Stead Air Force Base in Nevada. We spent the first five days on interrogation techniques, including how to behave if we went down in the Soviet Union and were captured. We spent the remaining five days on evasive/survival techniques. Our aircrews were taken some twenty miles into the mountains and given parachutes and survival kits, precisely what we would have in our possession if we went down in the USSR. Each crew had to survive for the next four days by living off the land. On the fifth and final night, the aircrews were given a rough map of the area. Their job was to find their way back to base camp, which included using the night stars for navigating, while at the same time evading the enemy (instructors acting as the enemy trying to catch as many crew members

Figure 32. B-47 Stratojet. Courtesy of the USAF.

as possible before they reached home base). This exercise lasted through the night and ended at 6:00 A.M.

My crew was successful in evading the "enemy" and reached base camp at 5:30 A.M. All of the crews were completely worn out and obviously quite hungry upon the completion of the twelve-hour exercise. We were served steak and eggs for breakfast, all we could eat. After breakfast and some nine hours of sleep, we showered, shaved, dressed up in uniform, and went to Reno for fun (drinking and gambling).

THE B-47

I returned to Lockbourne after completing the Survival School program in late November 1956. The final phase of training was a two-month B-47 advanced flying course at McConnell Air Force Base in Wichita, Kansas, which I began in February 1957. Up until this point, I had flown only single-engine and twin-engine planes. Flying a six-engine jet bomber, the B-47, was an entirely new experience. Even getting into the plane was different. The copilot and I climbed up a set of ladders and steps just to reach the rear and front cockpits (I was seated in the front). The navigator went down into the nose. Passengers (an extra pilot, the crew chief, etc.) could sit in the aisle.

The first time out in this huge airplane was a little intimidating. It was one of the few times that I was happy to have an instructor pilot with me.

At first my depth perception, which had always been excellent, didn't seem to be worth a damn. On the first practice landings, my instructor kept telling me I was high, and "to ease off the power and allow the plane to settle down," or he would say I was "way too high," in which case he told me to "go to full power and take the plane around for another final approach." I needed to develop a feel for the appropriate airspeed and correct landing position coming down final approach for landing. It just took practice. On my second flight, I was more comfortable, and by my third flight, I was making good landings.

Without a doubt, the B-47 was the most difficult airplane I ever flew. Because it was the first big jet bomber, it was designed with much redundancy to make it as safe as possible. This also increased the complexity of the aircraft. There was a primary system, a secondary system, and in a few cases, an emergency system for the most critical systems in the aircraft. If one system failed, another system took over. The big joke was that we needed a pilot up front and engineer in the backseat. The copilot had numerous panels and switches to control these systems.

The B-47 carried no fuel in its wings. The long cigar-shaped body carried all the fuel in its seven fuel tanks. It was critical that each time, before we flew, we computed the weight and balance of the aircraft. The copilot knew the slip stick, which was used for that computation, as well as he knew the back of his own hands.

Takeoff roll, including barometric pressure, runway altitude, runway temperature, and the plane's gross weight, had to be computed for each flight. On hot summer days, takeoff rolls could not proceed if they exceeded 90 percent of available runway (12,000 feet at Lockbourne). When we did begin our takeoff roll and our airspeed began to increase, the wing tips would rotate up a full eighteen feet from where they sat when we were parked until we became airborne. As we continued our flight, burning off fuel, it was important to keep the fuel distributed so that the center of gravity of the plane remained within safe limits. The copilot made fuel transfers as needed from auxiliary tanks to the three main tanks.

COMBAT READY

On returning to Lockbourne in March 1957, I selected my crew and we became N-02 (Non-Combat Ready with the crew number of 02). From day one of selecting my crew, I made it clear that our crew, through hard work and persistence, would obtain "select" crew status faster than any crew in the squadron had ever done.

I had one advantage over many of the other pilots. Since my flying background included many flight hours as a fighter pilot, I was extremely proficient in flying "tight" formation. This made the B-47 in-flight refueling procedure relatively easy for me. After my first refueling flight, the instructor pilot flying with me was ready to sign me off as being fully qualified in daytime refueling. The same was true of my first night refueling flight.

The ultimate determiner of the rating of a crew's status was the Standardization Board (Stan Board). Periodically the Stan Board, made up of "Select" crew members, rode for a full mission with the various crews to determine their proficiency in every in-flight procedure, from takeoff to landing. After about two months of training as N-02, my crew and I passed our Stan Board and we were moved to R-02 (Combat Ready).

When my crew and I moved from N-02 to R-02 in July 1957, we became a member of the SAC arsenal and began flying training missions as part of the 91st. These photo recon training missions were long and intense. The 91st flew a number of missions from England into the USSR. Occasionally, Soviet MiG fighters would intercept a 91st photo recon plane, and would direct it to turn around and head back to England. At times, the MiGs would fly formation with the photo plane until it was out of the USSR territory. We did a similar thing with the Soviet's photo recon planes. It was like a gentlemen's agreement and fortunately there was never a shooting incident.

ELECTRONIC COUNTERMEASURES

The 91st was inactivated in January 1958 at Lockbourne. The B-47 was no longer used for photo recon because faster and higher-flying planes were taking its place. The 376th Bomb Group took the place of the 91st and began flying a B-47 that was equipped differently for a new mission: electronic countermeasures. Our Emergency War Operations Plan (EWOP) was to provide a blanket of electronic countermeasures to block out all radar systems on the ground, thus allowing our bombers to go undetected to bomb their targets. Under the EWOP, for each mission every crew in the 376th was assigned a target. We planned out all the decision points—where refueling would occur, where we would abort the mission if an engine went out or if we lost the radar, etc. All the materials needed to go to war—target information, maps, code books, go–no go decision points—were kept inside a large metal can that looked like a briefcase. All cans were classified as top secret and kept secure.

We also participated in a one-time exercise of the Weapons Systems Evaluation Group (WSEG). We flew one mission per week for several weeks that included both the 376th and the 301st Bomb Groups. We took off about 9:00 P.M. and flew in our assigned flights up into Canada and then to Hudson Bay. From Hudson Bay, we would fly special routes down toward Detroit and Chicago. Two other bomb groups would send several planes each with Detroit and Chicago as the target areas. The mission was planned so that the 376th and 301st would saturate the air while the bombers came in at a lower level to "bomb" targets in Detroit and Chicago. A successful mission would be if our electronic countermeasures blanketed the area sufficiently so that the bombers would not be detected by ground radar. Such missions were extremely useful in designing new equipment and in laying out new Electronic Counter Measures (ECM) coverage.

FLYING INTO A STORM

I had one interesting experience while on a systems evaluation mission. We were heading north up into Hudson Bay when we spotted numerous thunderstorms in the area. The flight leader, instead of circumnavigating the storm, flew directly into it. One directive of CINCSAC was that we were never to fly through thunderstorms; we were instructed to always go around them, because the airplane could break up in flight due to extremely violent vertical turbulence.

On this night, the flight leader chose to ignore the other three of us aircraft commanders when we told him not to fly through the thunderstorms. Upon entering the storm, we immediately encountered extremely heavy updrafts. Even though I was holding the aircraft's nose 10 to 15 degrees below the horizon, the rate of climb indicator showed that the plane was climbing between 4,000 and 6,000 feet per minute. After flying for less than a minute in this updraft, we encountered a heavy downdraft. I rotated the aircraft's nose 10 to 15 degrees up in an effort to hold the plane level, and it still dropped 4,000 to 6,000 feet down. We went through two cycles of up and down before we broke out of the clouds and out of the thunderstorm.

After we got on the ground, we raised hell about the decision the flight leader had made, reporting him to the operations officer. The flight leader told us that he thought the mission was too important to deviate from the course, but the rest of us thought he had made one dumb-assed decision.

In-Flight Refueling

A critical part of almost every mission was refueling. The navigator would plan the mission to be at the refueling area at the designated rendezvous time, usually within the first two hours of the mission. The KC-97 tanker, with its four reciprocating engines (props), would be flying at 200+ knots per hour at an altitude of 15,000 to 16,000 feet, while the B-47 was at 400+ knots at 28,000 to 30,000 feet. In other words, we were flying twice as high and twice as fast in the B-47, so refueling had to be well planned.

At about 21 miles behind the tanker, the navigator would direct our aircraft to descend to the tanker's altitude and airspeed. I would then reconfigure the plane for slow flying (back our power off in the engines and 20 percent flaps down). I would bring the plane in under the tanker, ease the aircraft into formation, advise the tanker of my position, and let him know that we were ready for refueling. The boomer operator would then "fly" his boom into my fuel receptacle. My copilot would confirm the boom was attached and that our fuel tanks were open. The boomer operator would then begin pumping fuel. I had to fly the plane in perfect formation until the refueling was complete. If not, the boom would automatically disconnect. With a disconnection, I would have to reposition my plane into formation and start the refueling process again.

As my B-47 took on fuel, it became heavier, so I had to increase my speed to avoid stalling the aircraft. I would call the tanker on the radio and ask for more airspeed. The tanker pilot would respond as best he could by adding power. When he reached full power, the only thing we could do was to begin a slight descent in order to increase his speed. At this point, refueling could become quite difficult, especially if the tanker were off-loading 40,000 to 50,000 pounds of fuel.

Alert and Reflex Duty

Besides training missions, the other primary function for members of the 376th was Alert Duty, which occurred for a week at a time about four times per year. When we were on alert, our planes were fully loaded with fuel and ready to go to the Soviet Union. Alert Duty crews were subject to practice alerts at all times. We were allowed to leave our alert crew quarters and go to the Base Exchange store one crew at a time. We could go to the front of the line for check out to expedite the exchange trip. I recall those days with some ambivalence. We would sit around for seven days waiting for the horn to blow, sending us off to war, while at the same time hoping and praying that it would never happen.

There was also Reflex Duty to England, which occurred once or twice a year. There were about 1,500 B-47s in SAC around the world and one third of them were on alert at any given time. We had airplanes in England, which was our reflex site. We would periodically fly from Lockbourne to Upper Heyford, England, and stay for three weeks. We would leave at 9:00 P.M., do an in-flight refueling over Newfoundland, and continue on to England. The flight lasted about ten hours or so, depending on the wind. We arrived around noon in England. We would stay on alert for one week, then we would get a week off, stay on alert for the third week, and then take our airplanes off alert and fly back to Lockbourne. During our week off, we could spend our time in England or across the Channel in mainland Europe.

SELECT CREW

My crew established a history of disciplined performance and proficiency through Stan Board "rides." After becoming R-02 and with multiple months of additional flying, we became L-02 (Lead Crew). Finally, our crew moved to S-02 (Select Crew). In fact, we met my goal of moving from "Non-Combat" to "Select" faster than any other aircrew in the bomb group at that time.

"Select" was the highest rating a crew could achieve and affected the rank of its crew members. When a team achieved "Select" status, each member received a "spot" promotion. I had already achieved the rank of major when my crew became "Select" or I would have been promoted at that time; my copilot and navigator immediately moved from second lieutenant to first lieutenant.

Shortly after making "Select" in 1959, I was chosen by squadron operations to be trained as an instructor pilot on the B-47. Only a handful of us were included in this prestigious group. For two weeks, I attended the Central Flight Instructor School. I flew the B-47 from the backseat, the copilot's seat, until I became proficient flying the plane from that position. The pilot being instructed flew from the normal pilot's position up front.

About this time, the squadron commander also designated me as an instrument examiner. Every pilot in the squadron had to have his instrument rating certified annually by an instrument examiner. Only a few instructor pilots were qualified for this designation.

JOINING THE COMMAND POST

I stayed on crew duty until March 1961, at which time Colonel Alan F. Adams, commanding officer of the 376th, selected me to become a SAC controller. As part of the process, on April 19, 1961, I gave up my crew and went into the command post (CP). A SAC controller was handpicked by the wing commander to work in the command post and then approved by the commanding general, a three-star, of the Eighth Air Force. This selection required a personal visit with the commanding general.

The command post was the operational center of the bomb group and was located in a windowless room next to the group commander in the interior of the building. There was a single entry door with a small window that was always locked. Entry required identification, even for the group commander. Colonel Adams came to the command post frequently on the mornings after we had a heavy schedule of night flying. Even though I knew it was he, I would ask for his photo identification. He would reply, "Let me in, you SOB. What have you done to my fleet of airplanes? Did all of the planes complete their training missions or did you screw up and land the aircraft at bases all over the country?" This was typical of how Colonel Adams talked, but in reality, we had a good relationship.

The command post was manned 24/7 by six teams of controllers. Each team consisted of one officer and a senior enlisted man. Shifts were twelve hours long, from 7:00 P.M. to 7:00 A.M. or from 7:00 A.M. to 7:00 P.M. Each team of controllers was fully armed with .45 caliber pistols. The controllers controlled the EWOP and were the only ones who could send planes to war. Not even the wing commander could send an airplane off to war.

The controllers monitored daily flight operations from takeoff to landing. Any changes or deviations in the schedule—due to weather, aircraft problems, or changes from group operations—were handled by the command post. We were also responsible for assisting aircrews in cases of emergencies, minor or major. If we could not resolve a problem, we could request assistance from the Eighth Air Force Command Post. Numbered air forces also had access to Boeing aircraft experts. At times, it would be a beehive of activity and very exciting, but at other times there was little or nothing to do. As controllers, we would use these quiet periods as opportunities to review and study the numerous regulations and procedures that governed our responses to all situations.

Another responsibility of the command post was to control the alert force, which was in a steady state of readiness for launch. In the alert crew building there was a briefing room, which contained a map of the United States, Europe, and the USSR. Daily crew briefings included a worldwide weather review and the EWOP flight plan from takeoff to the air refueling area, to the target in the USSR, to the point of fuel exhaustion, where the crew would either crash-land or bail out of their airplane. There would also be briefings on "what if" situations.

It was quite common for CINCSAC or one of the numbered air forces to exercise the alert force with practice alerts. In each command post, there was a red phone that communicated all items of importance from the air forces and CINCSAC directly to the two SAC controllers through green-dot messages. Red-dot messages were restricted for imminent war; green-dot messages were for peacetime. Both controllers had to record and decode all red- and green-dot messages. After comparing their messages to ensure correctness, the officer controller would take action and sound the horn in the alert crews' quarters. The aircrews would race to their jeeps, drive down the flight line, board their airplanes, and listen to the command post for further instructions. The officer controller would then transmit a coded message to the crew, generally announcing: "This is a practice alert; return to your quarters."

If there had been a red-dot message, aircrews would have been instructed to start their engines, proceed to takeoff runway, and prepare for takeoff. The closest CINCSAC ever came to using red-dot messages to launch the fleet for nuclear war came during the Cuban Missile Crisis.

SAC AIR BASE EVALUATIONS

SAC Air Base evaluations were unannounced and occurred once every two or three years. The evaluation team was so large that it required two KC-97 air transports to move the team to the various airbases. It was not unusual to have over ninety men as part of the evaluation team.

The team would depart from CINCSAC in Omaha without filing a flight plan with Air Traffic Control (ATC). Normally, all flights within the United States and beyond were under control of ATC, but in this instance, their destination was kept secret until they arrived. The evaluation team consisted of experts in every operational phase of the airbase and bomb group stationed there. One of their favorite stunts was to attempt to gain access to the command post without proper identification. They could arrive any day at any time, but they often arrived at midnight to surprise us. We would hear a loud knock on the door. We went to a small window and asked the team members to show picture IDs. If the IDs matched the people, we let them in. Otherwise, we would deny entry.

The evaluation team did its job very thoroughly. It would randomly select aircrews and critically evaluate them while on training missions. The evaluation team also spent time in the command post observing and evaluating command post procedures. Each CP team took written tests; 100 percent was the only acceptable grade. The alert crews were verbally questioned about the EWOP from takeoff to target; they, too, were tested by written exams and again the 100 percent rule applied. All maintenance records and procedures were thoroughly reviewed. In a nutshell, nothing was left to chance.

After two or three days of such rigorous inspection and testing, the team would review its final report with the various commanders and then submit it to the appropriate numbered air force and to CINCSAC. Bomb group commanders were known to have lost their jobs over poor performance as reported by the evaluation team. It was critical that those in charge knew how to react to a war or to start one.

22

CRISES IN AMERICA AND MY DECISION
TO LEAVE THE MILITARY

DURING MY CAREER IN THE COMMAND POST, there were two incidents that
resulted in CINCSAC placing SAC on an alert status. The first was the Cuban
Missile Crisis, and the second was the assassination of President Jack Kennedy.

In October 1962, a U-2 spy plane photographed a Soviet ballistic missile
being assembled in Cuba. This sighting initiated a fourteen-day confrontation
that was the closest the Cold War came to escalating into full nuclear war.

President Kennedy called a meeting of all of his advisors, including the
Joint Chiefs of Staff, who advised the President to authorize a full-scale attack
and invasion of Cuba. General LeMay strongly pushed for allowing the SAC
command to strike the USSR. Soviet commanders in Cuba appeared prepared
to use battlefield nuclear weapons to defend the island of Cuba, if it were invaded by the United States.

The US armed forces were at the highest state of readiness. CINCSAC
placed the entire SAC fleet of aircraft on alert. All flight training in SAC
ceased. SAC had some 1,400 B-47s, more than one hundred B-52s (the first
and the only eight jet-engine bomber), and an Intercontinental Ballistic Missile (ICBM) system—all in place and ready to attack the USSR. The Soviets
did not have a comparable bomber fleet, nor did it have an ICBM system that
could reliably reach the United States. The longest-range missile the Soviets
had was a short-range, 2,800-mile missile, which could not reach the United

States from Russia. Clearly the Soviet Union was outgunned, and General Le-May made sure that the Soviets knew it.

Additionally, we had missiles in Turkey aimed at the Soviet Union; this is the primary reason the Soviets took the gamble to put missiles in Cuba. They really had nothing to lose if they could complete the deal with their missiles ninety miles from Florida. It would have given them an interesting bargaining chip. If the United States would remove its missiles from Turkey, then the Soviets would remove theirs from Cuba.

President Kennedy decided against attacking the Soviets with SAC's bomber fleet and opted instead to enact a naval blockade around Cuba. He made it clear that the United States was prepared to use its military force if necessary to neutralize this threat to our national security. B-52 bombers went on continuous airborne alert and were sent to orbit points within striking distance of the Soviet Union so that the Soviets would observe that the United States was serious. B-47s were dispersed to various military and civilian airfields and were made ready to take off, fully loaded, on fifteen minutes' notice. One-eighth of the SAC B-47 fleet was on airborne alert. SAC also had all of its serviceable planes ready to launch.

Initially I thought the Soviets would back down immediately and in a few days it would all end. The negotiations became tenser, however. After the first seven days, I was becoming doubtful that the Soviets would cave in. They might even take it to the brink. I was also beginning to doubt President Kennedy's ability to negotiate with Khrushchev, because of Kennedy's youth and lack of experience. There was a time when I asked myself: "Will I be the controller on duty to issue the red-dot coded message launching all of our B-47s on alert—sending them off to war?"

As the Soviets reached the naval blockade, the tension grew. President Kennedy told good old Khrushchev, "This is what you are facing." When they called his bluff out there in the Atlantic Ocean, I said to myself: "Are these fools really going to challenge the blockade?" CINCSAC had notified all command posts that if the Soviets attempted to breach the blockade, their ships would be sunk and the war would be on. The standoff continued until a deal was found. If any ship had attempted to breach the blockade, the full might of SAC would have been unleashed and only God knows what might have been the result.

We were ready to go. Most of our B-47 bombers carried a 1.1 megaton hydrogen weapon that just fit in the bomb bay. As a point of comparison, each of our bombs was fifty times more powerful than the atomic bomb dropped on

Hiroshima. There was also a lot of "overtargeting" built into the Emergency War Plan. There might be one important target with ten airplanes assigned to that target. Even if some of the bombers were shot down, there were enough others to ensure that at least one bomber hit that target.

Along with the other missiles and the powerful B-52s, one can scarcely imagine the firepower and consequent devastation that we could mobilize. If I were to speculate, the United States would have taken a few nuclear hits, but the USSR would have been completely wiped off the face of the planet. However, there is little consolation for me in knowing that. It was certainly not worth the trade-off.

The confrontation ended on October 28, 1962, when Kennedy and the United Nations Secretary General U Thant reached an agreement with Khrushchev. The Soviets would dismantle all offensive weapons in Cuba and would return them to the Soviet Union, subject to United Nation's verification and in exchange for a US public declaration and agreement not to invade Cuba.

After removal of the missiles and base bombers from Cuba, the United States formally ended the blockade at 6:35 P.M., EST, on November 20, 1962. During the crisis, as controllers in the command post, we were on pins and needles. All SAC aircrews breathed a sigh of relief that it was over.

The other major crisis that occurred while I was in SAC was the assassination of President Jack Kennedy.

There was a rule that bomb group commanders could only fly with an instructor pilot because they did not fly the B-47 on a regular basis. This could become a real challenge for many group commanders. I was a good friend of our base commander, Colonel Adams. When he needed some flying time and he saw my name was on the schedule, he would come out and get in the front (pilot's) seat. I would kick my copilot out of the backseat and get in it myself as the instructor pilot.

One of those days was November 22, 1963. We were near Atlanta, Georgia, on a seven-hour training mission, when Lieutenant Burris, who was sitting in the aisle, picked up a recall message. There were certain frequencies that every SAC aircraft was required to monitor at all times, in case a need for recall should arise. Such was the case this day.

The copilot was monitoring the radio when he received a recall message: "Hey, Harold, I think I just got an emergency message."

"Okay, what is it?" We tuned in the recall frequency, and it was a recall to all SAC aircraft: "Return to base." Recall coded messages were clear and required immediate action.

I informed Colonel Adams, saying: "Colonel, we've got to go back to base immediately."

He said, "What the hell is going on?" Colonel Adams instructed Lieutenant Burris to find out what was going on. He was unsuccessful; all he could receive was the recall message.

Colonel Adams, frustrated by the reply, instructed the copilot to tune into the radio broadcast band, because if something were going on, the regular broadcast band would be one of the first to broadcast it. Following instructions, Lieutenant Burris informed us that President Kennedy had been assassinated. Everything changed from training mode into work mode. If the Bear (Russia) had killed the President, then we had to be prepared to go to war. All flight training was stopped, and SAC was placed on alert because we didn't know what was going on.

SAC remained on alert until the death of President Kennedy was declared not to be an act of aggression by a foreign power. When the alert was lifted, we in the military returned to our normal duties, while the rest of the nation mourned.

ENDING MY CAREER IN THE MILITARY

While at SAC as a controller, I was offered the opportunity to go to Vietnam and was told that I would likely become a full colonel, but there were no guarantees. I was flattered by Colonel Adams's respect and confidence in my ability, but I decided to refuse. For some time I had begun to think about ending my military career.

Several factors helped me decide to leave the military. First of all, over time I had lost some of my enthusiasm for flying the B-47. It felt like I was taking a bus into the air. The B-47 weighed about 85,000 pounds without fuel. The plane, when fully loaded with fuel, weighed 215,000 pounds. That's 130,000 pounds of fuel.

Once I got the plane airborne, I would just sit there, flying straight from one heading to another. It was just a big machine. In a fighter I could do turns, loops, formation flying, or other fun stuff. This was like sitting in an office.

The tedious repetition of planning for and executing B-47 flights was another factor. The day before flying was spent in flight-planning the mission, which would normally take about four to six hours. The training mission would take about eight to nine hours to fly with only one in-flight refueling. Longer missions of eleven to thirteen hours included two in-flight refuelings.

Also, after two decades in the military, I had more than fulfilled my child-hood dream of being a military pilot. I had flown and maintained currency in twenty types of aircraft—a feat that few, if any, other Tuskegee pilots could claim to have accomplished.[1]

I had started my flying career in single-engine fighter aircraft. Flying them was fun—doing steep turns, climbing, diving, and executing every aerobatic maneuver imaginable. The flights were short, one to two hours on average, and required a minimum of flight planning. I just strapped on my chute, buckled up in the plane, and off I went, usually with two or three other planes. Flying them was great sport!

During my next five years in the military, I moved to a new and different kind of flying. No more fighters—twin engines became the norm. These were longer flights—six to seven hours—and for a definite purpose. The end of my flying career, the final ten years, was spent in SAC flying the B-47, a six-engine bomber. The progression of aircraft seemed very appropriate in that as I grew older and acquired more and more experience and flying time, the planes I flew similarly progressed from single-engine, to twin-engine, to six-engine bombers. Bigger, more expensive, but not more fun to fly.

Finally, I was not interested in further overseas duty. I had already had two overseas tours and my next assignment would probably have been to fly the B-52, a bigger eight-engine bomber. In the end, the decision was taken out of my hands, when the Air Force selected reserve officers to retire after reaching twenty-two years of service. I was in that category.

A New Direction

I had started taking correspondence courses back in 1948. I had no academic credentials beyond high school and knew I needed to better myself. In Hous-ton in the early 1950s I had taken mostly math courses on campus at Texas Southern. During the early 1960s, I was trying to get my baccalaureate degree so that I would have it by the time I retired. I knew I would need that creden-tial when I started looking for a job.

My initial hope was to get into the Air Force Institute of Technology in Day-ton, Ohio. I applied repeatedly but was told that I had a critical job specialty. Instructors in electronics who were officers were preferred to teach the stu-dents in Navigator/Bombardier School because the students were going to be commissioned when they completed training. That is, officers were desired to teach future officers. There were never enough electronics officers to meet the need, so I could not be approved to go to the Air Force Institute of Technology.

I continued to apply until I was assigned to SAC at Lockbourne. I contacted the Institute again and was refused because I was on my way to becoming a B-47 aircraft commander. Finally, I drove over to Dayton to speak with officials directly, and was told: "Harold, you are now in SAC and there is no way SAC will ever release you to go to school. Just forget it."

I had begun taking courses offered on the base by Ohio University located in Athens, Ohio. When I got close to retirement, I took my transcripts down to OU and was told that I could finish my degree in one year if I could get from Lockbourne to campus, because there was a residency requirement of a year. That meant that I had to take the courses that I needed on campus and they were offered only during the daytime. It still took me nearly a year to get those few courses. I also took two courses in engineering physics in my senior year. That was not easy.

Being in the command post in SAC provided me with an advantage. We normally worked twelve-hour shifts. I was on duty for three days, then off for three days. In order to not have breaks in my classes, I had to trade my day shifts for night shifts. All the guys gladly accommodated that request. I worked all-night shifts, 7:00 P.M. to 7:00 A.M., for a straight year. At 7:00 A.M. on Monday, I would jump in the car and drive to OU, where I'd spend seven hours in classes. That was my toughest day. I was up almost twenty-four hours. This was not the smartest thing in the world—I can remember getting drowsy on the way home and putting the window down to help me stay awake, regardless of how cold it might be.

I also had flying duties on my days off because I was an instructor pilot and instrument check pilot. There were always pilots in need of one service or the other. That's how I finished up my final year at OU. I got my bachelor's in mathematics almost at the same time as I retired in May 1965. I left the service on May 31, 1965, at forty years of age and with approximately 6,500 hours in flying time.

It was time to branch out into a new field. My military experience motivated me to go into education. I had seen how important education was, and I had neglected it during my military career. After retiring, I made education my primary goal. I was fortunate enough to be able to work with the new and upcoming college concept called the community college—I grew as it grew.

23

A NEW CAREER IN HIGHER EDUCATION

THE TRANSITION FROM THE MILITARY TO TEACHING in a two-year college was fairly easy. I had spent much of my military career as an instructor pilot and three years as an electronics instructor in the Air Force Training Command Navigator School.

Before I left the military, I visited with officials from the Columbus Public School System to see if they planned to start any of the two-year colleges that I had been reading about. Such colleges were very successful in California and Illinois, but I had heard little about them in Ohio.

I did not want to go into high school teaching. Because of my military training, I knew that I could not tolerate some smart-assed kid mouthing off to me. If he did, I would have kicked him out of my class and he would have gone home to tell his daddy. His daddy would have showed up in my class, raising hell with me. A big argument would have resulted and then my principal would probably have had to fire me. "No thank you," I said to myself. "I don't need that kind of aggravation at this time in my life."

During my visit to the Columbus Public Schools, I was surprised to hear that the district was just starting a school, the Columbus Area Technician School (CATS), grades 13 and 14. It was located in the basement of Central High School, where I went to speak with the director, Clinton Tatsch. At the time, CATS had three programs with just sixty-seven students and twelve instructors. I had finished my bachelor's degree in mathematics at OU and also had a lot of coursework in the physical sciences. The CATS folks said: "Boy, you are just what we're looking for."

I signed the contract in March 1965, just prior to my May retirement from the Air Force. That summer, because I had nothing better to do, I went down to the school and familiarized myself with the program. It was during that summer that CATS relocated to the old Aquinas High School building, which remains the site of what is today Columbus State Community College.

I began my teaching career in the fall of 1965, teaching eighteen hours of math and physics. Halfway through the term, our two electronics instructors received offers from North American Aviation. President Kennedy had promised that America would get to the moon before the decade ended so the possibilities in aerospace seemed endless. In 1965, regular NASA rocket shots were very big in the news. That was the best advertisement for the programs at CATS. A rocket shot would go off on one day and the next day we were hammered with students trying to get into school, because we were very big in engineering technologies. We had programs in electronics, mechanical, chemical, and civil engineering. We also had a program in architecture.

When those two instructors left, Clinton Tatsch asked if I wanted to take over as the chair of electronics engineering. I had taught in the military and said: "Yeah, I can take it over. There's nothing but a handful of students—maybe fifty or sixty." In the military I was responsible for a whole electronics school for navigators, which included nearly fifteen hundred students. I took over the electronics program and taught the two first-year electronics courses, each of which was eleven hours. I was able to find some graduate students from Ohio State University to teach the second-year students.

Besides being the administrator of the program, I still taught my classes, plus those of the two instructors who had left. I was teaching a full forty hours per week in the classroom plus grading student work, preparing for class, and meeting with students. This is a little different from teaching in today's world. The average college faculty member teaches fifteen or fewer hours per week in the classroom and has similar out-of-class duties. Even though the workload was heavy, I saw this as an ideal opportunity to advance.

I also met with parents and prospective students on a fairly regular basis. I don't think that students then were much different than students today. The parents, often the mother, would answer the questions that I asked of their son. It went something like this: Mom would come in with little Johnny. I'd ask him what he liked to do, what his goals were, and what decisions he had made about his future. The mother would begin responding to the questions that Johnny should have been answering. On more than occasion, I would very politely ask the mother to please let Johnny respond so that I could hear what Johnny thought and not what she was planning for Johnny.

On a few occasions, I even politely asked the mother if she would object to stepping out and letting me chat with Johnny a bit, privately, to see if I could learn directly from him about his goals. Most were more than willing to do so. In many cases, Johnny had no idea what he wanted to do. I often suggested to both Johnny and his parents that he might go into the military for four years or so. When he came out, he would have his education paid for. He would have matured a bit and would be much better positioned to come into school at that time, rather than now when he was eighteen and had no idea what he wanted to do. I told them that he was only going to school because they were insisting that he do so. On numerous occasions, I saw those students when they came back from military service. They often reminded me that they had taken my advice and that now they were really ready to go to school and had the money to pay for it. In every case that I can remember, they did extremely well, were good students, worked hard, and got the maximum out of their two years working with us on their associate's degree.

I had originally intended to get my master's degree in mathematics, but my advisor asked me if I intended to stay in the field of higher education and to advance in that field. When I said that that was my intent, he then suggested that I get my master's in vocational-technical education. Our governor, Jim Rhodes, provided significant funding for VoTech. He often said publicly: "General Education only leads to general unemployment."

At that time, there was great growth in the industrial sector in many states, but especially in Ohio. High school graduates needed technical training beyond grade 12, but not necessarily a bachelor's degree, to get good jobs and to further the economic needs of the state. There was also the GI Bill, which helped fund the tuition for many of the vets who had come into the workforce. I began my master's at Ohio State in 1967 and graduated in 1968. I began working shortly thereafter on my PhD in vocational-technical education.

COLUMBUS TECH

In the 1960s and '70s, Columbus Technical Institute was an exciting place to be. Two-year colleges were a growth industry without the strictures of a traditional university. We had no esteemed faculty with tenure, no curriculum that had been in place for decades. We developed programs quickly if there was a local need for trained technicians. Our sole focus was instruction.

Our students in electronics in those years were all placed upon graduation in good jobs in companies ranging from Bell Laboratories to Western Electric to Ohio Bell, electronics companies in Ohio at that time. We were growing so fast that we were advised in 1966 to go under the Ohio Board of Regents, which governed all institutions of higher education in Ohio. If we had remained under the Columbus Public School System, we would not have had adequate funding to support our growth. We changed our name to Columbus Technical Institute in 1967.

With my other administrative duties, I began to pursue accreditation for our two-year electronics program. Most of the four-year engineering programs already had been accredited by the Accreditation Board for Engineering and Technology (ABET). None of the two-year colleges, with one exception, had this prestigious standard of excellence. That exception, our primary competitor, eventually became DeVry University. The owner of that school was killing me with his advertisements, which stated that his school was the only one that was accredited in the Columbus area. Even though DeVry was private, I felt that it was cutting into the market of students who should be attending a public college, if for no other reason than we were much less expensive. It took eighteen months and a site visit to provide all the data that was necessary to be granted accreditation. We were the first two-year public college to gain this accreditation in Ohio.

The college began to grow very rapidly. Within three years, by 1968, it had grown to nearly nine hundred students. Most of our programs focused on engineering technologies. We had some programs in business and computers, but electronics was, by far, the largest. The administration decided to create three divisions. I was allowed to choose which division I wished to direct. I chose engineering technologies, of course.

The Final Push on the Educational Ladder

The military had prepared me well for my future career in higher education. Through the GI Bill, the government also paid for my entire higher education, every dime of it. I ran out of funded money exactly when I finished the last hour of my dissertation for my PhD.

The doctoral degree required approximately 135 hours of advanced study; 45 of those hours I had earned in my master's program, which counted toward the total. I took 9 to 12 hours of classwork, a minimum of three classes, almost every quarter for four quarters. I went to class after work almost every night of the week. I sometimes left work early to pick up an extra class.

The first summer after I completed my regular coursework for the PhD, I asked to take what were called my "General Exams." I told my advisor that I was as smart as I was ever going to be so I might as well take the exams now. The exams required twenty hours of writing in five 4-hour sessions. Each exam day I walked in with only a pencil and pad. I was given an envelope that included three to five questions, each written by a member of my graduate committee. Not long after I completed my written work, I met with my committee for three hours to discuss my responses. At this meeting I would learn whether my work was good enough for me to move to the final step in completion of my degree, the dissertation. I passed that oral exam and was on my way.

During my tenure as director of the Engineering Technologies Division, we were placing all of our graduates into excellent jobs. Unfortunately, very few black kids were taking advantage of the excellent opportunities the two-year colleges provided. I spent much time trying to encourage black kids into our program with little success. The few who did enter the program were not completing it. I decided to tackle this problem as my dissertation project. I looked at all the possible variables, especially the way that the students viewed themselves and why that might prevent them from coming into engineering technologies.

It took almost two and a half years to get the approval from Columbus Public Schools to test black students in the tenth, eleventh, and twelfth grades in predominately white schools and compare the results to students at the same grade level at predominantly black schools. My students at CTI, who had successfully graduated, were used as the standard for comparison. Work on the dissertation lasted from 1968 to 1973, when I was awarded my doctoral degree.

A Time of Expansion

By the early 1970s, the college was still growing and had reached close to 2,000 students. I was asked to be the Vice President of Academic Affairs in April 1974 and remained in that position until I retired.

In the mid-1970s we began offering health programs, such as Nursing, Medical Laboratory Technology, Emergency Medical Technology, Mental Health and Retardation, Hearing and Visual Impairment, and Optometric Assistant (jointly developed with Ohio State University). With new programs such as these, our enrollment rapidly grew from 2,000 to almost 8,000 students. Along with the growth in student numbers, we were constructing new buildings, such as the one depicted in Figure 33.

Figure 33. The growth of Columbus Tech. From left to right: Vice President Mike Leymaster, President Harold Nestor, and I review a model of the soon-to-be constructed Franklin Hall.

CHAPPIE JAMES DIES

During those years at Columbus Tech, a significant event occurred that drew me back to my military roots. In 1978, at age fifty-eight, General Chappie James, a legendary Tuskegee Airman, collapsed of a heart attack. It was devastating news for everyone who had known him. I attended his funeral in Washington, DC.

After attending Central Instrument Instructor School together in 1946, we had each gone our own way. Chappie had been assigned to Korea, where he distinguished himself as a pilot during the Korean War. When he came back, he was made the CO of an F-94 outfit at Otis Air Force Base in Massachusetts.

The stories about Chappie were legendary and were recalled during the course of his funeral service. A couple of those follow. Chappie made national news when he was at Otis AF Base. He was flying a F-94C up front and had a radar officer in the backseat when they had engine problems. Chappie first said to bail out, but they had trouble with the ejection of the canopy. Chappie then said: "No sweat. We'll just land it on the freeway," which he did. He dead-sticked the landing in his F-94 with complete engine failure.

In Vietnam, Chappie was named wing vice commander under Colonel Robin Olds. He and Olds were known for their willingness to take on dangerous missions. Chappie called the two of them Black Man and Robin after the famous duo Batman and Robin. Here are these two full colonels, the commander and the deputy commander, flying as many missions as the regular pilots. On one special mission designed by Colonel Olds, Chappie had one group of pilots and Olds had the other. They shot down seven MiG fighters on what became "the largest, most successful American fighter victory in the Vietnam War."[1]

After his service in Vietnam, Chappie was a CO over Wheelus Air Force Base in Libya. One story, about Chappie's confrontation with Colonel Muammar Khadafy, has been told over and over again. Chappie had been instructed to stay on the base, lock it up, and maintain control of it. Then, according to J. Alfred Phelps:

> Khadafy dispatched a column of Libyan halftracks which literally ran through American gate guards . . . and through the housing area of the base at full speed. Chappie James was called to the main gate, where he shut the gate barrier down. . . . Col. Muammar Khadafy himself stood a few yards beyond it, a fancy gun and holster hugging his hips. Khadafy stood there, wide-legged, his hand resting on his gun as he stared down Chappie James. . . . Chappie faced him down, his .45 glinting the Libyan sun. "Move your hand away from that gun!" Chappie growled. . . . Chappie James was as serious as death. Later he recalled: "I told him to move his hand away. If he had pulled that gun, he never would have cleared his holster! They never sent any more halftracks."[2]

That was the Chappie we all remembered. Chappie became a four-star general in 1975. He was one of the most respected airmen in the Air Force.

Change Comes for Columbus Tech and for Me

Shortly after Chappie's death, there were some major changes at Columbus Tech. In April 1978, our president retired and I applied for the job. The search was whittled down to twelve candidates. It was then narrowed to five individuals; I was not selected to be one of those to appear before the board. I asked a close friend on the committee why I had not moved forward. His response somewhat surprised me. He claimed that the committee was fearful of my becoming president with my military background.

I said: "As well as you know me—we all started here together in 1965— we've known each other for thirteen years—why would that make a difference?"

He responded: "Well, you were not the top dog. You were not in command during that time. Now, if you became the president, we are looking at a different animal—a president with a military background."

I said "Okay. If that was the reason, fine."

After I lost the presidency at Columbus Tech, I pursued one other in Chicago. I interviewed with the YMCA Community College, which had 20,000 students and twenty separate campuses. I was one of two final candidates but was not offered the job. This experience really had an impact on my thinking. The search consultant told me that the search committee had waited and waited for me to come forward and say that I really wanted the job.

As I learned and have said numerous times since to others: "When you are going for the top job, sooner or later you must make the move to go to them. You will never be so big or so important that they will come to you and say, 'We want you so badly.' At some point you have got to indicate to them that, without question, you want the job and say: 'Hey, I'll be on the job tomorrow morning!' You need to say: 'This is the job for me.'" I never really said that I wanted the job, and it was not offered to me.

Columbus Tech continued to grow exponentially. By 1983, the campus was serving almost 10,000 credit students and 3,500 noncredit students. Two-year colleges in urban areas, in particular, grew rapidly, since most students attended the college closest to their home.

In Figure 34, I am participating in a commencement ceremony with President Harold Nestor in 1984.

It became apparent that if we wanted our college to continue to grow, we needed to expand its mission from being a technical college to becoming a community college—an institution that would still offer its technical majors

Figure 34. President Harold Nestor and I stand at the podium at a Columbus Tech Commencement.

but also offer transfer programs. I assisted in the early stages of this process.

At a certain point, I began to feel that I had run out of ideas. I had been the vice president for twelve years and felt that it was time to move on, so in 1986, I retired from Columbus Tech shortly before it became Columbus State Community College.

After leaving Columbus Tech, I went on to be a consultant on various projects in the community college system, including longer-term ones as the interim Vice President of Academic Affairs at Clark Technical College (Springfield, Ohio) and Gaston College (Dallas, North Carolina). In fact, I met my future wife, Marsha, in 1987 at Clark Tech. She had recently taken an administrative position at the college and was asked to help write the proposal that would move the college from a technical college to a state community college. Her writing skills would prove invaluable, much later, as she put the book together that you are reading. Marsha went on to become the Vice President of

Academic Affairs at Clark State Community College and eventually the president of Terra State Community College in Fremont, Ohio. Over the years Marsha became my closest confidant and the love of my life.

In my years after Columbus Tech, I also had a long-term contract with Ohio's State Proprietary School Board as its curriculum specialist. The Board regulates for-profit institutions in Ohio. I frequently made site visits and met with the owners to make sure that the programs were offering a quality experience for students. I retired from the Proprietary School Board after twenty-six years of service, at age eighty-eight, at the same time my wife, Marsha, retired from her position as president of Terra State Community College in 2012.

Tow Head

In October 2014, shortly after I had turned ninety years of age, I was contacted by one of my former students, Greg Taylor, who had begun Columbus Area Technician School (CATS) in 1965 and graduated in its first class in 1967. Greg was fondly nicknamed Tow Head for his blond hair. We had not seen each other since graduation nearly fifty years before.

Greg was fairly typical of many two-year college students. He had a love of a particular subject, electricity, but was not interested in English or history. Through a variety of circumstances, he ended up at CATS, almost by default. Then we met. I was able to get him engaged in the classroom and hired him to be my lab assistant. Greg credited me and CATS with helping him to build a successful career. He even claimed that I "played a pivotal role in his life."

In his initial correspondence, Greg wrote:

> Dr. Brown,
> I know you'll recall me, Tow Head, from the early years at Columbus Area Technician School/Columbus Technical Institute (CATS/CTI), class of '67.
> I went on to finish my BS/MBA and eventually an MS, and had a pretty decent career in Aerospace/Defense with Honeywell, Sperry Univac, Loral, etc., and eventually retired from Lockheed Martin with my last job being on air defense radars. That career likely would not have happened without you.
> You probably don't remember my story, but my father was in the Navy and visited Nagasaki shortly after the bomb was dropped. He died of cancer when I was 5. My mother died when I was in high school and I

lived with my grandmother. I grew up in front of a black and white, tube-based television in the 50s. My grandmother's television was a bit older and prone to burnt out tubes. Needless to say, it was the end of the world when it failed. Fortunately, in small town Fremont, Ohio, where I grew up, a family friend was in the television repair business. He went the extra mile to explain how the picture came through the air and into the wire. The rest was tubes and magic. At that age, it captured my curiosity.

While I developed an interest in science and electronics, I had no use for education in anything I wasn't interested in, so I fell short of average as a high school student. I had an amateur radio Novice license as a junior so I had some potential, but I was unprepared when I started at Ohio State in the Electrical Engineering program. . . . I guess I was a year or two behind.

I flunked out after two quarters, and found my way to the office of the president of CATS, Clinton Tatsch. He encouraged me to join his Electronics Technician program. I don't know what would have happened to me without that lifeboat. The Vietnam War was ramping up and I would likely have been drafted. Anyway, I jumped into the program with enthusiasm. Smaller classes with a lab environment let us get acquainted with each other and our instructors faster and better than OSU's amphitheater approach.

I grew up pretty fast in that environment. I snagged a summer job as lab assistant, with you keeping me busy calibrating equipment and working on a variety of projects. You were a great instructor and mentor. Perhaps I can characterize your approach to educating and mentoring us as tough love, . . . but that doesn't do it justice. You knew we would be released into the industrial world in a wide variety of responsible positions. How do you mold some tow head for that? Maybe by continually raising the bar.

We know there are hundreds of variables that shape a person's paths, and I had often wondered why mine was notably different from my best friends growing up since we went to the same school, same teachers, essentially similar grades, same neighborhood . . . different family situations.

With all respect to those friends who stayed in Fremont for various reasons—one a retired electrician, one a retired tool maker, one working at Heinz—I left for OSU with a best friend and we both flunked out early. I visited CATS and Clinton Tatsch, the president. He picked up the pieces of me, and you put me together and helped launch me . . . a good career and good life with no shortage of great moments. I have been grateful all these years and I also know you changed a whole lot of lives. I wish you the best!

Tow Head '67

Greg Taylor

24

FAME

THE TUSKEGEE AIRMEN, HBO MOVIE, 1995

THE TUSKEGEE AIRMEN AND OUR ACHIEVEMENTS remained relatively obscure until 1995, with the release of the HBO movie *The Tuskegee Airmen*. Many of us had gone on to successful careers in a variety of arenas. Our acts of courage before and during the war were simply forgotten with the passage of time. It was only due to the persistence of one Tuskegee Airman, my friend Bob Williams, that the Tuskegee story was not lost.

Bob and I began training together at Tuskegee Institute in 1943. We were together through every phase of training. Bob was one of the best pilots in our class. Bob was a very popular guy—he was known as the "glamour boy" of our group. Bob could smell a camera from a mile away. If a camera came out, Bob was out front.

Just a few weeks after I was shot down, on March 31, 1945, Bob was among a group of twelve who shot down thirteen enemy planes in a dogfight. Bob shot down two German FW-190s (Focke–Wulfs).[1] Bob and I were not reunited until we were both back at Tuskegee as instrument flight instructors. He left the military when Tuskegee began to close down and went on to UCLA, and then had a successful career in marketing and some acting. He had a part in the movie *Pork Chop Hill* and was a regular on *The Phil Silvers Show*.

One of Bob's goals was to write his autobiography and to describe his experiences of World War II. He sent me the manuscript for review. Bob's original notion to make his autobiography into a film became a reality when a screen-writer helped shift the story line away from Bob's own life to a greater focus on the Tuskegee Airmen as a group. The film became more generic, with B. O. Davis being the only "real" personality to be featured in the film. The movie does begin, however, with a reference to Bob, who had grown up in Ottumwa, Iowa, where he had learned to fly. A plane is seen taking off from a field and is depicted as the one that Bob's father had flown and in which he taught Bob to fly. To see the beginning of the movie was, for me, like seeing "a touch of Bob."

One of the interesting facts about the movie was that it showed politicians as the ones fighting this whole experiment when in reality it was the generals who were totally resistant. However, the film was being produced on an air base in Oklahoma and the military staff were reported to have said: "Now, look, you can't talk negatively about our generals. Here we are out here, giving you all this assistance; you just can't talk about them that way." The general consensus was that it would work out even better to use politicians.

When the movie came out, Bob was seventy-three years old. He was quoted in *Time* magazine as saying: "Not even flying 50 missions, shooting down two Germans and getting the Distinguished Flying Cross from the President . . . compares with getting this movie made."[2] Bob had spent over four decades overcoming obstacles to getting the movie launched. He "started pitching his airmen movie script to studios in 1952. . . . A 1977 film about the airmen, starring Henry Fonda and Billy Dee Williams, fell apart because of financing problems. Steven Spielberg toyed with the project. . . . Finally producer Frank Price, who had carried the Williams script with him from one studio job to another since 1984, struck a deal with HBO. Even with a modest $8.5 million budget, the television project had no trouble attracting major talent."[3] Laurence Fishburne, Cuba Gooding Jr., Andre Braugher, and other well-known actors were all part of those who portrayed the airmen.

Five decades after their experiences in World War II, many of the Tuskegee Airmen recalled the price of being accepted and being successful in the military. At age twenty, Bob recalled applying for military service and was told by the white recruiter: "The Air Corps is not taking niggers."[4] At that time among the military brass, "There was a general consensus that colored units are inferior to the performance of white troops, except for service duties," as was included in a 1942 memo to General Dwight D. Eisenhower.[5] The idea of blacks flying planes was even more preposterous.

Charles Dryden, age seventy-four when the movie first came out, recalled

Figure 35. Bob Williams, me, and Bubba in Los Angeles, late 1980s.

"traveling in the South with his fellow airmen and being forced out of his seat and into the Negroes-only car at the front of the train, where the soot and smoke were thickest, to make room for German POWs." He also recalled "being barred from the cafeteria at military bases, where Italian POWs were served hot meals."[6]

The movie certainly documents the various trials that the Tuskegee Airmen had to overcome to be successful. In a few cases there were inaccuracies in timelines and personalities. For example, Eleanor Roosevelt actually flew with Chief Anderson, not a cadet, and the P-51 was not flown at Tuskegee. However, as I reflected upon the movie, only someone from that era would have recognized such errors. Most importantly, without the movie, the achievements of the Tuskegee Airmen would never have come to light.

Bob Williams and I kept in touch over the years. Figure 35 is a photo of Bob, me, and my brother, Bubba, on a visit to see Bob in Los Angeles in the late 1980s.

Bob remained my closest friend from Tuskegee. He called me shortly before his death from prostate cancer in 1997 to say goodbye.

I would never have believed that a movie about the Tuskegee Airmen would bring so much attention to my life. Before that HBO movie was released, many people had never heard of a Tuskegee Airman. What happened after 1995 up to the present time has been nothing less than amazing. Now it is a common occurrence for me to be invited to make public presentations and to make appearances at air museums, air shows, universities, and so forth. It is just unbelievable.

RECOGNITION LONG OVERDUE

In 1998, Marsha and I received a call from the White House. When she told me who was calling, I jokingly responded: "And this is the black house." Marsha told me that she thought that I should take this call, because this was the *real* White House trying to reach me. As I walked over to pick up the phone, I wondered: "Why in the world would the White House be calling me?" The woman on the phone said that I was invited to the White House for a ceremony during which President Bill Clinton would advance B. O. Davis to four-star general. I had ten seconds to decide to accept the invitation.

I knew that legislation had been proposed to bring B. O. Davis out of retirement and put him on active duty for a day to be made a four-star general, but I did not know the legislation had passed the Senate. A ceremony was being planned on December 9 at the White House. I don't know how the caller got my name or why it appeared on that list. There was only room for about 164 people, and more than half of them were politicians. That left space for just about 60 Tuskegee Airmen.

Those invited were all in the original 99th Fighter Squadron. There were a few of us still alive and able to travel to Washington. Charles McGee, who was president of our national organization, Tuskegee Airmen Incorporated, played a role in the ceremony. Other people like myself were pretty ordinary. I saw only a few guys that I knew or with whom I was close during the war.

I had to submit some personal information so I could be put on the official list, and when I arrived, I had to go through considerable police protection to be admitted. I entered through a side door to the White House. People invariably ask how it felt to be a guest in the White House. All I can say is that it wasn't that big of a deal. We were in one of the many meeting rooms. The original members of the 99th were all sitting on the stage, and the rest of the people were out in the audience. Most of the military, the Chief of Staff and all of the staff members, and all the big wheels were there. A number of politicians, including many black politicians, attended.

B. O. had retired as a three-star general. I can only assume that Senator John McCain, who initiated the process, felt that B. O. deserved the fourth star—that some sort of injustice had been done by not giving it to him earlier.

Figure 36. With B. O. Davis in Washington, 1998. General Davis is seated to the left of me.

It may have been that the assignments B. O. had been given in the military did not call for a four-star general. He may not have been put in a position to get that kind of promotion.

After the ceremony, we all retired to a reception in another room down the hallway, where I spoke with Senator McCain. I introduced myself and told the senator who I was, and that I was a Red Tail fighter pilot. I told him: "I, too, was a prisoner of war. There were thirty-one Tuskegee Airmen who had been shot down and taken prisoner during the war. Of course, you spent six years as a POW. That was a big difference. I only spent six weeks as a POW, and you went through much more pain than I did." After a little more chitchat, the senator told me that he was glad things had worked out for me.

I joined a line of well-wishers waiting to congratulate B. O. Davis. He was sitting down as he shook hands with those in line. Interestingly enough, when I came up and introduced myself, he said: "I remember you, Harold H. Brown. You were a lieutenant then."

I said, "Yes, sir, I was." We chatted a bit and then he said, "I think you were

Figure 37. With George Taylor and Marsha at the Congressional Gold Medal ceremony.

shot down." I told him that I was. I was somewhat surprised that, at eighty-eight, B. O. still remembered details about my service. We talked about that for a few seconds.

He then asked: "Are you now retired?" I told him I had retired as a lieutenant colonel, gotten my doctorate, and had pursued a career in education.

He said, "I'm happy for you," clearly pleased that I had achievements beyond the military.

Figure 36 is a photo taken from the ceremony. B. O. Davis is seated to the left of me.

THE CONGRESSIONAL GOLD MEDAL

On March 29, 2007, the Tuskegee Airmen, as a group, were awarded the Congressional Gold Medal, the nation's highest and most distinguished civilian award. The US Congress gives this medal to individuals or groups for exceptional service to our country. Individuals having received this award include numerous US Presidents, the Wright Brothers, Charles Lindbergh, Colin Powell, and Nelson Mandela.

This event brought together many of those who had supported me over the years, including my brother, Bubba.

Figure 38. Before the Congressional Gold Medal ceremony.

ELECTION OF BARACK OBAMA

Reflecting back on the Presidential campaign leading up to the election, I would describe my feelings as ambivalent. The campaign was a contest of "first" candidates, a white woman and an African American man—each seeking to be the Democratic Presidential candidate. The prospect of a woman

President was almost as appealing and important to me as an African American President. However, as the campaign continued, I finally concluded that the election of an African American would be a far greater accomplishment for the people of our country than the election of a white woman.

When Barack Obama captured the Democratic candidacy, the idea that an African American might win the election was still a dream and I could not completely accept the idea. I had seen too many instances in which black victories seemed assured, but failed to happen. I guess I was being overly cautious in not setting myself up for another gigantic flop. I also questioned whether the people of this great country could honestly accept a black man with a Muslim name like "Barack Hussein Obama" as its President. I had considerable doubt in my mind, right up until the day of the election.

On November 4, 2008, the impossible became reality. The American people had looked past the color of his skin and had elected a man based on his merit, knowledge, and ability to serve as the most important and powerful person in the world. As happy as I was for this event, my underlying feeling was one of caution—there were far too many people who would *never, ever* accept a black man as the President of the United States.

JANUARY 20, 2009

Never in my wildest dreams would I ever have believed that I would attend the Inauguration of an African American man as President of the United States of America.

I received word in early December 2008 that the original Tuskegee Airmen would be invited to attend President-Elect Barack Obama's inauguration ceremonies at the Capitol on January 20, 2009. The invitation arrived with the gilted gold seal of the President.

Marsha and I flew into Washington, DC, on January 19 and went to our hotel on the other side of the Potomac River. It was one of the few hotels left when we made our reservation. We had to arrive at Bolling Air Force Base by 6:00 A.M. the next morning, the day of the inauguration. At the base we would be served breakfast and assigned to one of twelve buses that would take us to the Capitol, where we would be escorted to our designated seats in the security area.

When we first arrived at the hotel, Marsha tried repeatedly to reach various numbers for transportation for the next morning, but cell service in the city had totally broken down because of the massive overload of people making calls. To complicate matters even more, we discovered that many of the crossings of the Potomac to the Capitol would be closed for security reasons on the day of the inauguration.

We then discussed our situation with the front desk and were informed that our only option was to be down at the desk by 3:45 A.M. and try to flag down a cab, if we could find one. Many of the cabbies, who were men of color, were taking the day off to witness the inauguration of the first black President. If we found a cab, we would need to cross the river some thirty miles south of the Capitol and then be on our way back up to Bolling Air Force Base.

As we planned for the day ahead, we laid out layer after layer of clothing— long underwear, double pairs of socks, multiple sweaters, military boots. Temperatures were well below zero, and we would be outside for hours in the frigid cold. At 3:30 A.M. we made the trek to the lobby and were excited that the bellman was able to hail a cab.

The trip ahead, however, was not like anything I have ever experienced. First, the cabbie was an Ethiopian who was new to the Capitol. He had no idea of the detours and spoke very broken English. It was his first day on the job. Our hopes were dashed again. I was wise enough to get the directions to the air base, just in case the cab driver did not know the detoured route. This turned out to be a lifesaver, because the cabbie had no idea how to get to the air base using the special detour.

We departed the hotel and within minutes were on a 60-mile-an-hour highway. Shortly thereafter, we arrived at a "Y" in the road. We told him to take the right lane; instead he took the left. He immediately realized his mistake, stopped the car, and began backing up on the high-speed highway. We were terrified. Some higher authority took care of us. The cabbie successfully backed up to the intersection and took the correct lane without causing an accident. Surely we were the luckiest people driving that morning.

We arrived at Bolling AFB without further incident and joined a crowd of several hundred other Tuskegee Airmen with wives and relatives. It was a great reunion with old friends and close buddies. There were many bear hugs and handshakes. I saw Colonel McGee and Leo Gray, two friends I had recently spent much time with at various events related to the Red Tail Project.

We boarded the buses and left Bolling AFB with an escort of police officers in cars and motorcycles. The route to the Capitol was extremely crowded. It became quite obvious why we needed a police escort to travel through the crowded streets. We arrived at the entry gates, disembarked from the buses, and walked into the fenced-off area to our designated seats. We were seated very close to the large platform in front of the Capitol, where the members of Congress, the Supreme Court, and other dignitaries from the United States and from around the world were seated. And it was cold! We huddled all together in our seats.

Looking behind our seats, we could see the entire mall area back to the Lincoln Memorial. Some two million people were standing there, hoping to get a glimpse of the inaugural proceedings.

After several hours of festivities, we boarded the buses, where we were warmed and served box lunches. We sat on the buses for a full three hours, and only found out some time later that the procession down Pennsylvania Avenue had been held up because Teddy Kennedy had had a seizure. By the time we got back to our hotel, it was late afternoon.

The next day we stayed in Washington, since we could not get a flight out until the following day. Marsha wanted to visit the National Gallery of Art, but I convinced her that we needed to visit the National World War II Memorial, and of course, the National Air and Space Museum. While at the latter, I met some of the band members from the previous day's festivities. They were eager to talk to a Tuskegee Airman from a prior period in history.

RED TAILS, THE MOVIE

When *Red Tails* was released in 2012, there was quite a stir in the nation. Many of the remaining Tuskegee Airmen were invited to private showings of the film and were invited to share their opinions about the movie.

I was invited to the Rave Cinema in Toledo, Ohio, where the theater was closed to the public. The local National Guard, elected officials, and other invited guests saw the first showing. After the movie was over, several reporters and local television personalities interviewed me. As I said then and have repeated since to many others, the movie is not a documentary, but a film designed primarily to entertain. The words at the beginning of the film, after all, state that the film was "inspired by true events," not that events are necessarily truthful. However, Mr. George Lucas, of *Star Wars* fame, who put up the full $57 million to pay for the movie, did a good job of telling our story.

Some of the scenes were based on specific missions, such as the mission to Berlin in March 1945, and to that extent the movie is factual. However, the presentation of the missions is very spectacular. We could never have flown like that. The congestion in the skies was not nearly what was portrayed in the movie—that was nothing more than gimmicks, trick photography, and animation. We flew at such high speeds that there was no way we could have gotten so many planes in such a small space. It just wouldn't have happened. On most missions we also had radio silence and there was very little chatter. The only radio transmissions we heard came either from the lead aircraft or else the squadron leader. Otherwise, it was silent.

Some other portions of the movie were also not factual. The love affair between the hot rock pilot and the Italian woman may or may not have happened. I am not aware of any love affairs, but considering the number of pilots and ground support, I would suspect that there could have been some serious affairs. That aside, in one scene the pilot throws kisses from his plane to the Italian woman hanging out laundry, and she appears to see him in the cockpit. That would be next to impossible.

The portion of the movie when Colonel B. O. Davis returned to the United States to meet with the generals was largely historically inaccurate. Davis did return to the United States, but the dialogue, dramatically portrayed, would not have happened. Military men don't talk that way. Colonels listen when generals speak. The real dialogue would have been dull. The movie added spice to it.

I think I can speak for most of the Tuskegee Airmen in saying that we really appreciated Mr. Lucas's effort to tell our story, and we realize that he had to add some spectacular details to make the movie sell.

25

GIVING BACK

The Red Tail Project

In 1997, I was invited, along with four other Tuskegee Airmen, to participate in a fund-raiser in Minneapolis–St. Paul, Minnesota, in support of the Red Tail Project. This project, the restoration of a P-51C Mustang, was undertaken by a chapter of the Commemorative Air Force located at Fleming Field in South St. Paul, Minnesota. When I first saw the plane, it was just five piles of junk. The chapter had to manufacture a lot of parts just to put it back together again.

The project was an idea conceived by Don Hinz, a retired Navy commander. In restoring a P-51C aircraft, the signature aircraft of the Tuskegee Airmen, Don Hinz believed that the achievements of the Tuskegee Airmen, despite all the obstacles related to the color of their skin, would be the perfect symbol to encourage the youth of our country to strive to become the very best that their God-given talents would allow. Don Hinz took his idea to the Minnesota State Legislature, which funded the project with seed money of $100,000. It was a start for the chapter that was now faced with the task of raising another $2 million to complete the project. The invitation to us five Tuskegee Airmen to come to Minneapolis–St. Paul was the beginning of the effort to raise the $2 million.

UNVEILING OF THE P-51

The next time that I heard from the chapter was four years later in 2001, when I was invited to participate in the July Fourth celebration leading the military veterans in the holiday parade in Edina, Minnesota. I arrived on July 1, 2001, and was taken to Fleming Field, where we were met by a crowd of about six hundred people. What I did not know was that the chapter was using this occasion for the first public display of the P-51C.

The P-51C was nothing less than breathtaking. The chapter had done an outstanding job of restoring the aircraft. It brought back happy memories of another time, when I arrived at Ramitelli, Italy, home of the 332nd Fighter Group as a twenty-year-old replacement pilot. Figure 39 is a photo of the P-51 as restored by the Commemorative Air Force (CAF).

After a brief ceremony, which included short talks by Don Hinz and me, Don announced to the crowd: "Doug Rozendaal, chief pilot of the P-51, and Colonel Brown will now take a flight in the aircraft." I would be the first passenger to fly in the plane! A seat had been created behind the pilot in place of a fuselage fuel tank.

After Don's announcement, I put on a concerned look and said: "Wait a minute, Don. Did you just say that Doug and I were going to fly that P-51? I saw that airplane when it was five piles of junk! If you think that I am going to fly in that plane, you're crazy!" Of course, I was only joking—but it caught everyone by surprise, to say the least. Poor Don was caught off guard, totally unprepared for my remarks. So there Don stood, nearly speechless, trying to explain to me that the aircraft had been safely flown and certified for flight.

There was a little snotty-nosed kid about six or seven years old in the front of the crowd, frantically waving his hand at me, so I glared at him and asked: "And what do you have to say?" His response was classic: "What's the matter, Mr. Old Man? Are you too old to climb into the airplane?" Well, that did it. I couldn't contain myself any longer and broke into laughter.

I responded to the youngster: "Too old? You just watch me."

After climbing into my flight suit, I looked at the youngster and said: "Watch this!" I then placed one foot on the main gear and jumped up on the wing! I looked back at the kid and smugly announced: "How did you like that?" The crowd who had witnessed the event thoroughly enjoyed my clowning around with Don and the youngster. They burst into a loud cheer.

We climbed into the P-51, started the engine, and taxied out to the runway. While waiting for the engine instrument to come up in the green, I

Figure 39. CAF P-51 Mustang. Courtesy of Robert Bell.

commented to Doug: "I feel so comfortable in this aircraft. I really believe I could safely fly it right now!" Doug's response was: "Not today, Harold. Just sit back and enjoy the ride." And I did. It was a wonderful 45-minute ride.

The aircraft soon joined the airshow circuit, appearing around the country at every opportunity. It did not take long for our P-51 to gain great popularity as the second P-51C flying in the United States. The other P-51C was a replica of Colonel Lee Archer's airplane.

In 2004, Don Hinz was participating in an airshow in Red Wing, Minnesota, over Memorial Day. Don was flying the Tuskegee P-51C, alongside a P-51D named *Gun Fighter*. Don had approached me earlier in the day and asked me if I wanted to ride with him. Since I had flown in the airplane once before, he assumed that I would want to go up. I told him, "No, I have to leave later this afternoon and need to go back with my brother." It was only later that I would realize how I had narrowly missed being part of the tragedy that occurred.

The two P-51s had completed their flights and were preparing to land. The *Gun Fighter* was the first to land with our plane, *Tuskegee*, behind on the downwind leg. *Tuskegee* turned base leg before final approach. After rolling out of base leg, Tuskegee had complete engine failure. Don was faced with

Figure 40. With the restored P-51, 2001. Courtesy of the *Minneapolis Star Tribune*.

houses, high-tension wires, and a rough terrain—most of which he avoided. He managed to land the plane as safely as possible on the hilly terrain. The plane was heavily damaged, and Don was unconscious after the crash.

I was standing close to Don's wife when the first P-51 landed and as the group of us near the *Tuskegee* tent waited for Don to land. Very shortly after the first arrival, we heard the on-ground crash equipment, with their sirens screaming, heading out toward the runway and we knew something bad had happened. I remember saying: "If the landing site is reasonably soft, Don will be okay." With Don's wife standing there, we knew that this would be a long night. Don never regained consciousness and died within twenty-four hours. His two sons, Kelly and Ben, both Marine pilots stationed in San Diego, were notified immediately after the crash. They made it to his bedside before Don died.

In retrospect, it was fairly clear what had caused the crash. The P-51 has a timing mechanism, almost like a timing belt, that keeps everything in time. As the experts inspected the engine after the accident, they saw that apparently the nut that holds the mechanism in place had backed off; there was supposed to be a cotter pin to hold the nut in place. It wasn't clear if the cotter pin had broken off or if someone forgot to put the cotter pin through the bolt. When the nut came off, the plane experienced horrific engine failure. Don was already below a thousand feet since he was coming in to land. With the crash, he experienced a lot of traumatic injuries from which he didn't recover. Sadly, if that plane had run another twenty seconds, Don could have landed and would have taxied off the runway at the time of engine failure. All of us pilots knew that there was some danger in flying vintage aircraft, but we sure hated to see Don's life end in such tragedy.

After Don's funeral, the chapter was faced with the question: "Where do we go from here?" The answer was quick and unanimous: "Don would want us to rebuild the aircraft and continue the mission we started. Nothing less would be acceptable." The decision was made and the aircraft restoration began immediately, all with the blessing of Don's wife and sons. Unfortunately, his older son, Kelly, was on a mission about a year later in Iraq, had a collision, and was killed. The younger son, Ben, considered giving up his career as a pilot, since his mother had been through so many tragedies. She had much earlier lost her father in an air accident. However, she urged Ben to stick with his career. They remained supportive of the Red Tail Project. They attended several events related to the Red Tail Project and Ben once remarked: "It is sometimes said that suffering makes a person stronger. . . . My mother and I are strong enough now."

RED TAIL REBORN

The restoration of the P-51C, *Tuskegee*, began within a matter of weeks. Tri-State Aviation, located in Wahpeton, North Dakota, the same organization that did most of the work on the original P-51, accepted the task of the rebuilding the P-51.

It was clear in the original project that public access to our project would be limited primarily to airshows, since we only had the P-51 to showcase. Even at that time we had discussed that we would like to have a broader exposure to the concepts exemplified by the Tuskegee Airmen, but we did not have sufficient funds.

Over time, a solution emerged. After we acquired the needed funds, we decided to convert a semi-truck trailer into a theater for showing a short documentary on the history and values of the Tuskegee Airmen. The film encourages young people to overcome obstacles that they may face in their own lives. The semi-truck was a valuable addition to the project. It accompanies the P-51 to airshows and, additionally, has the flexibility to visit schools, which was the primary purpose of the project.

The restoration of the P-51C and the acquisition of a semi-trailer truck were completed in July 2009. The exhibit was appropriately named "Rise Above." It is owned and operated by the Commemorative Air Force (CAF), a national organization that owns and operates a number of vintage aircraft, primarily from the World War II era. There are a number of original Tuskegee Airmen, like myself, who have been involved with the CAF Red Tail Squadron. They include Charles McGee, Hiram Mann, Leo Gray, George Hardy, and Alexander Jefferson. We have made numerous guest appearances, participated in fund-raisers, and are on-call for other activities as needed.

The CAF Red Tail Squadron is doing a remarkable job in taking the story of the Tuskegee Airmen to the general public. More importantly, the exhibit spends a significant amount of time visiting schools from the East Coast to the West Coast, delivering the message that Don Hines expressed as the reason for developing the exhibit.

The success of the exhibit is measured in several ways. The numbers of people who come to visit are extraordinary. Since the Rise Above Exhibit started coming to Port Clinton, Ohio, near my home in 2012, nearly a thousand visitors have come each year to see the plane and to watch the documentary movie. At least half of that number is made up of local schoolchildren who have been bused in from their schools.

The Rise Above Exhibit began traveling from coast to coast in 2011. By the end of 2015, over 170,000 had visited the exhibit. Well over half of those have been children. Who knows what a difference it might make in the lives of individual students who are struggling with adversity in their own lives? If the Tuskegee Airmen could succeed through determination and courage, might they also?

All the schoolchildren who see the *Rise Above* movie receive a free inspirational dog tag that features the six guiding principles of the CAF Red Tail Squadron's Rise Above educational program. These principles reflect how the Tuskegee Airmen rose above all the obstacles they faced in order to fly and fight for America. The dog tags read: *Aim High, Believe in Yourself, Use Your Brain, Never Quit, Be Ready to Go, Expect to Win.*

The hundreds of letters from teachers and children following their visit to the education programs are perhaps the best indicator of the exhibit's success.

Here are a few examples of their comments:

> Just wanted to let you guys know—I am a middle school teacher of special needs students. . . . I gave one of your dog tags to each student in my class this year. It is our class motto. . . . I asked if anyone had ever told them they couldn't do something—of course, all replied yes. They have their dog tags and they wear them with pride. . . . I wear mine with pride, too!

> One thing I learned was, when the black people asked to join the Tuskegee Airmen, the government said that black people can't fly planes and all of the black people said, "Watch me!!" Then they flew the planes. God Bless America, the land that I love. Thank you for standing beside her Tuskegee Airmen and for guiding her. I hope to be like you.

> It made me feel so proud. I like when they protected the bombers even when the men would not bunk with them or eat with them. My favorite part was when Mrs. Roosevelt flew with one of the airmen and the picture was shown across the world.

> On this field trip I learned many things. . . . But most importantly I learned the six Tuskegee principles. The Tuskegee principles will guide my life as long as I live because I know they will help me accomplish my dreams.

26

BREAKING PAR

There I was, standing over a ten-foot putt for birdie on a long and difficult par five at the country club where I belong. Birdies had become quite rare for me in my advanced years. It seemed that every year I would lose some distance and my short game was not nearly as good as it once was. So shooting bogie golf, which I had done regularly some years ago, had now become a major challenge every time I teed the ball up.

On this day, on this hole, I had one of those long beautiful drives down the middle of the fairway. It had been a long time since that had happened. My second shot was a four hybrid, which I caught right on the sweet spot and it ended up about a hundred yards from the green—two of the best back-to-back shots I've had since I can hardly remember when. The old adrenaline was really flowing as I approached my third shot. I had a clear view to the pin, no bunkers or water in my way, so I decided to punch a little eight iron, pitch the ball about sixty yards, and let it roll the remaining forty yards to the pin. I remember telling myself as I stood over the ball, "Commit to the shot and be aggressive." The third shot came off well and left me about ten feet for the birdie.

I viewed the hole from all directions, decided on my line, took two practice swings, and then putted the ball. From the moment I swung I knew it was a well-struck putt, and it went straight into the middle of the cup. It was a good feeling, made even better when my three partners all said in unison, "Great birdie, Brown!" It may not have been the best hole of golf in my life, because I've had some great holes, but coming at this time in my life, it was most gratifying. After all, in a few weeks I'd turn ninety-one.

MY INTEREST IN GOLF STARTED WHEN I was around fifteen years of age when I served as a soda jerk at the local drugstore. Occasionally, the owner of the drugstore would take off to play golf in the summer. Sometimes he took me out with him to be his caddie. During the first few times I was caddying, I had no idea what was going on, but the owner began to teach me the fundamentals of golf. Eventually, I was given the opportunity to hit the ball. I was introduced to the five iron, how to hold it and how to swing it. That was the full extent of my early exposure to golf. I couldn't afford golf clubs, but it was enough to whet my appetite for the rest of my life.

I bought a brand-new set of clubs—cheap—while I was in Japan, but I didn't really start playing regularly until I had finished my doctorate and had moved up to the VP job at Columbus Tech. I began to seek out colleagues in our two-year college system who also liked to play golf. About that time I got a membership at Ohio State's golf course and began playing quite regularly—close to three times a week. At that point it was only a game, but a game that I had fallen in love with, for all the right reasons.

Golf became my favorite pastime when I retired from Columbus Tech. Golf provides challenges and rewards, and keeps me doing something. I walked and carried my bag until I was seventy-two, and enjoyed it. A person can play golf as long as he/she can swing a club and get to the cart. Golf is a wonderful game. I will never give golf up willingly—I will die a bad golfer!

Golf is also an individual sport, and I like that. It's just me against the golf course. Golf is a little like flying a single-engine plane. I am in the plane by myself, I make my own decisions, and my life depends on me. On the golf course, I have to hit the ball and make the putt; no one else can do it for me. When I blow a shot, I may call myself some choice names, but by the time I get to the next hole, I have put that behind me and that's the end of it. I face the challenge of the next hole. Just like a poor landing. The next one will be better. In golf, it is important to remember that no one really quite masters the game. Just when you start to have some consistency, you can wind up with a triple bogie or worse on the next hole.

As I have grown older, my golf ability has seen some decline and my handicap has risen. I have suffered from spinal stenosis and was physically forced into using a cane, but I know what happens when a person becomes sedentary and I plan never to go down that slippery slope. I only had one alternative at that point and that was to get myself back into shape so I could play golf again. There was water therapy, land therapy—I took it all seriously. My therapist told me that to get back into golf, I should first practice swinging the club

Figure 41. Putting out for the win.

but without a ball, then practice with a plastic ball, and then put a tee down with no ball on it and hit the tee off the ground. The last thing I was told to do was take the tee and put a ball on top of it and hit away. There had to be a progression so that I didn't start swinging too soon and wind up right back in therapy. In time, I was back to playing eighteen holes a day—not bad for being over ninety years of age.

After my golfing partner Barry Hall and I won the Fremont Memorial Invitational (Ohio) in 2010, Barry described my golf game as follows:

Harold is, of course, passionate about the game. He has a very smooth and consistent swing. I have always said that from twenty yards away, if I told someone his age and they watched him swing a club, they would call me a liar. He is a first-class gentleman on and off the course.

Harold is also very competitive. He plays against two in every round, his opponent and his own score.

When Harold and I played and won the Memorial Tournament, I will never forget the last round that got us into the shootout. On #14, a long par 3 hole with water all along the left side, Harold hit a great shot onto the middle of the green. As we were going up to the green, Harold said that he thought he would just make the putt. Now what was so special about this was that at that time Harold had a 36 handicap, which means he got two strokes on each hole. He had about a twenty-five-foot putt and I'll be darned if he didn't make it. That not only put the nail in our opponents' coffin, but he had called it. That actually gave him a zero for the hole, because he was in the cup with just two strokes. I have never seen a zero for a score on a card before.

In retrospect, that play seems indicative of Harold's life in general: He called the play and then made it happen.

27

THE FOURTH QUARTER

As I reread my autobiography, in the twilight of my life, I was struck by the one consistent theme in the narrative: I was constantly setting goals for myself.

As soon as I had successfully achieved one goal, I would immediately set another one, which again would require meaningful effort, plain old-fashioned hard work, and flat out stubbornness to refuse anything less than a successful outcome. I am not sure where or how I developed this trait in my life, but I did.

My mother worked hard all of her life. She only had a sixth grade education, so her success was not through inspiration but through perspiration. Perhaps some of the hard work that characterized her life rubbed off on me.

Then there was Dad, the quiet one, who insisted that my brother and I finish high school—who refused to allow my brother to travel south to go to college and insisted that he select a college in good ole Minnesota. He preached independence and refused to accept government or any other kind of handout. Perhaps I acquired some of his independent spirit.

For whatever traits that have been instilled in me by my parents, there was always the idea that failure was not an option.

The traits that perhaps best summarize my success and my life are embodied in the six principles of the Rise Above Exhibit. Each principle begins with an action-oriented verb.

1. Aim High

When I was in the sixth grade, I became hooked on airplanes. I decided at this very young age that I would become a military pilot. In America in the 1930s, this was quite a lofty goal for a young colored boy, especially when there were virtually no black pilots. My friends teased me that I wouldn't even be allowed to wash one of those planes, much less pilot one. In spite of all the teasing, nothing anyone could say or do could persuade me from abandoning my goal of becoming a military pilot.

2. Believe in Yourself

When I was in high school, I became well aware that the military would not accept persons of color for pilot training. Some people told me that I was just wasting my time. My response was always the same: "When I finish high school and college, the problems will have been worked out and the door to flight training will be opened for me." I refused to give up on my dream of becoming a military pilot.

3. Use Your Brain

When I graduated from high school in 1942, I learned that the Army Air Corps was seeking high school graduates to fill the pool of eligible candidates for flight training. I immediately applied for the required mental and physical exams. I had studied pretty hard in school, especially in mathematics and physics. When I took the mental test, I scored fifth out of 100-plus students. It was important to develop the mental aptitude required long before I took that test.

4. Never Quit

The flight training for the Tuskegee combat pilots occurred in Alabama, where we had to deal with the distractions of a segregated environment, all while we were training in an extremely rigorous and quota-controlled flying program. We faced numerous obstacles, even after we had successfully completed flight training and were commissioned officers with pilot's wings. This was a way of life for black pilots until we were integrated. Even then, the life of black officers on a white base presented its own set of problems. Yes, it would have been easy to quit, but success does not lie in quitting.

5. BE READY TO GO

Jet fighters replaced the older World War II reciprocating engine fighters in the 1950s during the Korean War. The F-86 was the hottest and best plane to fight the MiG 15. When I had the opportunity to become jet qualified, I jumped at the chance. In short order I became current in the four jet fighters that made up the current fleet of fighters. I was ready to go.

6. EXPECT TO WIN

Throughout my career in the military, as well as my career in education, I was always well prepared for the next assignment. More importantly, I was confident of my ability to perform at a high level. General Chappie James said it best: "The power of excellence is overwhelming. It is always in demand, and nobody cares about its color."

NOTES

Preface

1. Joseph Caver, Jerome Ennels, and Daniel L. Haulman, *The Tuskegee Airmen: An Illustrated History: 1939–1949* (Montgomery, AL: NewSouth Books, 2011), 156.

2. Ibid., 198.

3. J. Todd Moye, *Freedom Flyers: The Tuskegee Airmen of World War II* (New York: Oxford University Press, 2010), 12.

4. Daniel L. Haulman, "Tuskegee Airmen in Combat," April 8, 2009, 6–7. A later version of this article was published in *Air Power History* 57, no. 3 (Fall 2010), 14–20.

5. Ibid., 8.

Part I. The Early Years

1. The narrative throughout this book is based on multiple interviews, oral histories, and lectures. Because they often overlap, no specific sources are quoted. Some are credited in the acknowledgments.

Chapter 1

1. Comments from Lawrence Brown, Harold's brother, come from a variety of sources, including the short autobiography that he wrote for his family: *Race: Human Lest We Forget* (Golden Valley, MN: Recollections—A Portrait of a Life, 2009). No attempt has been made to document particular sources.

2. Jack B. Martin and Margaret McKane Mauldin, *A Dictionary of Creek/Muskogee* (Lincoln: University of Nebraska Press, 2000), 170.

3. Henry Louis Gates, "High Cheekbones and Straight Black Hair," *The Root*, April 21, 2014, www.theroot.com/authors.henry_louis_gates_jr.html.

4. Benjamin O. Davis Jr., *Benjamin O. Davis, Jr., American: An Autobiography* (Washington DC and London: Smithsonian Institution Press, 1991), 11.

5. Isabel Wilkerson, *The Warmth of Other Suns: The Epic Story of America's Great Migration* (New York: Vintage Books, 2010), 174.

6. Ibid., 410.

7. Ibid., 8.

8. Ibid., 53.

9. Ibid., 54.

10. Ibid., 8.

11. Ibid., 10.

12. "Rediscovering Michigan's Rural African Americans," interview with Dr. Benjamin C. Wilson, *Found Michigan*, June 21, 2012.

13. Hortense Powdermaker, quoted in Wilkerson, 54.

14. An Alabama official, quoted in Wilkerson, 162–63.

15. *The Tragedy of Lynching*, quoted in Wilkerson, 39.

16. Ibid.

17. Ibid., 178.

18. "Command of Negro Troops," War Department Pamphlet No. 20-6, February 29, 1944, 2.

19. "History," Archer Daniels Midland Company, www.adm.com/en-US/Pages/default.aspx.

20. "Capital Punishment," Minnesota Historical Society Library Guides, libguides.mnhs.org/capital punishment.

21. "Part I: History of the Death Penalty," Death Penalty Information Center, deathpenaltyinfo.org.

22. Wilkerson, 366.

23. Wilkerson, 24–25.

24. Donald Holley, quoted in Wilkerson, 97.

25. Ibid.

Chapter 2

1. Isabel Wilkerson, *The Warmth of Other Suns: The Epic Story of America's Great Migration* (New York: Vintage Books, 2010), 261.

2. Ibid.

3. *The Heart of Bassett Place: W. Gertrude Brown and the Wheatley House. A Documentary*. Written and directed by Mick Caouette, 1999. DVD.

4. *A Century of Population Growth in Minnesota*, The University of Minnesota Agricultural Experiment Station, 1954. (Available from the Minnesota Historical Society.)

5. Wilkerson, 528.

6. A full description of the Wheatley House can be found in *The Heart of Bassett Place*.

7. A copy of this speech was found in Bubba's effects after his death.

Chapter 3

1. Benjamin O. Davis Jr., *Benjamin O. Davis, Jr., American: An Autobiography* (Washington DC and London: Smithsonian Institution Press, 1991), 17.

2. US Army War College, "The Use of Negro Man Power in War," November 10, 1925, www.fdrlibrary.marist.edu/education/resources/pdfs/tusk_doc_a.pdf.

3. J. Todd Moye, *Freedom Flyers: The Tuskegee Airmen of World War II* (New York: Oxford University Press, 2010), 19–20.

4. Ibid., 24.

5. Ibid.

6. Ibid.

7. Ibid., 25.

8. Ibid., 25–26. Moye gives a full description of the lobbying effort on these pages.

9. Ibid., 27.

10. Joseph Caver, Jerome Ennels, and Daniel L. Haulman, *The Tuskegee Airmen: An Illustrated History: 1939–1949* (Montgomery, AL: NewSouth Books, 2011), 155.

11. Ibid., 156.

12. Ibid.

13. Daniel L. Haulman, "Misconceptions about the Tuskegee Airmen," October 22, 2015, 84, www.spiritof45.org/Misconceptions%20About%20the%20Tuskegee%20 Airmen.pdf (accessed December 2015).

14. Moye, 29.

15. Ibid., 30.

16. Caver, Ennels, and Haulman, 156–57.

17. Moye, 36.

18. Caver, Ennels, and Haulman, 156–57.

Chapter 4

1. Isabel Wilkerson, *The Warmth of Other Suns: The Epic Story of America's Great Migration* (New York: Vintage Books, 2010), 145.

2. Joseph Caver, Jerome Ennels, and Daniel L. Haulman, *The Tuskegee Airmen: An Illustrated History: 1939–1949* (Montgomery, AL: NewSouth Books, 2011), 11.

3. Rick Atkinson, *The Day of Battle: The War in Sicily and Italy, 1943–1944* (New York: Henry Holt and Company, 2007), 383.

4. Ibid., 381–82.

5. "The Use of Negro Man Power in War," no page given.

6. "White Attitudes Toward Negroes," Intelligence Report Prepared for the Director of the Office of War Information, August 5, 1942, 5.

7. Ibid., 14.

Chapter 5

1. J. Todd Moye, *Freedom Flyers: The Tuskegee Airmen of World War II* (New York: Oxford University Press, 2010), 67.

2. Ibid., 30.

3. Ibid., 79.

4. Ibid., 77.

Chapter 6

1. J. Todd Moye, *Freedom Flyers: The Tuskegee Airmen of World War II* (New York: Oxford University Press, 2010), 105.

Chapter 7

1. Joseph Caver, Jerome Ennels, and Daniel L. Haulman, *The Tuskegee Airmen: An Illustrated History: 1939–1949* (Montgomery, AL: NewSouth Books, 2011), 196–97.

2. Ibid., 187.

3. Ibid., 193.

4. Rick Atkinson, *The Guns at Last Light: The War in the Western Europe, 1944–45* (New York: Henry Holt and Company, 2013), 25.

5. Ibid., 85.

Chapter 8

1. J. Todd Moye, *Freedom Flyers: The Tuskegee Airmen of World War II* (New York: Oxford University Press, 2010), 58–59.

2. Benjamin O. Davis Jr., *Benjamin O. Davis, Jr., American: An Autobiography* (Washington DC and London: Smithsonian Institution Press, 1991), 48.

3. Moye, 59.

4. Ibid., 96–98.

5. Ibid., 99.

6. Ibid.

7. Ibid., 101.

8. Ibid., 102–3.

9. Ibid.

10. Davis, 115–16.

11. Ibid., 118.

12. Ibid.

13. Ibid., 119.

14. Ibid., 118.

15. Ibid., 122.

16. Ibid., 121.

17. Daniel L. Haulman, "Misconceptions about the Tuskegee Airmen," October 22, 2015, 9–10, www.spiritof45.org/Misconceptions%20About%20the%20Tuskegee%20Airmen.pdf (accessed December 2015).

18. Ibid., 8.

Chapter 9

1. Rick Atkinson, *The Guns at Last Light: The War in the Western Europe, 1944–45* (New York: Henry Holt and Company, 2013), 350.

2. Charles E. Francis, "Tuskegee Honor Roll," in *The Tuskegee Airmen* (Boston: Branden Publishing Company, 1988).

Chapter 10

1. The quotes from the various monthly histories of the 332nd Fighter Group were provided courtesy of the Air Force Historical Research Agency, Maxwell Air Force Base, Alabama.

2. J. Todd Moye, *Freedom Flyers: The Tuskegee Airmen of World War II* (New York: Oxford University Press, 2010), 118.

3. Rick Atkinson, *The Guns at Last Light: The War in the Western Europe, 1944–45* (New York: Henry Holt and Company, 2013), 354.

4. Ibid., 353.

5. Barrett Tillman, *Forgotten Fifteenth: The Daring Airmen Who Crippled Hitler's War Machine* (Washington DC: Regnery History, 2014), 5.

6. Atkinson, 350.

7. Ibid., 351.

8. Ibid., 350.

9. Joseph Caver, Jerome Ennels, and Daniel L. Haulman, *The Tuskegee Airmen: An Illustrated History: 1939–1949* (Montgomery, AL: NewSouth Books, 2011), 193.

10. Comments about the Eighth Air Force are based on the United States Air Force Fact Sheet, Headquarters Eighth Air Force, Office of Public Affairs, Barksdale AFB, LA).

Chapter 11

1. Benjamin O. Davis Jr., *Benjamin O. Davis, Jr., American: An Autobiography* (Washington DC and London: Smithsonian Institution Press, 1991), 131.

2. Ibid.

3. Ibid.

4. Rick Atkinson, *The Guns at Last Light: The War in the Western Europe, 1944–45* (New York: Henry Holt and Company, 2013), 412.

5. Ibid., 421.

6. Ibid., 488.

Chapter 12

1. Kenn C. Rust, *Fifteenth Air Force Story . . . in World War II* (Temple City, CA: Historical Aviation Album, 1976), 40.

Chapter 13

1. Joseph Caver, Jerome Ennels, and Daniel L. Haulman, *The Tuskegee Airmen: An Illustrated History: 1939–1949* (Montgomery, AL: NewSouth Books, 2011), 191.

2. Ibid.

3. Quoted in Thomas Saylor, *Long Hard Road: American POWs During World War II* (St. Paul, MN: Minnesota Historical Society, 2007), 3.

4. Ibid., 6.

5. Ibid., 5.

6. Ibid., 130.

7. Nicole-Melanie Goll and Georg Hoffman, *Missing in Action—Failed to Return: Members of the American and British Air Forces Killed in the Air War Over Present-Day Austria (1939–1945): A Memorial Book* (Austria's Federal Ministry of Defense and Sports, May 2016), 12.

Chapter 14

1. Thomas Saylor, *Long Hard Road: American POWs During World War II* (St. Paul, MN: Minnesota Historical Society, 2007), 40.

2. Joseph Caver, Jerome Ennels, and Daniel L. Haulman, *The Tuskegee Airmen: An Illustrated History: 1939–1949* (Montgomery, AL: NewSouth Books, 2011), 192.

3. Saylor, 6.

4. Caver, Ennels, and Haulman, 194.

5. Nicole-Melanie Goll and Georg Hoffman, *Missing in Action—Failed to Return: Members of the American and British Air Forces Killed in the Air War Over Present-Day Austria (1939–1945): A Memorial Book* (Austria's Federal Ministry of Defense and Sports, May 2016), 12.

6. Ibid.

7. Rick Atkinson, *The Guns at Last Light: The War in the Western Europe, 1944–45* (New York: Henry Holt and Company, 2013), 534.

8. Daniel Haulman, "Target: Berlin," May 25, 2012, 1, tuskegeeairmen.org/wp-content/uploads/Target-Berlin.pdf (accessed June 26, 2012).

9. Ibid., 2.

10. Ibid., 3.

11. Ibid., 6.

12. Ibid.

13. Ibid., 6, 8.

14. Caver, Ennels, and Haulman, 189.

15. Ibid.

Chapter 15

1. Thomas Saylor, *Long Hard Road: American POWs During World War II* (St. Paul, MN: Minnesota Historical Society, 2007), 155.

Chapter 16

1. Ian Kershaw, *Hitler: A Biography* (New York and London: W.W. Norton & Company, 2008), 12.

2. Atkinson, *The Guns at Last Light: The War in the Western Europe, 1944–45* (New York: Henry Holt and Company, 2013), 423–25. Atkinson gives a full rendering of this story in these pages.

3. Ibid., 466.

4. Harold Brown Interview with Thomas Saylor, *Minnesota's Greatest Generation: Oral History Project* (St. Paul, MN: Minnesota Historical Society, 2003), 47.

5. Atkinson, 611–12.

6. Ibid., 612.

7. Ibid., 614.

8. Ibid.

9. Ibid., 616, 626.

Chapter 17

1. Introduction to "The Cigarette Camps," compiled by the US Army Military History Institute Reference Branch, 1984, www.skylighters.org/special/cigcamps/cigintro.html.

Chapter 18

1. Daniel L. Haulman, "Misconceptions about the Tuskegee Airmen," October 22, 2015, 78, www.spiritof45.org/Misconceptions%20About%20the%20Tuskegee%20Airmen.pdf (accessed January 15, 2016).

2. Joseph Caver, Jerome Ennels, and Daniel L. Haulman, *The Tuskegee Airmen: An Illustrated History: 1939–1949* (Montgomery, AL: NewSouth Books, 2011), 11.

3. Benjamin O. Davis Jr., *Benjamin O. Davis, Jr., American: An Autobiography* (Washington DC and London: Smithsonian Institution Press, 1991), 146.

4. Ibid., 140.

5. Ibid., 148.

6. Ibid., 151.

7. Ibid, 152.

Chapter 19

1. J. Todd Moye, *Freedom Flyers: The Tuskegee Airmen of World War II* (New York: Oxford University Press, 2010), 158.

2. Benjamin O. Davis Jr., *Benjamin O. Davis, Jr., American: An Autobiography* (Washington DC and London: Smithsonian Institution Press, 1991), 165.

3. Lieutenant Colonel Charles W. Dryden, *A-Train: Memoirs of a Tuskegee Airman* (Tuscaloosa, Alabama: University of Alabama Press, 1997), 238.

4. Davis, 164.

Chapter 22

1. These include the PT-17, BT-13, AT-6, P-40, P-47D/N, P-51C/D, F-80, F-84, F-86, F-94, C-45, C-47, T-29, B-25, B-47, and Army aircraft, L-5, L-16, L-17, L-19, and L-20.

Chapter 23

1. J. Alfred Phelps, *CHAPPIE: America's First Black Four-Star General. The Life and Times of Daniel James, Jr.* (Novato, CA: Presidio Press, 1991), 229.

2. Ibid., 255.

Chapter 24

1. Joseph Caver, Jerome Ennels, and Daniel L. Haulman, *The Tuskegee Airmen: An Illustrated History: 1939–1949* (Montgomery, AL: NewSouth Books, 2011), 193.

2. Christopher John Farley, "Winning the Right to Fly," *Time* magazine, August 28, 1995, 62.

3. Ibid., 64.

4. Ibid., 62.

5. Ibid.

6. Ibid.

INDEX